A Cotswold Miscellany

ALLAN JONES

1937 - 2001

A Cotswold Miscellany

ALLAN JONES

BREWIN BOOKS

First published by
Brewin Books Ltd, 56 Alcester Road,
Studley, Warwickshire B80 7LG in 2003
www.brewinbooks.com

ISBN 1 85858 225 3

A Cataloguing in Publication Record
for this title is available from the British Library.

Typeset in Times
Printed in Great Britain by
Henry Ling Limited.

AUTHOR'S ACKNOWLEDGEMENTS

I wish to thank the many persons - some living a long way from the Cotswolds - without whose help this book could not have been written. Their advice and support have been invaluable. I am particularly grateful to the following for the time they have spent and care they have taken in reading particular sections. Thanks to their diligence a number of errors have been averted, though if any remain the responsibility is entirely mine: Seumas Stewart (Dover's Games); Earl Bathurst (Cirencester Park); Dr. Henry Rack of the Department of Religions and Theology at Manchester University (John Wesley); Rev. Ralph Mann of Broadwell (Warren Hastings); Hugh Greenhalf (John Keble); the late Dr. A.R. Dufty of Kelmscott (William Morris); Mary Greensted of Cheltenham Art Gallery and Museum (Gimson and the Barnsleys); Felicity Ashbee (C.R. Ashbee and the Guild of Handicraft); Trevor Chinn of the Gordon Russell Trust (Gordon Russell); Myfanwy Thomas (Edward Thomas and W.H. Davies); Geoffrey Handley-Taylor (John Masefield); Colin Matthews of the Holst Foundation (Gustav Holst); Penny Ely (Ivor Gurney); Elizabeth Pooley of the Finzi Trust and Christopher Finzi (Gerald Finzi), and Dr. Jim Hoyland and Geoffrey Hoare, both of Painswick (C.W. Orr).

I wish also to thank the following, who in their various ways kept me 'pointing in the right direction': Graham Baker of Gloucester City Library; Dr. Stephen Banfield; Joyce Banks of Westminster College, Oxford; Keith Clark; Alan Crawford; Dr. E. Dorothy Graham of the Wesley Historical Society; Robin Herbert; Frank Johnson of the Guild of Handicraft, Chipping Campden; Fiona MacCarthy (Lund Humphries Publishers Ltd.); Rev. Dr. Henry McKeating of Wesley College, Bristol; Diana McVeagh; Alyson Rogers of the National Monuments Record, Swindon; Edward Eastaway Thomas; James Walkely; Rona Woodruff.

I am grateful to the staff of the British Library, the Bodleian Library, Oxford, and the Gloucestershire Record Office who responded to my many enquiries. Without their help my task would have been much harder.

Allan Jones - Cheltenham 2001

EDITOR'S FOREWORD

This book was written by the late Allan Jones, my cousin's son, before his sudden and untimely death in September 2001, and to me fell the task of preparing the manuscript for publication. Fortunately the text was complete and posed few problems, though I have taken the liberty of doing a little judicious pruning in places in the interests of conciseness. Everything that appears in the text, apart from a few 'footnotes' located at the end of each chapter, was written by Allan.

One of the definitions of 'miscellany' given in the Oxford Dictionary is "a literary work or production containing miscellaneous pieces on various subjects", and that is exactly what this is - a collection of vignettes of places and personalities connected in some way with the Cotswolds. In some cases the Cotswold connection is rather tenuous, but no matter: what Allan has done is to write about people who interested him and who he thought would interest others. In this I believe he was remarkably successful, and this book constitutes a fitting memorial to his memory.

The illustrations, however, did pose severe problems. Allan had planned a very large number, of which barely one half could be found in his files. I have managed to locate or find elsewhere what seemed the more important ones, and have added a few which I came across in my searches and which seemed interesting and relevant. I can only hope that the results will be deemed satisfactory.

To the best of my knowledge, apart from a few short quotations of minor importance, I have been able to trace all the copyright holders of illustrations and quotations and have obtained the necessary permissions. Anyone claiming the copyright on any quotation that may have slipped through the net should get in touch with me so that I can make amends.

Apart from the acknowledgements made by Allan, I should like to express my own personal thanks to Felicity Ashbee, Myfanwy Thomas, Lord Bathurst, Anthony Boden, Trevor Chinn, Philip Errington and Frank Johnson for clarifying obscurities in the manuscript or for helping me with copyright problems, and to Harold Jones for using his digital wizardry in adapting to a more suitable format the photograph of Allan that forms the frontispiece. Finally, I must acknowledge the continued help and encouragement given by Allan's fiancée, Valerie Smith, both to Allan during the writing of the book and to me during the subsequent preparation of the manuscript.

Emlyn Rhoderick - Ilkley 2002

CONTENTS

LIST OF ILLUSTRATIONS

COLOUR

BLACK & WHITE

1. THE COTSWOLD SCENE: WOOL AND AFTER

The boundaries of the 'Cotswold region' are imprecise. They certainly extend beyond the Cotswold Hills, for cottages of the distinctive honey-coloured limestone are to be found both in the Vale of Gloucester and in the Upper Thames Valley. Beyond Horton and Badminton in the south west the character of the Cotswold countryside dies away toward Bath, and in the north east the colour of the stone deepens to dusky orange as one approaches the ironstone country around Banbury.

For the purposes of this book, William Cobbett's 'Rural Rides' supplies an 1826 definition which is as good as any:

> ...At Dodeswell [Dowdeswell] we came up a long and steep hill, which brought us out of the great Vale of Gloucester and up upon the Cotswold Hills, which name is tautological, I believe; for I think that wold meant high lands of great extent. Such is the Cotswold, at any rate, for it is a tract of country stretching across, in a south easterly direction, from Dodeswell to near Fairford, and in a north easterly direction from Pitchcomb Hill in Gloucestershire ... to near Witney in Oxfordshire. Here we were, then, when we got fairly up on the wold, with the Vale of Gloucester at our back, Oxford and its vale to our left, the vale of Wiltshire to our right, and the vale of Berkshire in our front: and from one particular point I could see a part of each of them.

In Richard II (Act 2, scene iii) William Shakespeare has the Earl of Northumberland complaining, after a journey across the Cotswolds to Berkeley Castle, that:

> These high wild hills and rough uneven ways
> Draw out our miles and make them wearisome.

but Cobbett was more forthright, if less poetic (Hazlitt described his style as "plain, broad, downright English"):

> This wold is, in itself, an ugly country... as there are for a mile or two together, no trees to be seen, and as the surface is not smooth and green like the downs, this is a sort of country having less to please the eye than any other that I have ever seen, always save and except the heaths like those of Bagshot and Hindhead.

On another occasion he writes in similar vein:

In leaving Cirencester ... I came up hill into a country, apparently formerly a down or common, but now divided into large fields by stone walls. Anything quite so ugly I have never seen before ... Anything quite so cheerless as this I do not recollect to have seen; for the Bagshot country, and the commons between Farnham and Haslemere, have heath at any rate; but these stones are quite abominable.

One wonders if Cobbett ever met his contemporary, the Reverend Sydney Smith, (who called Cobbett "that consummate villain"[1]). Smith was a man of letters, a humane and kind writer and cleric, and a Whig. He held the livings of parishes in Yorkshire and Somerset before becoming a canon of St. Paul's Cathedral in 1831. Although Lord Byron called him 'smug Sydney' he was a doughty campaigner against many laws which he saw as illiberal, including transportation and slavery. His numerous writings show Smith to have been a great wit, but his description of a journey through the Cotswolds is as charmless as Cobbett's.

You travel for twenty or five-and-twenty miles over one of the most unfortunate, desolate counties under heaven, divided by stone walls and abandoned to the screaming kites and the larcenous crows; after travelling really twenty and to appearance ninety miles over this region of stone and sorrow, life begins to be a burden and you wish to perish. At the very moment when you are taking this melancholy view of human affairs and hating the postilion and blaming the horses, there bursts upon your view, with all its towers, forests and streams, the deep and shaded Vale of Severn.

In 1832, writing from Newcastle during his Northern Tour, Cobbett recalled his Cotswold visit in more generous terms:

Lord John (Scott Eldon)'s brother William, (who has some title that I have forgotten) has taken up his quarters on the healthy and I say beautiful Cotswold of Gloucestershire...

For more than a thousand years the English wool trade was centred on the Cotswolds; the very name derives from the Saxon 'cote', a sheepfold. On the large monastic holdings, belonging to such abbeys as Gloucester, Winchcombe and Cirencester, Italian merchants and Flemish cloth-makers competed to buy the heavy white fleeces even before the animals had been shorn. A saying among twelfth century European weavers went:

In Europe the best wool is English,
In England the best wool is the Cotswold.

Mansions were built, and churches rebuilt, from the riches acquired by such local merchants as Thomas Fortey and William Midwinter of Northleach, John Tame of Fairford and William Grevel of Chipping Campden. Grevel's memorial brass in Campden church describes him as "the flower of the wool merchants of all England".

The distinctive local breed of sheep, with its white face and prominent forelock, (Plate I), was nicknamed the 'Cotswold Lion'. (A probable ancestor was the longwool breed brought over by the Romans.) Michael Drayton[2] described it well in 'Polyolbion':

> No browne, nor sullyed black the face or legs doth streak,
> Like those of Moreland, Cank or the Cambrian hills
> That lightly laden are: but Cotswold wisely fills
> Her with the whitest kind: whose browes so woolly be,
> As men in her faire sheepe no emptiness should see.
> The staple deepe and thick, through, to the very graine,
> Most strongly keepeth out the violentest raine:
> A body long and large, the buttocks equal broad;
> And of the fleecie face, the flanke doth nothing lack,
> But every-where is stor'd; the belly, as the back.
> The faire and goodly flock, the shepeards only pride,
> As white as winters snowe, when from the rivers side
> He drives his new-washt sheepe...

It is likely that cross-breeding has changed the appearance of the animal over the centuries; as a result of the work on selective breeding by Robert Bakewell (1725-1795) and others, the Leicester longwool was crossed with the Cotswold to produce a larger animal with greater meat production. Cobbett describes the breed thus:

> And here has come down to us, from a distance of many centuries, a particular race of sheep, called the Cotswold breed, which are, of course, the best suited to the country. They are short and stocky, and appear to me to be about half way, in point of size, between the Rylands and the South Downs. When crossed with the Leicester, as they are pretty generally in the north of Wiltshire, they make very beautiful and even large sheep; quite large enough, and, people say, very profitable.

The demand for local wool and cloth saw a decline in the eighteenth and early nineteenth centuries for which several reasons have been given. The finer wool produced by Spanish merino sheep was finding increasing favour among the clothiers. The irony of this did not escape Daniel Defoe:

> Hence we came to the famous Cotswold-Downs, so eminent for the best sheep, and finest wool in England: It was of the breed of these sheep. And fame tells us that some were sent by King Rich. I into Spain, and that from thence the breed of their sheep

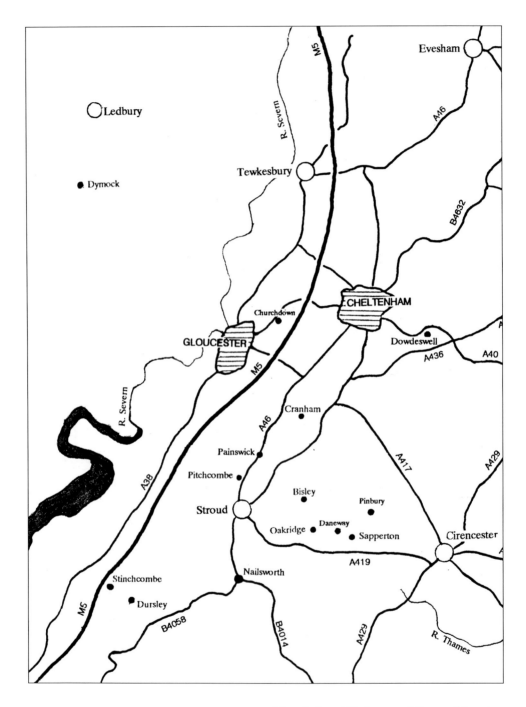

Map I. Simplified map of Cotswold region

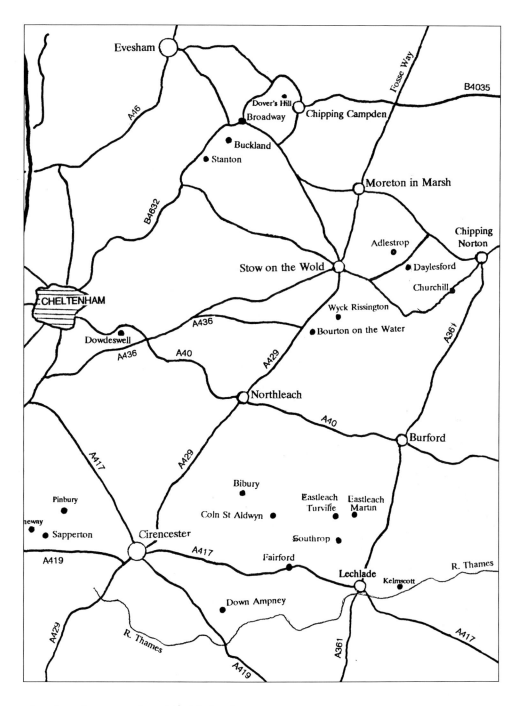

showing places mentioned in this book.

was raised, which now produce so fine a wool, that we are oblig'd to fetch it from thence, for the making our finest broad cloaths; and which we buy at so great a price.

The selective breeding noted by Cobbett was in any case favouring mutton rather than fleece. As cloth prices fell, cottage weavers found it increasingly difficult to obtain adequate payments for their work, and life for them became hard. Introduction of power-looms in the Stroudwater mills met with strong local opposition, and strikes, arson and violence were common.

The early years of the nineteenth century saw a frantic building of mills, both great and small, along every stream and river around Stroud, Dursley and Nailsworth as clothiers invested in new machinery. Intense competition both at home and abroad lowered profit margins, and bankruptcies were inevitable. Cottage weavers who were still able to sell their work received a diminishing return, and life was grim. Cobbett came this way in 1826:

> These villages lie on the sides of a narrow and deep valley, with a narrow stream of water running down the middle of it, and this stream turns the wheels of a great many mills and sets of machinery for the making of woollen-cloth. The factories begin at Avening, and are scattered all the way down the valley. There are steam engines as well as water powers. The work and the trade is so flat that in, I should think, much more than a hundred acres of ground, which I have seen today, covered with rails or racks, for the drying of cloth, I do not think that I have seen one single acre where the racks had cloth upon them...
>
> At present this valley suffers; and though cloth will always be wanted, there will yet be much suffering even here, while at Uley and other places they say the suffering is great indeed.

(The mill at Uley closed in 1837, putting 1000 people out of work. Some of these sought employment in the Yorkshire mills, but over 100 emigrated to Australia and America).

In Stroud Museum is an oil painting of the Stroudwater Canal, painted about 1785. In the fields close to the mills and the clothier's houses can be seen 'tenter-racks' of red and white cloth. (Plate II).

Between 1820 and 1844, 78 mills closed in the county and the number of handlooms halved. Cloth production held its own, though; the industry concentrated in a few large mills whose owners could afford up-to-date machinery, operated by former handloom weavers who surrendered their independence to avoid penury. By 1850 the Inspector of Factories was able to report prosperity in these remaining mills. Broadcloth enjoyed a temporary return to fashion after 1848: in the Great Exhibition of 1851 the Gloucestershire manufacturers earned several prize medals.

Several of the mills were fine, large buildings of architectural merit. Dunkirk Mill, near Nailsworth, (plate 1) was enlarged between 1800 and 1820. The oldest part is said to be the mill described by Amberley resident Mrs. Craik in "John Halifax, Gentleman" (1856):

Through [the mill meadows] the stream on which the machinery depended was led by various contrivances, checked or increased in its flow, making small ponds, or locks, or waterfalls. We used to stay for hours listening to its murmur... He [John] was setting up that wonderful novelty - a steam engine. He had already been to Manchester, and elsewhere, and seen how the new power was applied by Arkwright, Hargreaves and others...

The number of mills continued to decrease as the larger of them installed more machines. Eighty mills were operating in the county in 1850, but only forty nine in 1861. At the same time, the number of powerlooms increased from 224 to 618, devoted mainly to the manufacture of worsteds and tweeds, while the work-force fell from over six thousand to something over four thousand. Many of the redundant workers found jobs in new industries which moved into the vacant mills. These enterprises were often related to cloth manufacture, and included the production from woollen rags of shoddy and flock - the former for making cheap cloth and the latter for filling mattresses. Carpet-making, silk-weaving, stocking-knitting, elastic manufacture and dyeing were other clothing-related businesses which by diversification helped economic stability. To them were added paper-making (also based on cloth waste), furniture manufacture and engineering. One of the largest of the mills, Mrs. Craik's "Enderly", suffered such a fate when in 1891 Dunkirk Mill became a hosiery factory.

1. Dunkirk Mill, near Nailsworth.

In 1871 William Morris came to live in Kelmscott, (Chapter 7) and the Arts and Crafts movement had arrived in the Cotswolds. Ernest Gimson and the Barnsley brothers Ernest and Sidney moved to the Frome valley in 1892 to make good, plain furniture and metal work, and in 1902 C.R. Ashbee brought his Guild of Handicraft to Sheep Street in Chipping Campden, to "do good work, and to do it in such a way as to conduce to the welfare of the workman... to produce honest craftmanship with or without the aid of machines." Such men were the first of many artists and craftsmen to settle in the towns and villages of the region. Their disciples are still occasionally to be found in cottage studios and workshops producing pottery, paintings, cloth, silverwork and wrought iron of the highest quality. Meanwhile, the automated factories of the southern Cotswolds continue to provide much-needed employment.

Two World Wars have had little lasting effect on the Cotswold scene (other than leaving a few airfields, some derelict, some still in use). In 1955 Professor W.G. Hoskins was able to claim that the "landscape of the Cotswold uplands... was even in late Saxon times much as we know it today", but the expansion of private car ownership since then has had a major impact. Tourism is now a major source of local revenue, and many old cottages have become 'second homes'. Sydney Smith's "region of stone and sorrow" was in 1966 designated an Area of Outstanding Natural Beauty. Such protection as this affords may help protect the famous 'Cotswold Downs', but constant vigilance is necessary, or Cobbett's "ugly country" could become a reality.

Chapter 1 - FURTHER READING

Cobbett, William: *Rural Rides*. Penguin (1985).
Defoe, Daniel: *A Tour Through the Whole Island of Great Britain*. Dent (1974).
Drayton, Michael: *Polyolbion*. (1612).
Finberg, Josceline: *The Cotswolds*. Eyre Methuen (1977).
Hoskins, W.G.: *The Making of the English Landscape*. Hodder & Stoughton (1955).
Woodman, Marian: *Cotswolds to Calais*. Corinium Museum (Cirencester)/Sabra Productions (1978).

[1]Letter to Lady Grey, January 12th 1819.
[2]Michael Drayton (1563-1631), prolific writer of historical and religious verse. *Polyolbion* (1622) (from the Greek 'having many blessings'), a topographical poem, is probably his best-known work. It consists of thirty 'Songs', in which the author describes the geographical features and beauties of the English countryside.

2. ROBERT DOVER AND THE 'COTSWOLD OLIMPICKS'

"This was the man, Dover, that first these noble sports began."

West of Chipping Campden is a grassy plateau, Dover's Hill, (plate 2), which commands a fine view over the Vale of Evesham to the Welsh Mountains, Long Mynd and Wrekin. Fore more than two hundred years the Cotswold Games or Cotswold 'Olimpicks' were held here annually, attracting competitors and spectators from as far afield as the Midlands and the south-west.

Robert Dover was born in Norfolk in 1582. In 1611 he came to live in the village of Saintbury, where his brother-in-law was Rector. Dover was an attorney, a Royalist and a friend of Michael Drayton, Ben Jonson and other, lesser, poets of the day. These were friends, too, of William Shakespeare, and it seems likely that the Bard of Avon was at least acquainted with Dover, particularly as the latter received his legal training at Gray's Inn, where Shakespeare was a frequent visitor.

Robert Dover, like his King, James I, despised Puritanism, and the denunciations of neighbourhood festivities and revelries which thundered from local pulpits cannot have escaped his attention. Anthony à Wood describes him as "full of activity, and of a generous, free, and Public Spirit", and perhaps it was in defiance of Puritan doctrine that Dover involved himself in the organisation of country sports in the area - so involved, indeed, as to inaugurate an annual Whitsuntide meeting which became known as the 'Cotswold Olimpicks' or 'Dover's Games'. One wonders what his brother-in-law had to say.

The first of these events seems to have been held in or about 1612. Rustic sports had taken place, in one form or another, for perhaps a thousand years, and were referred to by Shakespeare in 'The Merry Wives of Windsor' (Act 1, scene i) - written in about 1599. Mr. Justice Shallow's cousin Slender asks:

How does your fallow greyhound, sir? I heard say he was outrun on Cotsall.

They were picturesquely described by Drayton:

But Muse, returns to tell, how there the sheepeard's King,
Whose flock hath chanc't that yeere the earliest lambe to bring,
In his gay bauldrick sits at his low grassie bord,
With fawns, curds, clowted-crème, and country dainties stored:
And, whilst the bag-pipe playes, each lustie jocund swaine
Quaffes sillibubs in kans, to all upon the plaine,

And to their country-girles, whose nosegays they doe weare,
Some roundelayes doe sing: the rest, the burthen beare.

Wood is not, perhaps, accurate, when he writes that Dover "did *select* a place on Cotswold
Hills in Gloucestershire whereon these games should be enacted". Whitfield points out
that the road along the top of the hill forms a boundary between the parishes of Weston
and Campden, that the nearby Kiftsgate Stone had been a meeting place since Saxon
times, and that it is likely, therefore, that some kind of festivity involving the two parishes
had taken place here for centuries before Dover inaugurated his 'Cotswold Olimpicks'.

Dover received support and encouragement from two public figures. One was Sir
Baptist Hicks (whose fine monument has its own chapel in Chipping Campden church).
The Royalist Hicks owned much of the land around Campden and was probably
instrumental in Dover's gaining the King's permission to hold his Games - permission
likely to have been obtained easily in view of the King's general support for such
recreational pursuits. Hicks's goodwill, though, was essential; he owned part of the land
on which the Games were to be held, though there is no evidence that he took any
interest in the Games himself.

The other important figure was Endymion Porter of Aston-sub-Edge, a distant
relative of Dover, for whom the latter acted as agent while Porter was in London or
abroad on Court duties or errands for his master, the Earl of Buckingham. Wood records
that Porter, "a servant of the King, a person also of a most generous Spirit, did, to
encourage Dover, give him some of the King's old cloathes with a Hat and Feather and
Ruff, purposely to grace him and consequently the Solemnity".

In 1636 Mathewe Walbancke, an old Gray's Inn friend of Dover, published a
volume of collected poems, "Annalia Dubrensia[1]", written by no less than thirty-three
of Dover's friends. Affectionate and acclamatory in tone, they suggest that Dover was
indeed "of a generous, free and Public Spirit". Chief among the contributors were
Drayton and Ben Jonson, and it may well have been Drayton who instigated the project;
certainly it is his poem which appears first, with the dedication "To my Noble Friend
Mr. Robert Dover on his brave annual Assemblies upon Cotswold". In like vein,
Jonson's short contribution is "An Epigram to my Jovial Good Friend Mr. Robert
Dover, on his great Instauration of his Hunting and Dancing at Cotswold". The final
poem is by Dover himself: "A Congratulatory Poem to my Poetical and Learned Noble
Friends, compilers of this Booke". He can barely conceal his pride at being the subject
of such adulation:

... Yet I was bold, for better recreation,
T'invent these sports, to countercheck that fashion;
And blesse the troope that come our sports to see,
With hearty thanks, and friendly courtesie!
I never thought that any one of you,
In written poems would the same allow,

DOVER'S HILL & THE LYNCHES: THE CENTRE OF THE VILLAGE COMMUNITY OF WESTON SUBEDGE WHERE THE COTSWOLD GAMES

WERE PLAYED. CAMPDEN & ASTON SUBEDGE LIE ON THE OTHER SIDE OF THE HILL, AND THE VALE OF EVESHAM IS IN THE DISTANCE.

2. *Dover's Hill (drawing by EH New, 1904).*

Nor did I thinke the same could ere have wonne
The general approbation it hath done,
And much it joyes me, you of such great fame,
Have undertaken thus to praise the same...

The frontispiece to "Annalia Dubrensia", (plate 3), depicts some of the sports which comprised the "Cotswold Olimpick Games", and Wood describes them thus:

... men playing at cudgels, wrestling, leaping, pitching the bar, throwing the iron hammer, handling the pyke, leaping over the heads of men kneeling, standing upon their hands, etc. Also the dancing of women, men hunting and coursing the hare with hounds and greyhounds etc., with a castle built of boards on a hillock with guns therein.

In the foreground is Dover, mounted and attired as Wood describes him, with a "Hat and Feather and Ruff", while behind is the "famous and admirable Portable Fabricke of Dover Castle, her Ordnance and Artillery...". The firing of guns from this remarkable construction must have been a most alarming way to begin the day's activities.

Some of these contests were very fierce. On one occasion a backswords[2] player lost an eye, and a fortnight later his opponent died from his injuries.

The festivities were not confined to the hill; cock-fighting, plays, balls and concerts took place in Chipping Campden itself, and on the Saturday was held a Wake, with stalls, booths, roundabouts and divers amusements.

The Games stopped in 1653. This may in part have been due to a resurgence of Puritanism in the area, but the first battle of the Civil War had taken place the previous year at Edge Hill, just fifteen miles away, so local Royalist gentry perforce turned their attention from Dover and his Games to more pressing matters of state.

Robert Dover lived with his memories while the War went on around him, and died at his son's home in Barton-on-the-Heath in 1652. The Games were revived some little time after the Restoration in 1660, but it was not until 1725 that an advertisement for them again appeared, and that for 1806 is shown in plate 4. An 1819 advertisement shows that by that time horse racing had been added to the activities. The course led from the Hill south-west along the track now known as the Mile Drive. Through the 18th and early 19th centuries the Games became the scene of increasing disorder and violence. Gangs on the Hill organised protection rackets, and stallholders risked the wrecking of their stocks unless they paid up. (It is said that one lady was immune because she had done a 'service' for a gang member.)

By the 1840s the Games had become so objectionable that moves were made to stop them altogether. Pressure from local landowners and clergy was sufficient to have Weston parish included in the schedule to the 1850 Enclosure Act. One of the clergy, Canon Bourne, wrote that:

COTSWOLD GAMES.

3. Frontispiece from Annalia Dubrensia. The figure on horseback is Robert Dover.

Dover's Hill became a meeting of the lowest characters merely for debauchery. During Whitsun week the residuum of the black country came there. I have seen as many as thirty thousand, but I am told that many more were assembled. The whole district became demoralised and I determined if possible to stop this evil. An Act was passed for the division and enclosure of the hill and the last Dover's meeting was held in 1851.

The estimate of thirty thousand was almost certainly a gross exaggeration, but Bourne's efforts were successful. Dover's Hill was fenced off and divided into fields, and with no large area to hold the Games, they ceased, though the Wake in Chipping Campden continued. By 1887 this had become known as the Scuttlebrook Wake, after the Scuttle Brook which ran through part of the town. Records of early Wakes are unclear, and it is uncertain whether they took place during the Commonwealth, but it is probable that the Wake and the Games are of similar chronology.

Dover's Meeting, 1806.

On THURSDAY in the *Whitsuntide Week*, upon that Renowned and Celebrated Spot called DOVERS HILL, there will be a Purse of

Thirteen Guineas

to be Play'd for, at *Backswords* upon a Stage, by Eleven Men on a side, each side to appear by *Three o' Clock* in the afternoon, the Victors to receive TEN GUINEAS, the Vanquished THREE GUINEAS, also a GOLD LACED HAT to be Wrestled for by five Men on a side, likewise GLOVES and RIBANDS to be Danced for, a good pair of SHOES to be Jumped for in Bags by Men, with an infinite number of Ancient Pastimes for which this Meeting is so justly fam'd.

AND ON THE FOLLOWING DAY, FRIDAY,

The Sports will commence with a DONKEY RACE for a Prize of ONE GUINEA, the best of three, one Mile heats, and not less than three *Donkeys* to Start ; the same will be succeeded by a great variety of Rural & Athletic Sports, to enumerate which wou'd fill a Volume, the whole being calculated to create Mirth and Jollity to the Company, which is expected to be more respectable and numerous than any that have Assembled since the Institution of these Ancient Festivities.

☞ No Person to erect a Booth or Shed to sell Liquor in, without first Subscribing Ten Shillings and Six-pence, to be paid to the Conductors.

N.B. A Main of Cocks to be fought each Morning at the *Green Dragon*, in Campden, between the Gentlemen of Gloucestershire and Worcestershire.

An Ordinary each day at the Principal Inns ; and a Ball each Evening at the *George Inn*.

On Saturday, the WAKE will be held at Campden as usual ; the whole to be conducted by

Mr. Richard Andrews, Mr. Daniel Weston, and Mr Ebenezer Prestage.

Campden : *May 9th,* 1806. ——— *COX, Printer, Stratford-on-Avon.*

---

4. Advertisement for Dover's Games (1806).

In 1929, through the efforts of F.L. Griggs (p.91) the hill was purchased by the National Trust, averting the proposed building of a hotel on the site.

In the Wake's present form a procession, led by a band and folk-dancers, passes through the town from Littleworth to the Almshouses. The town Square en route is the venue for the crowning of the Scuttlebrook Queen, for maypole and morris dancing, and for the awarding of prizes for floats and fancy dress.

The 1951 Festival of Britain celebrations in Chipping Campden included a re-enactment of the 'Cotswold Olimpicks' on Dover's Hill. 'Robert Dover' attended in full attire, and a small wooden 'Castle' was constructed. Among the events were shin-kicking, boxing, tugs-of-war and 'bowling for a pig'. The evening concluded with a bonfire, fireworks, and a torchlight procession from Dover's Hill into the town.

In 1963 the Scuttlebrook Wake committee revived the Games as an annual event, and in 1965 arrangements were formalised with the establishment of the Robert Dover's Games Society.

Each year the Games, now usually held on the last Friday of May, and the Scuttlebrook Wake on the following day, attract large crowds. Michael Drayton's promise, in his contribution to "Annalia Dubrensia":

Go Dover, from these Games, by thee begun,
Wee'l reckon ours, as time away doth run.
Wee'l have thy Statue in some Rocke cut out,
With brave Inscriptions garnished about;
And under written, "Loe, this was the man,
Dover, that first these noble sports began."

has not been fulfilled, but on the site of the Games a National Trust plaque depicts the founder, complete with "Hat and Feather and Ruff".

Chapter 2 - FURTHER READING

Burns, Francis: *Heigh for Cotswold! A History of Robert Dover's Olimpick Games.* Robert Dover's Games Society, Chipping Campden (1981).
Drayton, Michael: *Polyolbion.* (1612).
Gissing, Algernon: *The Footpath Way in Gloucestershire.* Dent (1924).
Walbancke, Mathewe: *Annalia Dubrensia.* (1636) (See Whitfield, below).
Whitfield, Christopher: *Robert Dover and the Cotswold Games* (containing an edition of *Annalia Dubrensia*). (1962).
Whitfield, Christopher: *A History of Chipping Campden.* (1958).

[1] From *Dubris*, the Roman name for Dover.
[2] Fencing with basket-hilted wooden sticks. See front cover.

3. ALLEN, 1st EARL BATHURST, ALEXANDER POPE, AND CIRENCESTER PARK

"Teach us, Bathurst, yet unspoil'd by wealth... "

When Sir Benjamin Bathurst died in 1704, the Oakley land to the west of Cirencester passed to his son. Allen Bathurst, though, was barely able to enjoy his inheritance before the citizens of the town elected him, still a minor, as their Tory Member of Parliament. For seven years he represented them in the Commons, and seems to have involved himself in the work of the House with enthusiasm. However, in 1712 he was one of twelve Tories elevated to the peerage to persuade the House of Lords to accept the Treaty of Utrecht with Louis XIV. Two years later the death of Queen Anne and the accession of George I brought the House of Hanover to the Throne, the Whigs to power, and Bathurst the time to indulge himself as a landed gentleman (plate 5).

From his youth Bathurst had attracted a wide circle of friends, including major literary figures of the day. He was certainly an attractive man: cheerful, robust, energetic, shrewd, knowledgeable and amicable. Allen Bathurst enjoyed the 'good life' and the company of like-minded men. Alexander Pope (plate 6), Jonathan Swift, John Gay, William Congreve and William Cleland were among them, and his undoubted charm no doubt compensated for his impetuousness and his unpredictability.

Kip's engraving of 1712 (plate 7) gives some idea of the house and estate which Bathurst inherited, and on which he proceeded to spend so much time and energy. The seventeenth-century house, Oakley Grove, underwent drastic alteration; the wings were demolished to leave a plain, box-like building. "How comes it to look so oddly bad?" he asked of Alexander Pope, though perhaps he was not too concerned about the answer. Construction, or reconstruction, of country houses was certainly fashionable at that time, but in Bathurst's case the result was highly traditional, unlike the neo-Palladian mansions of his contemporaries.

To the west of the Bathurst estate, in the village of Sapperton, was the home of the historian Sir Robert Atkyns, author of 'The Ancient and Present State of Gloucestershire' (1712), which contains the Kip engraving. Following Atkyns' death, Bathurst purchased the land (Oakley Wood) between his own estate and Sapperton from Atkyns' executors, and immersed himself in the creation of a park, or rather a carefully planned and planted beech wood, with a scattering of oak, elm and other trees. Clearings in the wood were joined by 'rides', which converged on the Broad Ride (or Broad Avenue). A plan of the 'Home Park', as created by Allen Bathurst, is shown in plate 8, which is taken from Samuel Rudder's 'A New History of Gloucestershire', published in 1779 (4 years after the First Earl's death). The Broad Ride is shown about

5. Allen, 1st Earl Bathurst (portrait by Sir Godfrey Kneller, 1719).

6. Alexander Pope (portrait by Jervais, after Kneller).

a mile shorter than it is at present; it was lengthened by Henry, the Second Earl, and now extends in a direct line towards Cirencester Church Tower (not, as one might expect, towards Cirencester House). The First Earl also planted what has become the highest yew hedge in the world, to screen the House from the public gaze (Plate III).

The park was certainly of a revolutionary design. Just as he had deserted the neo-Palladian tradition in reconstructing the House, so Bathurst abandoned the formal rectangular gardens and neat hedges of European custom in designing the park. Instead, his guiding principle was Pope's "amiable simplicity of unadorned nature". Thus the long straight rides and broad vistas which he imposed on the landscape connect clearings among the trees, and winding paths through the woods follow the natural contours.

Pope's influence on the planning and design of the park was considerable. The poet made numerous visits to Cirencester, and his advice was sought and freely given. Following the first of such visits, in the summer of 1718, his letter of July 5th teases Bathurst thus:

> Woods are, not to be prolix
> Collective bodies of straight sticks;
> It is, my Lord, a mere conundrum

To call things woods, for what grows und'r 'em.
For shrubs, when nothing else at top is,
Can only constitute a coppice.

A resting-place constructed among the saplings of Oakley Wood was almost certainly Pope's idea. This 'Sylvan Bower' was an ideal spot for the poet to muse and to write, and his visits there must have been idyllic; on October 8th, 1718, he sent his friends Martha and Teresa Blount a most happy letter:

> ... I am with Lord Bathurst at my bower, in whose groves we yesterday had a dry walk of three hours. It is the place of all others that I fancy, and I am not yet out of humour with it, though I have had it some months: it does not cease to be agreeable to me so late in the season; the very dying of the leaves adds a variety of colours that is not unpleasant ... I write an hour or two every morning, then ride out ahunting on the Downs, eat heartily, talk tender sentiments with Lord B. or draw plans for houses

Cirencester the Seat of Allen Bathurst Esq:

7. *Kip's engraving of the Cirencester Estate as inherited by Allen Bathurst (1712).*

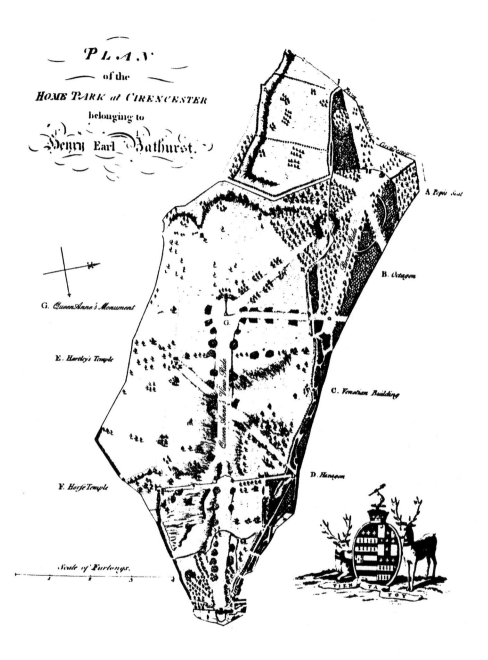

8. *Plan of the Cirencester 'Home Park' at the time of the 2nd Earl (1779).*

and gardens, open avenues, cut glades, plant firs, contrive water-works, all very fine and beautiful in our imagination. At night we play at Commerce,[1] and play pretty high: I do more, I bet too; for I am really rich, and must throw away my money if no deserving friend will use it. I like this course of life so well, that I am resolved to stay here till I hear of somebody's being in town that is worth coming after.

(Perhaps there is a hint in this last sentence of a less agreeable side to Pope's nature.)

Pope was not inexperienced in matters of landscape gardening: in 1716 he had bought a house and five acres of land at Twickenham. Horace Walpole describes how, in this garden, "Pope had twisted and twirled and rhymed and harmonised ... till appeared two or three sweet little lawns, opening and opening beyond one another, and the whole surrounded by impenetrable wood." The best known work there was the grotto, a short tunnel under the road which Pope lined with fragments of mirror and pieces of coloured rock sent by his friends from the mines of Derbyshire and Cornwall. "Complete with spars and gems", Walpole describes it, "the prototype of others of unbounded expense". If Pope tried to persuade the noble Lord to build a grotto in Oakley Wood he did not succeed, but he would have approved of the classical temples which embellished the rides. In a proud, excited letter to the Hon. Robert Digby in 1722 he offers to accompany Mrs. Digby on a visit:

> How much I wish to be her guide thro' that enchanted forest is not to be expressed: I look upon myself as the Magician appropriated to the place, without whom no moral can penetrate into the recesses of those sacred shades. I could pass whole days, in only describing to her the future, and as yet visionary beauties, that are to rise in those scenes: The palace that is to be built, the pavilions that are to glitter, the colonnades that are to adorn them; nay, more, the meeting of the Thames and Severn, which (when the noble owner has finer dreams than ordinary) are to be led into each other's embrace, thro' secret caverns of not above twelve or fifteen miles, till they rise and openly celebrate their marriage in the midst of an immense amphitheatre, which is to be the admiration of posterity a hundred years hence ...

Other minds must have been thinking of such a "marriage" even while Bathurst was alive; work on the Thames and Severn canal began in 1783, just eight years after his death, and the two and three-quarter mile Sapperton Tunnel between Daneway and Coates actually passes under Hailey wood, on Bathurst land.

In the early years of their friendship Pope teased Bathurst for "being immersed in your vast wood", and Bathurst wrote of "reports which have pierced even through Oakley Wood". He tells Pope:

> I would quit the finest walk on the finest day in the finest garden to have your company at any time. That is saying a great deal more than is commonly understood...

Pope was a diminutive figure, and never enjoyed good health. He had spinal curvature and tubercular infection. All his life he suffered headaches and general pain, and although he could ride, and loved travelling, he was forced to spend much of his time reading and writing. His friendship with Bathurst was therefore of immense value to the poet. As James Lees-Milne notes, "He found in the extrovert character, and the robust physique of the imperturbable Bathurst a refuge from the thoughts that racked his own misshapen body". There can be no doubt that he longed to be involved in the work which Bathurst was doing at Cirencester; he shows this in a letter of October 11th, 1730:

> I remember something you spoke of about buying elms at a nursery in Isleworth, which Gay told you of. Can I do anything in it?

The buildings which Bathurst erected in the park were a novel and motley collection. The Wood House, among the Oakley beeches, was begun in 1721, but for more than ten years it suffered alterations and additions. Jonathan Swift, Dean of St. Patrick's Cathedral in Dublin, lodged there and was lucky to escape with his life. Mary Pendarves (see page 27) records the incident in her letter to him from Gloucester on October 24th, 1733:

> My Lord Bathurst talked with great delight of the pleasure you once gave him by surprising him in his wood, and showed me the house where you lodged. It has been rebuilt, for the day you left, it fell to the ground; conscious of the honour it had received by entertaining so illustrious a guest, it burst with pride...

Much of the stone for the rebuilding came from Sir Robert Atkyns' old house at Sapperton which Bathurst had demolished. The resulting folly, complete with battlements, was described in Mrs. Pendarves' letter:

> My Lord Bathurst has greatly improved the wood house, which you may remember but a cottage, not a bit better than an Irish cabin. It is now a venerable castle, and has been taken by an antiquarian for one of King Arthur's, "with thicket overgrown, grotesque and wild". I endeavoured to sketch it for you, but I have not skill enough to do it justice.

Thus the building became known for a time as 'King Arthur's Castle', but was soon to be christened 'Alfred's Hall' after the Saxon king.

On the north side of what was to become the extended Broad Ride was built the Hexagon (Plate IV). Backed by trees, the three sides which are visible are open, and face down three rides. Much further to the west, Pope's Seat (Plate V) is a small stone pavilion which looks across a clearing, the Seven Rides, down an avenue to the distant Kemble church spire. Further still to the west Bathurst cleared a large area of the trees which he had planted as the site for three castellated buildings: the Square House, the Round House and the large folly Ivy Lodge. When Pope visited in 1728 he was disappointed to find that his friend was away from home, and was surprised by the work which had been done.

The four Epistles which comprise Pope's "Moral Essays" deal largely with ethical matters. Epistle III, 'Of the Use of Riches', is dedicated to Bathurst. It is in the form of a dialogue between the poet and his friend, and concerns extravagance and greed, the two forms which the 'use of riches' can take:

> To balance fortune by a just expense,
> Join with economy, magnificence;
> With splendour, charity; with plenty, health;
> Oh, teach us, Bathurst, yet unspoil'd by wealth,
> That secret rare, between th'extremes to move
> Of mad good-nature, and of mean self love.

These were dark days for Pope. His physical condition had worsened, friends had died (Congreve in 1729, Gay in 1732), and Swift was in Dublin. Pope expressed his feelings in a letter to Martha Blount on September 7th, 1733:

> You cannot think how melancholy this place makes me: every part of this wood puts me in mind of poor Mr. Gay, with whom I passed once a great deal of pleasant time in it, and another friend who is near dead, and quite lost to us, Dr. Swift. I really can find no enjoyment in the place...

If this pessimism was genuine, Pope seems quickly to have regained his enthusiasm; in July, 1734, Bathurst told Lady Suffolk:

> Pope endeavours to find faults here, but cannot; and instead of admiring (as he ought to do) what is already executed, he is every day drawing one a plan for some new building or other, and then is violently angry that it is not set up the next morning.

The following year, the noble Lord wrote to Jonathan Swift in Dublin. The Dean of St. Patrick's replied on October 21st, 1735, with a jocular reminder of Bathurst's unpredictability:

> My Lord,
>   What have I to do with a letter from Cirencester where Mr. Pope, poor John Gay and I were forced to lodge at one of your farmers and walk two miles to dinner, with your two thousand five hundred acres of garden, and not a codling to eat?

As though this complaint might be taken seriously Swift reassured him:

I am extremely obliged by your Lordship's remembrance, and I will tell you one thing that may possibly make you angry; but what care I? When I receive a letter from you, I summon a few very particular friends, who have a good taste, and invite them to it, as I would do if you had sent me a haunch of venison.

Bathurst was, at this time, in a state of some financial embarrassment; his spending on the park, and the demands of a wife and a large family, had strained his resources. Nevertheless, he continued to make plans for the park, and wrote of them to Pope in August, 1736. A lake was to be excavated, visible from the house. Its irregular shape was, like much of the estate, a rejection of the formal tradition adopted by his contemporaries. The hill beyond the lake was not to Bathurst's liking, so, nothing if not thorough, he proceeded to lower it and to level the top. This was to be the site for a memorial to Queen Anne. When Pope learned that an obelisk was proposed, he countered by suggesting:

> ...a solid pyramid of 100 ft. square, to the end there may be something solid and lasting of your works...

as if neither the buildings which Bathurst had erected, nor the park itself would survive as sufficient memorial to the noble Lord. Dismissing Pope's idea, Bathurst turned also from his own, and in 1741 raised, on a straight line from the church tower through the centre of the house to the top of the hill (the line of Queen Anne's View Ride), a Doric column on which was mounted a statue of the last Stuart sovereign (plate 9). Queen Anne's Monument could be seen, too, from Seven Rides, where Pope's Seat had been installed more than a decade earlier. The Eighth Earl Bathurst believes that the elms which had been obtained from "a nursery in Isleworth" were planted to make the splendid design of the Home Park in which, more than a decade later, Queen Anne's Monument was to be sited. The avenue leading from the House to the hill, now known as Queen Anne's View Ride and shown in Rudder's plan (plate 8), still exists, but the elms have long gone.[2]

9. Queen Anne's Monument.

Letters after this time are few; Pope's death in 1744 and Swift's in 1755 deprived Bathurst of close friends and confidants. Such evidence as exists indicates that he remained active to the end of his days, though his visits to London became less frequent. He continued to work on his park, and to ride among the groves of Oakley Wood, and would do so for another thirty years. Walpole would later describe how Bathurst's

> ...extreme longevity enabled him to enjoy, with philosophic calmness, the shade of those trees which he himself had planted half a century before.

The noble Lord would undoubtedly have been proud of his eldest surviving son; Henry Bathurst became Cirencester's Member of Parliament in 1735, and occupied the post until 1754. During these years he became, in succession, a barrister of Lincoln's Inn, a King's Counsel, solicitor-general and attorney-general, and in 1754 was appointed a judge of common pleas. All these events would have pleased his father immensely.

Bathurst senior continued the social round on his visits to London, and enjoyed the roles of host and guest as much as he had ever done. One such occasion is recorded in a letter from Laurence Sterne, the author of 'Tristram Shandy', to his daughter Eliza. He wrote:

> I got thy letter last night Eliza, on my return from Lord Bathurst's, where I dined, and here I was heard (as I talked of thee an hour without intermission) with so much pleasure and attention, that the good old Lord toasted your health three different times; and tho' he is now in his eighty-fifth year, says he hopes to live long enough to be introduced ... This nobleman is an old friend of mine. You know he was always the protector of wit and genius; and has had those of the last century, Addison, Steele, Pope, Swift, Prior, &c. &c. always at his table. The manner in which his notice began of me was as singular as it was polite. He came up to me, one day, as I was at the Prince of Wales's court. "I want you to known, Mr. Sterne... who it is that wishes this pleasure. You have heard," continued he, "of an old Lord Bathurst, of whom your Popes, and Swifts, have sung and spoken so much: I have lived my life with geniuses of that cast; but have survived them..." This nobleman, I say, is a prodigy; for at eight-five he has all the wit and promptness of a man of thirty. A disposition to be pleased, and a power to please others beyond whatever I know: added to which, a man of learning, courtesy and feeling.

On January 23rd, 1771, Henry Bathurst became Lord Chancellor, and entered the upper House as Baron Apsley (his mother's maiden name). Catherine Bathurst did not live to see her son occupy the Woolsack (she died in 1768), but the event would have brought great joy to the ageing Lord, who the following year was himself created the first Earl Bathurst by his sovereign, George III.

Bathurst died at Cirencester on September 16th, 1775, in his ninety-first year, and was buried beside Catherine in the north aisle of the parish church. On the west wall of the Trinity Chapel are their monuments, complete with busts by Joseph Nollekens. From the top of the church tower the view to the west (Plate III) is over the park which Bathurst loved so well, and which Pope did so much to fashion.

Chapter 3 - FURTHER READING

Curtis, L.P. (ed.): *The Letters of Laurence Sterne*. London (1935).
Lees-Milne, James: *Lords of Creation*. Century-Hutchinson/National Trust (1962).
Pope, Alexander: *The Works of* ... London (1876).
Pope, Alexander: *The Correspondence of* ... Vols. 1-5 (ed. Sherburn) (1956).

[1] A gambling card game.
[2] I am informed by Lord Bathurst that two American Hospitals were erected near Queen Anne's Monument during World War II, and many of the beech trees in the park were felled to make plywood for the skins of Mosquito fighter-bombers - Ed.

4. STANTON: JOHN WESLEY (1703-91)

"Dear delightful Stanton"

Over a period of some ten years John Wesley, the founder of Methodism, was a visitor to the villages of Buckland and Stanton, which lie at the foot of the scarp near Broadway. The Vale of Evesham is near, but the limestone cottages, with their mullioned windows and steep roofs, gabled and tiled, are as 'Cotswold' as any in the hills to the east. In the company of lively, cultured young people, Wesley found here friendship, relaxation and a willingness to discuss at length matters both spiritual and temporal; for at least one of the young ladies Wesley may well have entertained hopes of a deeper, permanent relationship.

John Wesley was born at Epworth, Lincolnshire on June 17th 1703, the son of Samuel Wesley, the Rector of Epworth, and his wife Susanna. At eleven years of age he went to Charterhouse School, and in 1720 to Oxford University. Here he lived an impoverished but industrious life as an undergraduate of Christ Church. After taking his bachelor of arts degree in 1724, Wesley remained at Oxford to take his M.A. and to plan his future, though it had long been taken for granted (by his parents at least) that he would be ordained into the Church. John was not averse to the idea, and he was ordained a deacon by the Bishop of Oxford on 19th September 1725. Samuel Wesley was keen that his son should now assist him as a curate; John, though, preferred to remain at Oxford in the hope of obtaining a college fellowship. This would end his days of penury, as it would provide him with free board and lodging and a small stipend, as well as giving him time to pursue his studies of Latin, Greek and modern literature. The opportunity came in 1725, when a fellowship became available at Lincoln College. John Wesley was elected a Fellow of Lincoln in March 1726.

He was introduced to the Cotswolds by a group of undergraduate friends. Robin Griffiths, son of the vicar of Broadway, was at New College. Edward Winnington of Trinity hailed from Broadway, and Harry Yardley, also of Trinity, from Notgrove. When Robert Kirkham came up to Merton in 1729 the Kirkhams were already good friends of Wesley.

The Rev. Lionel Kirkham, Rector of Stanton, had five surviving children: Robert, Bernard, Sarah (Sally), Elizabeth (Betty) and Damaris, all near Wesley's age. This was, by all accounts, a lively, friendly, articulate family, as ready to dance, play games or have a picnic as to engage in serious conversation about topics both religious and secular.

Close friends of the Kirkhams were the Granvilles from nearby Buckland. Colonel Bernard Granville retired from public life when the family moved to a house at Buckland called The Farm. His daughters Mary and Anne soon made friends with the

Rector, the Rev. Trethewey Tooker, the Rector's daughter Fanny, and inevitably with the Kirkhams across the fields in Stanton. In later years Mary Granville recalled her friendship with Sally Kirkham:

> She had an uncommon genius and intrepid spirit, which though really innocent, alarmed my father, and made him uneasy at my great attachment to her. He loved gentleness and reserve in the behaviour of women, and could not bear anything that had the appearance of being too free and masculine; but as I was convinced of her innocence, I saw no fault in Miss Kirkham. She entertained me with her wit, and she flattered me with her approbation, but by the improvements she has since made, I see she was not, at my first acquaintance, the perfect creature I thought her then. We wrote to one another every day, and met in the fields between our fathers' houses as often as we had an opportunity, thought that day tedious that we did not meet, and had many stolen interviews.
>
> Her extraordinary understanding, lively imagination and humane disposition, which soon became conspicuous, at last reconciled my father to her, and he never after debarred me the pleasure of seeing her, when it was convenient we should meet. My sister was at this time a plaything to us, and often offended at our whispers and mysterious talk.

Mary recalled her home at Buckland in fond terms:

> ...The Farm is a low house, with very good, convenient room in it, the outside entirely covered with laurel, the inside neat, furnished with fine china and prints. The front of the house faces the finest vale in England, the Vale of Evesham, of which there is a very advantageous view from every window: the back of the house is shaded by a very high hill which rises gradually; between lies the garden, a small spot of ground, but well stocked with fruit and flowers. Nothing could be more fragrant and rural...

Mary Granville, at the age of seventeen, was persuaded into marriage with a Cornish squire named Pendarves, who was fat, uncouth and more than forty years her senior. The couple lived in Cornwall and later in London. When, to Mary's relief, her husband died in 1724, Mary continued in the capital. Her mother and sister had moved to Gloucester on the death of Bernard Granville in 1723, and Mary visited them there. She maintained her friendship with the Kirkhams, and was a welcome visitor to Stanton when she came down from London.

It was the fashion at that time for friends to refer to each other by nicknames[1]. Thus, Mary became 'Aspasia', her sister Anne 'Selima', and John Wesley 'Cyrus'. His brother

Charles, who was an occasional visitor, was 'Araspes'. Several authors have believed 'Varanese' to have been Betty Kirkham. This is not correct. Betty died in 1733, but Charles Wesley's journal records that he met 'Varanese' in 1737, when he visited Stanton. This lady was certainly Sally Kirkham. The point is not trivial, as letters suggest that 'Varanese' for a time occupied a special place in John Wesley's affections. He was, after all, in his early twenties, and in affairs of the heart would have been as vulnerable as the next in spite of his puritanical background. Thus on April 14th 1725 he recorded in his diary "First saw Varanese. May it not be in vain!". He would have been more than a little sad when Sally married the local schoolmaster John Chapone in Stanton church that December. "May God give her the happiness she deserves" he wrote in his diary.

Wesley and Sally remained affectionate, though she reassured the newly-ordained clergyman:

> ... I would certainly tell you if my husband should ever resent our freedom, which I am satisfied he never will; such an accident as this would make it necessary in some measure to restrain the appearance of the esteem I have for you, but the esteem as it is founded on reason and virtue and entirely agreeable to us both, no circumstance will ever make me alter.

John Wesley may well, by his own lights, have loved Sally Kirkham, but he had not the maturity to cope emotionally with a permanent commitment of this kind; his religious upbringing brought little but guilt at such thoughts, and even as he saw her slipping away from him his diary recorded his confession of "lying, distraction, sin in thought".

Wesley stayed at Broadway in October 1726, and spent a few days with his friends, hunting on the hills with Edward Winnington or Robin Griffiths or visiting Sally, Betty, Damaris and the others at Stanton Rectory (plate 10). A favourite walk was on the hill called Horrell, to the south of Stanton, from where a good view of the village could be obtained; Wesley was to refer to it fondly in his later correspondence. He spent Christmas and the New Year, 1726-27, at Stanton with the Kirkhams (another guest was Mary Pendarves) and the gathering amused themselves in the usual ways. There seems little doubt that Sally was not the only lady to have found Wesley an attractive figure; Robert Kirkham wrote to him on February 2nd, 1727:

> With familiarity I write, dear Jack... You have often been in the thoughts of M.B. (Miss Betty) which I have curiously observed, when with her alone, by inward smiles and signs and abrupt expressions concerning you. Shall this suffice? I caught her this morning in a humble and devout posture on her knees... I must conclude, and subscribe myself, your most affectionate friend, and brother, I might wish to write,

> Robert Kirkham

10. Stanton Rectory (from an old print).

Betty's feelings, and Robert's fraternal wishes, would have arisen at least in part from sympathy; three weeks earlier, Wesley had preached at the funeral of his friend Robin Griffiths, who had died of consumption on January 10th. The happiness shared in the festive season had turned to melancholy, and Wesley went back to Lincoln College in a state of depression from which only his religious faith could lift him.

There can be no doubt that in matters of genuine love for a woman John Wesley was a soul tormented, and it is likely that he could not allow his feelings to carry him further than the "love" of one Christian soul for another, or the deep affection, devoid of romantic meaning, of two close friends. This may explain why his eventual marriage at the age of 48 to the widow Molly Vazeille was not a success.

On February 7th 1727 Wesley was being examined for his master's degree, which he duly obtained. Much of his time now was spent away from Oxford, mostly in Lincolnshire, where his father, still the Rector of Epworth, had in that year made John his curate at the neighbouring village of Wroot. Visits to Oxford and the Cotswolds were less frequent now, though he returned to Oxford for his ordination to the priesthood in 1728.

In the summer of 1729 Wesley visited the Kirkhams and spent his days in the usual ways. That autumn he was recalled to his statutory duties at Lincoln College, and Robert Kirkham became an undergraduate at Merton College. Wesley's own record shows that

In November, 1729, four young gentlemen of Oxford, Mr. John Wesley, Fellow of Lincoln College; Mr. Charles Wesley, Student[2] of Christ Church; Mr. Morgan, Commoner of Christ Church; and Mr. Kirkham of Merton College; began to spend some evenings in a week together, in reading chiefly the Greek Testament.

Though there does not seem to have been a formal structure to these meetings, the group, and their associates, were known as the 'Holy Club', and became known as 'methodists' from their methodical studies of the scriptures. As their numbers grew John's role may well have become of increasing importance. Thus were the foundations of Methodism laid.

Even for such a pious group, though, university life had its distractions; both Charles Wesley and Robert Kirkham had to discipline themselves (no doubt with John's encouragement) to work. Thus John Wesley wrote to his mother on February 28th, 1730:

...I have another piece of news to acquaint you with, which, as it is more strange, will, I hope, be equally agreeable. A little while ago Bob Kirkham took a fancy into his head that he would lose no more time and waste no more money; in pursuance of which he first resolved to breakfast no longer on tea, next to drink no more ale in an evening, or however but enough to quench his thirst, then to read Greek or Latin from prayers in the morning till noon and from dinner till five at night. And how much may one imagine he executed of these resolutions? Why, he has left off tea, struck off his drinking acquaintances to a man, given the hours above specified to Greek Testament and Hugo Grotius[3], and spent the evenings either by himself or with my brother and me.

Wesley was back in the Cotswolds in the summer of 1730, and the presence of Mary Pendarves (Aspasia) and her sister Anne (Selima) made his visit a particularly happy one. "I often pour out my heart by myself, when it is full of Selima and Aspasia and Varanese", he confessed. "Thus I endeavour to steal into their protection...".

Mary Pendarves heard Wesley preach in Stanton church (plate 11), and asked him for a copy of the sermon. On her return with Anne to her mother's home at Gloucester she wrote to him on August 28th, 1730:

Sir - I think myself extremely obliged to you for the favour of the sermon, and those letters that alone were worthy of the correspondence they maintained. I received them safe last week, and should sooner have made my acknowledgements for them but that I have been engaged with so much company since my return from dear, delightful Stanton, that till this moment I have not had time to express my gratitude for the elegant entertainment I have had, not only from the manuscripts, but in recollecting and repeating the conversation you and your brother made so agreeable, which I hope will soon be renewed...

On September 12th Wesley replied in affectionate terms which recalled the brothers' visit to the Cotswolds:

> Madam - I am greatly ashamed that I can only think how much I am obliged to you. Your last favour leaves me utterly at a loss, and even without hope of making any suitable acknowledgement at the same time that it convinces me of a mistake which I should not otherwise have so easily given up: it convinces me it was possible I should enjoy a higher pleasure than even your conversation gave me. If your understanding could not appear in a stronger light than when it brightened the dear hill, the fields, the arbour, I am now forced to confess your temper could: you even then showed but half your goodness...

ST MICHAEL'S CHURCH, STANTON

11. Stanton Church (from an old print).

In November that year Mary Pendarves and her sister travelled by coach from Gloucester to London, and stayed overnight at Oxford. John and Charles rode to Burford to meet the coach, and accompanied it to Oxford. In her letter to him of November 19th, Mary referred to:

> ...The pleasure you and your brother gave us of your conversation at Burford, the entertainment we had upon the road to Oxford, which neither the dirty way nor rattling wheels could entirely deprive us of...

Between Wesley and Mary, then, there was mutual admiration to the point of genuine affection, but there could never have been anything more; the devout clergyman knew little of the glittering social round of operas, balls, dinners and attendances at court which was so much a part of Mary's life in London, and could not have shared it. This beautiful, talented and much-admired lady (whom Edmund Burke declared to Fanny Burney was "the model of a perfect fine woman" (plate 12), and of whom Dean Swift wrote "a most lovely face of great sweetness") may have found in Wesley a respite from the heady and affected society which claimed much of her attention. She was at heart religious, and Wesley could advise her on matters of morality and Christian belief as they wandered on Horrell or sat in the rectory garden.

1730 was probably the last year in which the two were to meet, but Wesley recalled their conversations when he wrote to Mary (Aspasia) in June 1731:

> If Providence has used me as an instrument of doing any good to Aspasia, I had almost said 'I have my reward.' Some part of it I have, undoubtedly. The thought of having added anything to your ease will make many of my hours the happier. Yet, perhaps, I ought not to desire that you should be easy at the common conversation of the world; which, if once it comes to be indifferent to us, will scarce be long before it be agreeable...

and in July Aspasia confessed to Wesley (Cyrus):

> ...How ardently do I wish to be as resigned and humble as Cyrus! ...As you say, my lot is fallen among those who cannot be accused of too much strictness in religion. So far from that, that they generally make an open confession of having no religion at all. I can't observe my fellow creatures in such manifest danger, without feeling an inexpressible concern. But God in His good time may make them sensible of their blindness... I cannot always submit to this sort of life. It encroaches too much.

Wesley's visits to Stanton in 1731 lacked only the company of Aspasia, who was preparing to visit Dublin. On June 17th he wrote to Anne Granville (Selima):

> ...We had so much pleasure in the late hours we spent at Stanton that nothing could have added to it but Selima or Aspasia. All things else conspired to complete our happiness...

Mary Pendarves sailed for Ireland in September. There she met Jonathan Swift and the popular preacher and tutor of Trinity College, Patrick Delany, and at once involved herself in Dublin high society. So little time did she find for letter writing that her sister Anne in Gloucester seems to have been the only recipient. Although Mary asked Anne to give Wesley her address in Dublin, she did not reply to his letters, for which lapse she confessed her guilt to Anne in March 1732:

12. Mary Pendarves, formerly Mary Granville ('Aspasia'), as a young widow; subsequently Mrs. Delany. (Artist unknown).

Cyrus by this time has blotted me out of his memory, or if he does remember me, it can only be to reproach me; what can I say for myself?... I only am the sufferer, but I should be very sorry to have him think my silence proceeded from negligence; I declare 'tis want of time.

In the years 1732-34 Wesley was in the Cotswolds on several occasions, visiting the Griffiths family at Broadway and the Kirkhams at Stanton, being attracted by the company sufficiently to make the forty-mile journey across the windswept hills from Oxford even in the depths of winter. In the spring of 1733 Betty Kirkham (Mrs. Wilson) died. Wesley would have mourned the loss of a friend, but it is significant that his diary does not record Betty's passing.

He continued to visit other members of the Kirkham family, Damaris, Bernard and Sally (Mrs. Chapone), though the latter now had a large family to compete for her attention. Damaris, too, was soon to be married, and it will have been evident to Wesley that his visits to Stanton were drawing to a close.

Mary Pendarves returned to England in April 1733, and commenced a correspondence with Jonathan Swift and more particularly with Patrick Delany. (Ten years later he would come to England and make her his wife.) It was July 1734 before she set pen to paper to seek Wesley's forgiveness for her long silence:

I never began a letter with so much confusion to anybody as I do this to Cyrus... I am so sincerely sorry for the ill impression I have given you of myself that I shall shun you as a criminal would a judge.

Wesley's reply lacked the affection which once he had expressed at every opportunity; the flame was quite extinguished:

You do me no injury by your silence. It did, indeed, deprive me of much pleasure, and of a pleasure from which I received much improvement. But still, as it was one I had no title to but your goodness, to withdraw it was no injustice. I sincerely thank you for what is past... Adieu!

John Wesley would never again visit 'dear, delightful Stanton' nor tread the 'smooth turf' of Horrell. At Oxford, membership of the Holy Club[4] had grown, and Wesley was more involved in it than ever. Even so, his missionary zeal was soon, in 1735, to take the brothers to the newly-founded colony of Georgia in America. For several reasons the visit was not successful; Charles returned to England in December 1736 and John in February 1738. For the next fifty years the latter would travel the British Isles, preaching and founding Methodist societies where he could. (The portrait of him in plate 13 is dated 1742.)

The Wesley's Cotswold friends make a final appearance in Charles's journal in 1737. He visited Oxford that February, and met Robert Kirkham and his brother

Bernard, who was now an undergraduate of Corpus Christi College. On March 17th Charles visited Mary Pendarves at her house in Little Brook Street, London, where he met Anne Granville and her brother. The latter "pressed me to bear him company to Mickleton". They set out on March 22nd, together with Anne and her future husband John Dewes, stayed the night at Oxford and reached Mickleton the following evening, where "we passed the time agreeably enough in walking, conversing and reading." On March 30th he "rode over to Stanton, where they were all overjoyed to see me; especially my first of friends, Varanese."

When Charles Wesley left Mickleton for Oxford in April 1737 the last contact with the Cotswolds was broken. Robert Kirkham succeeded his father as rector of Stanton, but the precise date is unclear. He continued in this post until his death in 1767. Sally (Mrs. Chapone) busied herself with her large family and her schoolmaster husband, and played host occasionally to

13. John Wesley (portrait by John Williams, 1742).

her friend Anne Granville (Mrs. Dewes). Mary Pendarves became Mrs. Delany in 1743; as a friend of the Duchess of Portland and, later, a favourite of George III, she remained a significant figure in London society until her death in 1788.

In 1783 Mary Delany recalled her days at Stanton half a century earlier:

> Ah yes! She had known the Mr. Wesleys - the Methodist preachers; she knew them when they were young men... These brothers joined some other young men at Oxford, and used to meet of a Sunday evening and read the Scriptures, and find out objects of charity to relieve. That was a happy beginning, but the vanity of being singular and growing enthusiasts made them endeavour to gain proselytes and adopt that system of religious doctrine which many reasonable folk thought pernicious. Well, well! Perhaps they did some good to the common people...

Perhaps, too, the days when John Wesley journeyed to Stanton and visited "the dear hill, the fields, the arbour" with his Cotswold friends were a fonder memory for Cyrus than they were for Aspasia.

Chapter 4 - FURTHER READING

Green, V.H.H.: *The Young Mr. Wesley*. Edward Arnold (1961).
Johnson, R. Brimley: *Mrs. Delany at Court and Among the Wits*. Stanley Paul (1925).
Marshall, Dorothy: *John Wesley*. Oxford University Press (1965).
Vulliamy, C.E.: *John Wesley*. Epworth Press (1954).
Vulliamy, C.E.: *Aspasia: The Life and Letters of Mary Granville*. Geoffrey Bles (1935).

[1] It may help the reader to make a 'cast list' of these nicknames. - Ed.

[2] A Student of Christ Church is a junior Fellow; a Commoner is an undergraduate.

[3] Hugo Grotius (1583-1645): Dutch jurist, scholar, and theologian.

[4] Name given to a group of friends of John and Charles Wesley at Oxford who laid the foundations of Methodism. See the book by V.H.H. Green under 'Further Reading'.

5. DAYLESFORD: WARREN HASTINGS (1732-1818)

"A child's dream... never faded away."

The village of Churchill in the Evenlode valley has two claims to fame: it was the birthplace of William Smith (1760-1839), the 'father of British geology', commemorated by a monolith of local stone, and not far away, a house (Plate VI) bears a simple plaque recording the birth there in 1732 of Warren Hastings, the first and perhaps the greatest of the British Governors-General of India. When he died eighty-six years later Hastings was laid to rest in the churchyard of Daylesford, just over two miles to the north-west.

When Warren Hastings' great-grandfather, Penyston Hastings, died, the house and surrounding land at Daylesford passed to his son Samuel Hastings, Warren's great-uncle. Being in a state of penury Samuel sold the estate in 1715 to a merchant, Jacob Knight, who quickly demolished the decaying building. Penyston's second son (also named Penyston) had become rector of Daylesford in 1701, but moved to Churchill because, it was said, of differences with Knight over the payment of tithes, though he continued as Daylesford's rector until his death in 1752. He married and had three sons, Howard, who became a respected Customs officer, Samuel, who died without issue, and Penyston the third, of whom little can be said that is good. This Penyston married Hester Warren of Twyning near Tewkesbury in 1730, and in that year was inducted as vicar of Bledington, just across the Evenlode stream from Churchill. A daughter, Anne, arrived the following year, and on December 6th 1732 Warren Hastings was born in his grandfather's cottage in Churchill. Nine days later his mother died, and was buried at Daylesford. Not many months later Warren's father remarried and emigrated to Barbados, leaving the boy in the care of his grandfather at Churchill.

These, then, were the humble origins of this major figure of British Imperial history. He learned from his grandfather how the Daylesford lands were lost, and in later years Warren Hastings recalled to a friend the stirring of ambition:

> To lie beside the margin of that stream and muse was one of my favourite recreations; and there, one bright summer's day, when I was scarcely seven years old, I well remember that I first formed the determination to purchase back Daylesford. I was then literally dependent on those whose condition scarcely raised them above the pressure of absolute want; yet somehow or another the child's dream, as it did not appear unreasonable at the time, so in after years never faded away.

Thus was the resolution made. One day the dream would come true, though,

God knows there were periods in my career when to accomplish that, or any other object of honourable ambition, seemed to be impossible, but I have lived to accomplish it. And though, perhaps, few public men have had more right than I to complain of the world's usage, I can never express sufficient gratitude to the kind Providence which permits me to pass the evening of a long and I trust not a useless life, amid scenes that are endeared to me by so many personal as well as traditional associations.

Macaulay's oft-quoted version of the tale has the stream beside which the boy lay as flowing "through the old domain of his house". This is incorrect. G.W. Hastings points out that there is no such stream at Daylesford, and in any case the boy was then living at Churchill though probably he was driven on Sundays to his grandfather's church. The stream was probably the brook by Churchill Mill. (G.W. Hastings charges Macaulay with "infecting his Essay throughout with wide inaccuracy", and it certainly seems to be a most unreliable biographical source).

When Warren was eight years of age Howard Hastings decided to arrange the boy's education, and he was transferred from the charity school at Churchill to Newington Butts, and in 1743 to Westminster School. There seems little doubt that Howard was rich enough to be able to offer his nephew a comfortable life, at least in the holidays, and in old age Warren Hastings acknowledged that his uncle gave him "every care which good principle, unimpelled by natural affection, could dictate". Hastings made good progress at Westminster, and in 1747 headed the list of scholars. He excelled at sports, too, and it was under much protest from the headmaster, Dr. Nicholls, that he was removed in 1749. Howard had died and left Warren forty pounds a year in his will, placing the young man in the care of the Hon. Henry Vane (later to be Lord Darlington). Vane, though, whom Horace Walpole described as "a toad-eater and spy to all parties", wanted none of the responsibility which Howard had left him, and the guardianship transferred to another executor Joseph Creswicke. Creswicke proceeded to obtain for the young man a post as writer in the East India Company, and on January 22nd 1750 Warren Hastings sailed from Gravesend, bound for Bengal.

The staff of the East India Company with whom Hastings found himself working was composed largely of young English merchants devoted to the pursuit of profit both for the Company and (quite legitimately) for themselves. Disputes with the local Bengali administration were frequent, and Hastings could not but become embroiled in these affairs - to the extent, even, of a single brief period of imprisonment. Accounts of the time suggest that he had no liking for the ruthless methods by which his fellow Englishmen achieved their purposes. In a Memorandum of 1765 he was to complain of "a fierceness in the European manners, especially among the lower sort, which is incompatible with the gentle temper of the Bengalee."

Two years after Warren Hastings sailed for India the same journey was undertaken by a certain Philadelphia Austen. (Her brother, the Rev. George Austen, rector of Steventon in Hampshire, was to be the father of Jane Austen). It is likely that Philadelphia was sent to India for the sole purpose of finding a husband. Family conditions at home were such that she lacked a dowry, which made a marriage in England unlikely. On the other hand, the arrival of a personable young spinster among the many young Englishmen trapped by economic necessity in the Indian sub-continent made marriage there a virtual certainty. Thus it was that six months after setting foot in India Philadelphia Austen, aged 22, married a surgeon, Tysoe Saul Hancock, who was twenty years her senior.

Although Hancock's financial resources were limited, he was a loving and generous husband, but in the earlier years of her marriage Philadelphia's life cannot have been happy. For one reason or another she remained childless for eight years, and with no family, no work and no close friends of her own age she cannot have led a settled life among the quarrelling factions which comprised the Madras population.

In 1756 Warren Hastings married Mary Buchanan, widow of a Captain Buchanan who had died in the Black Hole of Calcutta. A son, George, was born in 1757. In the following year a daughter, Elizabeth, was born, but she lived for no more than two months; Mary died the year after. Hastings was now a widower with a three year old son to care for. It was at about this time that he met Tysoe and Philadelphia Hancock, who had been asked by General Clive to move to Bengal. Tysoe Hancock and Hastings became close friends and trading partners and Philadelphia's companionship, too, was very welcome. Hastings was about her age, and following the recent loss of both his wife and his daughter, he found consolation in her friendship.

Philadelphia gave birth to a daughter in 1761. Perhaps it is significant that she was named Elizabeth, as had been Hastings' own daughter. A hint of scandal was inevitable, but in 1765 General Clive, writing to his wife, was forthright: "It is beyond a doubt that (Philadelphia) abandoned herself to Mr Hastings". Tysoe Hancock ignored such whispers, if indeed he ever heard them. Hastings became godfather to the child, and would remain attached to her and give financial support for the rest of her life.

In the year that Elizabeth Hancock was born Hastings' own son George was sent home into the care of Philadelphia's brother, the Rev. George Austen, at Steventon in Hampshire. (Perhaps Philadelphia recommended him, though he was still a bachelor). Three years later the child died of "putrid sore throat", which was probably diphtheria. Hastings heard the news when he came home in 1765; it was to affect him for many years. The Hancocks returned too, but the journey, which cost £1500, left Tysoe's resources so reduced that after three years in England he was forced to obtain further employment in Bengal, and indeed to borrow the money for his fare from Hastings. When this venture of Hancock's was unsuccessful Hastings generously gave £10,000 in trust for Tysoe, Philadelphia, and, after their days, Elizabeth ('Betsy', as she was known). Tysoe Hancock did not see his wife again; having achieved little by returning to India he died in Calcutta in November 1775.

In 1769 Warren Hastings returned to India as second-in-command of the ruling council in Madras. Philadelphia and Betsy remained at the Steventon vicarage; when Philadelphia suggested that Betsy go to India, Tysoe reminded his wife of her own experiences:

You know very well that no girl, tho' but fourteen years old, can arrive in India without attracting the notice of every coxcomb in the place; you yourself know how impossible it is for a young girl to avoid being attached to a handsome man whose address is agreeable to her.

On the journey to India aboard the 'Duke of Grafton' Hastings met the Baron and Baroness von Imhoff. The Baron had been an army officer in Germany, and was proceeding to Madras to seek similar employment there. A friendship sprang up between Hastings and the Baroness, and when Hastings became ill in Madras, it was Anna Maria, Baroness von Imhoff, who nursed him back to health. (Hastings called her 'Marian'). In 1770 the Baron moved to Calcutta, leaving Marian in Madras.

Marian joined her husband in October 1771; at the end of that year Hastings was appointed governor of Fort William in Bengal, and in 1772 he too went to Calcutta. He had not forgotten Philadelphia, though; he wrote to her before he sailed from Madras:

Kiss my dear Bessy for me, and assure her of my tenderest affection. May the God of goodness bless you both! ...adieu, my dear and every-valued friend. Remember me, and make my Bessy remember and love her godfather and her mother's sincere and faithful friend.

In April 1772 Tysoe Hancock wrote to his wife. He told her of the affair between Hastings and Marian:

She is about twenty six years old, has a good person and has been very pretty, is sensible, lively and wants only to be a greater mistress of the English language, to prove she has a great share of wit. ...I should not have mentioned Mrs Imhoff but I knew everything relative to Mr Hastings is greatly interesting to you.

Was there, perhaps, a little sarcasm here?

At the time of Hastings' appointment the East India Company was in financial difficulty, and engaged in major revisions of its methods of revenue collection. Hastings undertook to reform the administrative and judicial systems, and in the face of much opposition he pushed ahead with these changes, though, he wrote, the effect was of "arming my hand against every man, and every man's, of course, against me". To another correspondent he bared his soul: "My whole time, and all my thoughts, I may add all my passions, are devoted to the service of the company". This cannot have been entirely true; his friendship with Baroness von Imhoff was intimate, to the point that in 1773 the Baron went to Germany to start divorce proceedings.

Hastings was now spending (and giving away) large sums of money. A new house was built for himself (and Marian?), complete with marble staircase. Goods were obtained from China, and from London he was ordering a substantial number of books on India, law, poetry, plays and history. To pay for all of these he had built up a lucrative private trade in opium and jewels, to supplement his income from the Company. In the midst of all these activities Hastings had not forgotten his life's ambition: in a letter to England he gave an instruction to buy any land "near Daylesford or along the Sarsbrooke".

In 1774 Hastings would have been pleased to receive three letters from the eminent Dr. Samuel Johnson, whom he had visited many years before. The first, and longest, letter, dated March 30th, was, at Johnson's admission, for no purpose other than recalling himself to Hastings.

> Sir,
>
> Though I have had but little personal knowledge of you, I have had enough to make me wish for more; and though it be now a long time since I was honoured by your visit, I had too much pleasure from it to forget it. By those whom we delight to remember, we are unwilling to be forgotten; and therefore I cannot omit this opportunity of reviving myself in your memory by a letter... That this is my only reason for writing will be too apparent by the uselessness of my letter to any other purpose... I can only wish for information; and hope that a mind like yours will find leisure, amidst the cares of your important station, to enquire into many subjects of which the European world either thinks not at all, or thinks with deficient intelligence and uncertain conjecture...

The remaining letters seek Hastings' favour for young men of Dr. Johnson's acquaintance. (The second letter accompanies a present of Johnson's "Journey to the Western Islands of Scotland").

It was not until 1777 that news reached Calcutta that Imhoff had obtained his divorce, and on August 8th that year Hastings and Marian were married. The marriage was a happy one and would last more than forty years.

In 1773 a new Regulating Act replaced the ruling council in Calcutta with a new council of four members, three of whom were to be sent out from England. Hastings was made governor-general of Bengal, with a large salary but only a casting vote in council. The councillors from England were not Hastings' friends, and made repeated attempts to prove bribery and corruption against him. Hastings fought off their attacks through lack of evidence, but the struggle left him embittered and defensive for the rest of his time in India. Without Marian's support he might have succumbed.

The East India Company had given Hastings explicit authority to review the legal and administrative systems of Bengal. "We now arm you" he was told "with full powers to make a complete reformation", and in 1777 he announced to Alexander Elliott his intention

> to make the British nation paramount in India, and to accept the allegiances of such of our neighbours as shall sue to be enlisted among the friends and allies of the king of Great Britain.

He told Elliott:

> On my arrival in Bengal I found this Government in possession of a great and rich dominion, and a wide political system which has since been greatly extended, without one rule of government, but what descended to it from its ancient commercial institutions, or any principle of policy but such as accident or the desultory judgement of those in actual power recommended. It was necessary to restore the authority of Government to the source from which its powers originated; to assume the direct control, instead of allowing it to act by a concealed and weakened influence; to constitute a uniform and effectual mode for the management and collection of the public revenue; to establish regular courts for the administration of civil and criminal justice; to give strength and utility to its political connexions, and to transfer a share of its wealth to Great Britain, without exhausting its circulation. This, aided by the abilities and superior knowledge of my associates in the Government, I attempted, because it was essentially necessary in itself; because it was my particular province, and because I was expressly enjoined to do it: and if I may judge by the present state of Bengal, notwithstanding the distractions which have prevailed in it for more than two years past, the measures which were adopted for these ends were as effectual as the means with which we were supplied could enable us to make them...

In all Hastings' dealings, then, the interests of the Company were paramount, but in his relations with Indian rulers and merchants his even-handed approach did, perhaps, invite the accusations which he was obliged to answer.

These were years of crisis for Hastings. Forces in many parts of India, supported by contingents of the French army, were forming alliances for the sole purpose of driving the British not only out of India, but out of the whole of Asia. British forces were ill-equipped to put down insurrection in the provinces, and Hastings was forced to divert limited resources and men to deal with the conflict. It was largely through his actions that a treaty was eventually concluded in 1783, which affirmed British supremacy in India and thus safeguarded the Company's interests in the sub-continent. These actions were not, however, above reproach from the Company directors. Philip Francis in particular was bitterly opposed to what the governor-general was doing. Matters came to a head when the two fought a duel. Francis was wounded, and returned to England planning his revenge.

Hastings was by now becoming increasingly despondent about what he could achieve as governor-general, though when Marian returned to England in 1783 he remained to welcome the Bengal army on its return from Madras, and to complete various matters of administration. As if by way of a legacy to his adopted country he helped to found the Asiatic Society of Bengal, and gave generous support for the furtherance of studies in Indian law and culture.

At the end of 1784 Hastings relinquished his office, and in February 1785 he finally embarked for England, setting foot on his native soil on 13th June.

Marian had not been idle during their separation. Amid the social round of dinners, dances, visits to Court and jaunts to fashionable spa towns she had found time to give instructions for the purchase of several acres of land around Daylesford. Soon after she and Hastings were reunited they went to Cheltenham to spend the summer and to take the waters. Hastings was active now in his pursuit of the Daylesford estate. He sought out the Rev. Thomas Knight of Castlemorton, Worcestershire, a grandson of the Jacob Knight to whom it had been sold by Hastings' great-uncle and tried unsuccessfully to persuade him to sell the Daylesford property. He went to Daylesford, walked by the Evenlode and rode on the estate (lodging at Adlestrop with the Rev. Thomas Leigh, a distant relative of the Austens). In London he and Marian took a house, dined in high society and saw the latest plays. They were seen at Tunbridge Wells and Bath, and Hastings went to Cirencester and rode in the second Earl Bathurst's great park. He was, in fact, living above his means; perhaps he was compensating for his failure to win Daylesford.

Immersed as he was in these activities, Hastings was becoming aware, too, that political forces were beginning to range against him. He knew little of English politics; after all, most of his career had been spent on the other side of the world. The activities of the East India Company, though, had become the subject of bitter debate between Whigs and Tories. His former enemy in the Calcutta Council, Philip Francis, had enlisted the aid of the Whig M.P.s Edmund Burke and Charles Fox, to whom Francis reported widespread oppression and corruption among the Company's employees. In 1783 Fox introduced his India Bill, which would have placed control of the Company firmly in England, where its employees would have been answerable to Parliament. The coalition government led by Fox and Lord North collapsed when Fox's Bill failed in 1783, and the Whigs found themselves facing a Tory government led by William Pitt ("Pitt the Younger"). In his attacks on the East India Company Burke turned his fury on Hastings. The latter found little support from Pitt's government; the public mood was generally to regard with disfavour newly-returned Company employees, and although Hastings was at present meeting with some acclaim, this could easily change, in which case the position of Hastings' supporters, too, would be compromised. Moreover, Pitt was jealous of Hastings' friendship with the Royal Family and the esteem with which he was held at Court. The man whom Hastings had assumed to be his friend was in the event easily persuaded to take sides against him.

For three years the accusations of corruption were dragged before the House, during which time Hastings and Marian moved to Windsor. There, Hastings busied himself with farming and gardening and with preparing his defence against the charges of Burke and Fox. On April 3rd 1787 the House voted for Hastings' impeachment by a majority of nearly three to one, and the trial before the House of Lords opened on February 13th 1788.

The scene was more like a pageant than a criminal trial. Westminster Hall was decked out for a public entertainment, though very few without reserved seats were able to get in. Queen Charlotte and the Princesses arrived for the start, together with the Prince of Wales and the Dukes of York, Cumberland and Gloucester. The novelists Fanny Burney (Madam d'Arblay) and Richard Brinsley Sheridan were there too, the latter in his role as an M.P. (During the trial he would vigorously support the attacks on Hastings). The gallery was filled by some two hundred Members of the House of Commons.

Hastings showed signs of strain. Fanny Burney described him as "pale, ill and altered". When his diminutive figure came to the Bar, the proclamation was read:

> Whereas charges of high crimes and misdemeanours have been exhibited by the knights, citizens and burgesses of Parliament assembled, in the name of themselves and of all the Commons of Great Britain, against Warren Hastings Esq., all persons concerned are to take notice that he now stands on his trial, and they may come forth in order to make good the said charges.

Hastings' answer was brief. "My Lords, I am come to this high tribunal, equally impressed with a confidence in my own integrity, and in the justice of the court before which I stand".

Burke's attack was vituperative.

> The crimes we charge are not the causes and effects of common human frailty, such as we know, and feel, and can allow for, but they are crimes which have their rise in avarice, rapacity, pride, cruelty, ferocity, malignity of temper, haughtiness, insolence - in short everything that manifests a heart blackened to the very blackest - a heart dyed deep in blackness - a heart gangrened to the core... a captain-general of iniquity, thief, tyrant, robber, cheat, swindler, sharper. We call him all these names, and are sorry that the English language does not afford terms adequate to the enormity of the offence...

He charged Hastings with having

> ...wasted the country, destroyed the landed interest, cruelly harassed the peasants, burned their houses, seized their crops, tortured and degraded their persons, and destroyed the honour of the whole female race of that country.

As Sir Nathaniel Wraxall noted in his Memoirs, (16th March 1787),

> Burke, while conducting the prosecution against Hastings, enjoyed the singular advantage of being surrounded by a constellation of extraordinary men, whose talents were devoted to his purposes, passions and prejudices. He had only to select his instrument, while he superintended the execution...

It was fortunate for all parties, such was the intensity of feeling, that the Court sat for only a few weeks each year; Hastings and Marian were able to get away to the country for much-needed respite. On August 26th 1788 Hastings signed the deed which at last gave him ownership of Daylesford. He agreed to pay the Rev. Thomas Knight a sum of £11,424 plus an annuity of £100 for life for the house and 650 acres of land. The house, which had never been completed, was so dilapidated that he ordered it to be demolished and a new one built on a different site. While this was being done he sold the house at Windsor and leased a property in Park Lane in Marian's name. It was from Park Lane that on December 2nd 1790 he wrote to James Boswell, the close friend of Dr. Johnson. Hastings had agreed to let Boswell have the three letters which Johnson had sent him in Bengal.

> ...my veneration for your great and good friend, Dr. Johnson, and the pride, or I hope something of a better sentiment, which I indulged in possessing such memorials of his good will toward me, having induced me to bind them into a parcel...

Boswell in turn was flattered to have had a letter from Hastings, who he saw as

> ...a man whose regard reflects dignity even upon Johnson; a man, the extent of whose abilities was equal to that of his power; and who, by those who are fortunate enough to know him in private life, is admired for his literature and taste, and beloved for the candour, moderation, and mildness of his character.

Meanwhile, the trial seemed interminable. Burke and Fox, urged on by Francis, pursued Hastings relentlessly, but in the few weeks each year that the court sat, neither the public nor the peers could maintain much interest in the proceedings. In a letter dated 21st April 1788, Philadelphia Walter, (Eliza's[1] half-cousin) told her brother

> I have once been to the trial which, because an uncommon sight, we fancied worth going to, and sat from 10 till 4 o'clock, completely tired, but I had the satisfaction of hearing all the celebrated orators, Sheridan, Burke and Fox. The first was so low we could not hear him, the second so hot and hasty we could not understand him, and the third was highly superior to either as we could distinguish every word, but not to our satisfaction as he is so much against Mr. Hastings whom we all here wish so well.

When, after three years of bitterness, contempt and unconcealed malice Burke finally ground to a halt, Hastings rose to defend himself. Over two years he refuted the charges in meticulous detail, ending angrily but proudly.

> To the Commons of England, in whose name I am arraigned for desolating their provinces in India, I dare to reply that they are the most flourishing of all the states in India. It was I who made them so. I gave you all, and you

have rewarded me with confiscation, disgrace, and a life of impeachment...

In the same month, June 1791, Hastings and Marian moved at last to Daylesford, though much building had yet to be done. They spent their days in riding, planning, and perhaps dreaming of India, while the lawyers made their final addresses to a sparsely attended court.

On April 23rd 1795 Hastings was acquitted of all the charges (his portrait, plate 14, was painted in that year). The trial had lasted for 145 days and had cost him £71,000. If it had not been for the Company's generosity in the matter of pension and loan, he would have been destitute. John Nicholls M.P. recalled meeting Hastings when it was all over.

14. Warren Hastings (portrait by Francis Abbott, 1795).

I was unacquainted with Mr. Hastings when these charges were laid on the table... When I examined them, I was disgusted with the unfair manner in which they were framed. This led me to take part in the debates; and after the session was ended, I became acquainted with Mr. Hastings. He appeared to me to be a man of a strong, vigorous, decisive mind; well acquainted with the character of the natives of India, and with the views and interests of its various Princes. He seemed to me to be a man capable of extricating himself from difficulties by his great resources and dauntless courage... I think that he was a man of the most powerful mind I have ever conversed with.

Jane Austen's brother Henry wrote to Hastings:

Permit me to congratulate my country and myself as an Englishman; for right dear to every Englishman must it be to behold the issue of a combat where forms of judicature threatened to annihilate the essence of justice.

In August 1795 Hastings and Marian were in Cheltenham, from where Hastings went to Cirencester. His diary records the visit:

Friday 19. Col. Toone and Maj. Scott, to Lord Bathurst's. At 1 met Lord Bathurst at the end of his Wood. All rode... saw the excavation of parkland...
20. At 11, all rode through the woods to Sapperton, saw the land and Tunnel.

At Daylesford Hastings was busy. While the surveyor for the East India Company, S.P. Cockerell, supervised the building of the house, Hastings extended his property by buying neighbouring farmland, and proceeded to develop the grounds of his estate. A lake was excavated, and boulders were brought from a hill at Adlestrop to make an island, and to build bridges and a grotto. The boulders had been known from time immemorial as the Grey Geese of Adlestrop, and had been associated with tales of witchcraft. It seems that Hastings was not superstitious. Stone for the house was of finer quality, coming from nearby Cotswold quarries and from Edge Hill, near Banbury.

By the time that all the work at Daylesford had been completed Hastings had spent a total of £60,000 on the property, including Cockerell's fee and the workmen's wages. The new house was not of great architectural merit, but it was home; Hastings' boyhood dream had been realized, and with Marian he would live out his days comfortably. Not idly, though; that was not his way. He experimented with breeding livestock and cereals. He planted trees in some places and cleared them in others. He rode to meetings in the nearby villages and to the races at Bibury. He took Marian on jaunts to the seaside and on trips to London. Although he was no longer a rich man he gave generously when he saw a need. S.C. Grier describes his philanthropy.

> He had always acknowledged an obligation of gratitude to his foster-mother, a poor woman named Ellis, living at Churchill, and her family, of which they kept him well in mind, and on the acquisition of Daylesford he became an earthly providence to every man, woman and child on the estate. In the severe weather at the beginning of 1795 he gave orders for the daily distribution of bread, to the value of 6d. a week per head of the poor inhabitants, but his later endeavours were directed rather to the inculcation of self-support. Mrs. Hastings taught the village girls sewing and straw-plaiting, and he chose out some of the boys to be sent to Joseph Lancaster's school for an industrial education. But the mothers were seized with the idea that they were to be taken for soldiers or sailors, and besieged him with tears to beg them off, so that the experiment came to an untimely end...

He nursed Marian when she was ill, and in 1800 he was able to write to a friend

> ...Daylesford is very much improved since you saw it, both in its ornamental acquisitions, its comforts and its husbandry. My beloved wife is what she was in her moral and spiritual substance, and I should and ought to be perfectly contented, if her health (which is not worse, but rather better) was more stable. The worst is, we live too much secluded from society, excepting that of our neighbours, and too remote from our friends; but our hearts turn to them with as much warmth as ever, and with as hearty an interest in their concerns.

In April 1801 Hastings confessed to his stepson Charles Imhoff "...I am scarce ever indoors, but to dress, eat, drink and sleep...", and in June 1802 he told Imhoff:

> ...As to myself, my dear Charles, if I live three years longer, and live as I have done the last 6 or 7, I shall be disqualified from any conversation but upon pigs, turnips and potatoes, and have lots and lots to say on them.

In his letter of 10th November that year Hastings was able to tell his stepson of other activities in the park and in the village.

> ...I forget in what state you left this place. The great pond has undergone another repair, and I hope an effectual and durable one. I have almost finished a very great and heavy work at Daylesford village. I have completely surrounded the churchyard, besides enlarging it, with a handsome circular wall; walled in a space between Bowles's farmyard and the street for a parish green; laid the new road over the Moor to join Mr. Leigh's road; cut off the end of a cottage which projected into the street so as to obstruct the carriages in their passage, and made the circuit easy, and even the road ornamental. The best of these improvements, the green, is the suggestion of Mrs. Hastings, and the finishing of it will be executed, as the past has been, according to her directions.

In August 1806 Jane Austen and her sister were taken by their mother, Cassandra, to visit the Rev. Thomas Leigh (p.42) at Adlestrop Rectory. Warren Hastings would undoubtedly have been well known to Jane, at least by reputation. Her cousin Eliza Hancock (Betsy) would have spoken fondly of her godfather, and in any case such an eminent elder statesman, a friend of her father and a neighbour of the Leighs would have been the subject of much conversation in the Austen household. It is hard to believe that Jane Austen and Warren Hastings never met, but there is no record that they did so. It would hardly have been on this occasion; the Rev. Thomas Leigh had recently and unexpectedly inherited Stoneleigh Abbey in Warwickshire, and the family group quickly moved there to view the new property. Perhaps they met through a mutual acquaintance, such as Fanny Burney (whose novels Hastings admired) or Jane's brother Henry. Henry Austen had known Hastings for some years, and when in 1813 his sister's "Pride and Prejudice" at last appeared, he sent a copy to Hastings. The latter responded enthusiastically, and on September 15th 1813 Jane Austen wrote to her sister from Henry's home at 10 Henrietta Street in London:

> ...And Mr. Hastings! I am quite delighted with what such a man writes about it. Henry sent him the books after his return from Daylesford, but you will hear the letter too... I long to have you hear Mr. H.'s opinion of P. and P. His admiring my Elizabeth so much is particularly pleasing to me...

That same year, the House of Commons considered the renewal of the East India Company's charter, and summoned Hastings as a witness. His appearance at the Bar of the House, twenty seven years after his first appearance there to answer Burke's charges, was greeted by the Members removing their hats, rising to their feet and remaining standing until he was seated. When he had finished his evidence the compliment was repeated. In May 1814 Hastings was made a Privy Councillor, and in June the Prince Regent presented Hastings to overseas sovereigns when they visited London. A friend of Hastings was prompted to write to Sir John D'Oyly of

> ...the triumph which our great friend has obtained over all his enemies. He has not, I believe, one remaining. Those whom death has spared, remorse has converted into friends, and I am most perfectly convinced there is not at this moment a Man in England the worth of whose private and public character is more universally and indisputably admitted than his is.

1816 saw the ageing (and ailing) Hastings embark on a remarkable project. He would demolish the old and decaying church in Daylesford and rebuild it. The rector was Hastings' nephew, the Rev. Thomas Woodman, who was also vicar of Brackley in Northants, about 20 miles distant. Daylesford was left in the hands of the Rev. Joseph Owen, curate of Daylesford and Oddington. Having persuaded the curate to hold all his Sunday services in Oddington church close by, Hastings began. As each stone was removed it was renumbered, and where possible was replaced in its original position. The foundations were preserved and the new building made as far as possible to resemble the old. His diary records his supervision of the work in detail.

> 8th July 1816: The workmen began to remove the pews (mine, of course, to remain so), desk, and pulpit, and to unslate the roof. The woodwork deposited in the stable. 9th: The rafters all removed, and lastly the belfry taken down. 10th, 11th, and 12th: Demolition... 20th: The church much impeded by yesterday's rain, but otherwise going on well... 23rd: The wall is above the window sills. The ladies went to see the church... 10th August: The principal rafters, and many of the smaller, and the wall tablets are fixed... 24th: Half the slating done, and 3ft of wall to the chancel... September 10th: All timbers and masonry of the chancel finished, and slating two courses done... 14th: The ridge laid, and the roof finished; the rubbish removed, and the floors swept. 23rd: Plastering finished; labourers unemployed.

The following month, Hastings records

> 8th December: This day, just five months from the demolition of the church, Divine service was performed by the Rev. J. Owen, curate, with a prayer and sermon for the occasion, most appropriate and impressive. A full congregation... Sunday 15th: We all went to church. 17th: My eighty-fourth birthday.

In the church was fixed a tablet to commemorate the rebuilding, and in the graveyard a new stone was placed over the grave of Hastings' grandfather, inscribed "The Rev. Penyston Hastings, B.A., Rector of this church, was buried here the 1st of October, 1752".

In March 1817 Hastings went to London for the last time, and stayed there till May, dining with friends including the Prince Regent. Hastings' health was failing, but his letters show that his mind was as active as ever, and current affairs still drew his attention. When in May 1818 Marian went to London he confessed to a friend that he had "the conscious satisfaction of having throughout allowed a bias in favour of every wish and opinion of hers, in preference to my own". In August he dictated a letter to the directors of the Company, appealing to them to maintain Marian when he was gone, as "she has been the virtual means of supporting the powers of life and action by which I was enabled to maintain their affairs in vigour, strength, credit and respect". He promised the directors that "my latest prayers shall be offered for their service; for the welfare of my beloved country, and for that also of the land whose interests were so long committed to my partial guardianship, and for which I feel a sentiment in my departing hours not alien from that which is due from every subject to his own".

Warren Hastings died at Daylesford House on August 22nd 1818. In all that he did in the service of his country Hastings was driven by honourable motives, though perhaps some of his actions in the employ of the Company showed a lack of judgement. He was generous to a fault, and indeed came perilously close to insolvency. His selflessness, though, was tempered by a strength of character which made him a formidable opponent when the way of life in which he believed was threatened. At the end, the greatest of the governors-general of India was laid to rest not among the great and the good in Westminster Abbey but in a Cotswold churchyard not far from where a boy had dreamed his dream, and had grown to make it come true. In Daylesford, Adlestrop, Oddington and Churchill the people mourned their loss, and in the house on the hill Marian Hastings was left to grieve for the man who had loved her.

Visitors to Daylesford will find little of the hamlet which Warren Hastings knew. G.W. Hastings notes that "much has changed, and that much includes what was characteristically his". The façade of the house has almost gone; the height of the elevation has been halved by a terrace built in front of it, and the entrance is now at the back. The church which Hastings so lovingly rebuilt was replaced in 1860 by a new building designed by J.L. Pearson, the architect of Truro Cathedral. Hastings' memorial tablet, though, was preserved and fixed on the north wall of the nave.[2] The eastward extension of Pearson's church covered Hastings' grave, so that his mortal remains lie beneath the present altar, but in the churchyard, below the chancel window, is a neo-Greek monument, a square Coade stone pedestal supporting an urn (Plate VII). The simple inscription is

WARREN HASTINGS 1818

Chapter 5 - FURTHER READING

Boswell, James: *Life of Johnson*, ed. G.B. Hill. Vol. IV. Clarendon Press (1887).
Chapman, R.W. (ed.): *Jane Austen's Letters to her Sister Cassandra and Others*. Oxford University Press, 2nd edition (1952).
Feiling, Keith: *Warren Hastings*. Macmillan (1954).
Hastings, G.W.: *A Vindication of Warren Hastings*. Henry Frowde (1909).
Macaulay, 1st Baron: *Essay on Warren Hastings*. Macmillan (1907).
Marshall, P.J. (ed.): *The Impeachment of Warren Hastings*. Oxford University Press (1965).
Turnbull, P.: *Warren Hastings*. New English Library (1975).

[1] Presumably Eliza (Betsy) Hancock, Hastings' goddaughter. - Ed.
[2] The reason for the replacement of Hastings' church only 44 years after it was rebuilt is given in this tablet as that the existing church was "found too small to accommodate the increased number of the inhabitants of the parish". However, David Verey, in his book *The Buildings of England - Gloucestershire: The Cotswolds*, suggests that an additional reason may have been that the new church, being more ornate than the one it replaced, was thought more in keeping with the spirit of the Oxford Movement. - Ed.

6. FAIRFORD AND BISLEY - KEBLE COUNTRY
John Keble (1792-1866) - Thomas Keble (1793-1875)

With the passing of Lord John Russell's Reform Bill in 1832, relations between the Church of England and the state became strained. Clergy, already alarmed by what they saw as threats from secular authority to their own order, were now required to accept Dissenters into the ranks of the House of Commons - men who could legislate on matters affecting the Established Anglican Church. The Reform Act was but one of a number of measures taken by Parliament which undermined the Church's authority: the Test and Corporation Acts, which made it mandatory for members of municipal corporations and holders of government offices to be communicants of the Church of England, had been repealed in 1828, and the passing of the Catholic Emancipation Act in the following year freed Roman Catholics from many of the restrictions which had been imposed on them. Amid these concerns, the Church was being forced to come to terms with the demands being made on it by the industrial revolution. A growing urban working class required a properly structured system of pastoral care, a whole new programme of church-building and an increased force of clergymen to minister to the needs of the expanding urban population.

The Church of England, then, was being made, whether it wished to or not, to examine the structure and organisation which it had evolved over centuries, and which had served a relatively small and rural population fairly effectively. Now that a significant number of Anglicans was beginning to re-evaluate traditions which had been matters of religious dogma for many hundreds of years, and even to raise doubts about the continued Establishment of the Church of England, High Churchmen were becoming increasingly anxious about the way in which their Church might develop. They were concerned to protect it from the predations of a liberal, Protestant, tendency and from undue usurping of its authority by Parliament. While preserving the traditions of the Anglo-Catholic church they had, though, to avoid endorsing all the tenets of the Church of Rome.

Such a numerically significant constituency needed leaders, and it found them in the common rooms of Oxford University. The traditional seats of learning of senior churchmen were the Universities of Oxford and Cambridge, and the proposal that Oxford should open its doors to Dissenters was bitterly opposed. High churchmen there were defending the Anglican Church against the actions of religious liberals both within the House of Commons and outside it. Inevitably a group of men emerged who would found the Oxford Movement, dedicated to asserting the Church's independence from Parliament, claiming that it alone taught Christian truth, and that its bishops could trace their authority in a direct line from the Apostles. The group included Hurrell Froude,

John Henry Newman (who subsequently converted to Roman Catholicism and became Cardinal Newman), Edward Pusey, Robert Wilberforce and Isaac Williams. The name generally associated with the Oxford Movement, however, is that of a Cotswold parson.

At the end of the eighteenth century Court Close, Fairford, was the home of the Rev. John Keble and his wife. Here were born to the couple five children, Elizabeth (1790), John (1792), Thomas (1793), Sarah (1796) and Mary Anne (1799). The girls received their education intermittently at a boarding school near Faringdon, but the father took upon himself the responsibility for tutoring his sons. Such were his considerable abilities that both John and Thomas obtained scholarships to their father's own Oxford college, Corpus Christi, at the then normal though tender age of fourteen - John in December 1806 and Thomas in March 1808. Four years later John was awarded double first class honours, and in the following year he was elected to a fellowship at Oriel College.

The Keble family was a closely-knit and self-sufficient group, with little need of friends. When the children were young they suffered little from living in the isolated rural environment of Fairford. Their playgrounds were the orchards, fields and streams around their village, where they rode their horses or played with their other pets. Here the flowers and animals gave John a love of nature which would last all his life. Central to his existence at this time (literally) was Fairford parish church, where, Rowell suggests, "the famous medieval stained glass, ...with its saints and biblical scenes, stamped on his mind the significance of symbol and imagery as channels of religious truth". Mrs. Keble does not figure prominently in the records of this period, but her husband was a powerful influence, and the children received a thoroughly Christian upbringing.

In later years John Keble would be a prolific writer of poems, many of which would appear in "The Christian Year" and "Lyra Innocentium". Professor John Shairp describes John's life thus:

> This strictly home training, in the quiet of a Gloucestershire parsonage, placed in the heart of rural England, under a roof where the old High Church tradition lived on, blended with what was best in modern piety, makes itself felt in every line the poet wrote...

John's reverence for his father was total. Shairp again:

> Unlike most sons distinguished for ability, John Keble never outgrew the period of absolute filial reverence, never questioned a single opinion or prepossession which he had inherited from his father. Some of his less reverential companions used to think that this was an intellectual loss to him.

In 1815 John was ordained a deacon, and in 1816 a priest, by Dr. Jackson, Bishop of Oxford. Before his ordination John wrote to his Oxford friend John Coleridge:[1]

Pray for me too: pray earnestly, my dear, my best friend, that He would give me His grace, that I may not be altogether unworthy of the sacred office on which I am, rashly I fear, even now entering; but that some souls hereafter may have cause to bless me. Pray that I may be free from vanity, from envy, from discontent, from impure imaginations; that I may not grow weary, nor wander in heart from God's service: that I may not be judging others uncharitably, nor vainly dreaming how they will judge me, at the very moment that I seem most religiously and most charitably employed.

During his undergraduate years John was a frequent visitor to Fairford, where Elizabeth was suffering from a bone disease in her leg which would eventually require amputation, and Sarah was in terminal decline. In 1814 John wrote to Coleridge:

(Sarah) used to uphold us all. It is so melancholy to have two out of three sisters to carry upstairs every night. Oh, what a day of joy a day of perfect health would be in this family! We are all so united, so fond of home, and just separated enough to make us know and value each other's society.

Sarah died in June 1814 aged eighteen. On May 20th 1815 John wrote to Coleridge:

On Sunday next I hope to be ordained, and on Monday I go to Fairford for the summer, having engaged myself for the next six weeks to take charge of two small parishes, the churches of which are as near as Oriel and Corpus chapels...

These were the hamlets of Eastleach and Burthrop (now Eastleach Turville and Eastleach Martin), within an easy ride of Fairford to the south west, and Coln St. Aldwyn (where John's father was the incumbent) to the west. The engagement had been intended to be for the six weeks only, to relieve the old man who was its Rector, but John stayed there for nearly eight years. Coleridge, in his Memoir, quotes a parishioner:

I well remember Mr. John Keble coming to Eastleach to do duty when the Rev. B. Boyes, through age and infirmity, was unable to do it. A very great change took place in the village; he commenced a Sunday School and the church (there) and at Burthrop was well attended... Mr. Keble used to ride to and fro from Oxford, and on Sunday used to dine at a cottager's, for which he paid, and used to charge them not to provide anything extra for him; that was the stipulation.

On August 1st that year John told Coleridge that his parishioners were

...quite as tractable and regular at church as I could expect in places much less neglected than they, I fear, have been lately. [They are] complete rough Cotswold: a hard work I have of it to make sermons plain enough for them.

Letters at this time portray the Keble family at Fairford as a devout group of people sharing the burden of ill health and bereavement, but not averse to a spot of fun. Fairford Fair and Bibury Races were rich sources of entertainment. On July 4th 1816 John wrote from Fairford to his brother:

> I assure you we have gone on very well in your absence and indeed have been quite gay - In the first place you know Mama went to the Races, where she and Mrs. Morgan met with a fine adventure tho' they did not get tipsy, but as I know that Mama depends upon the pleasure of relating it to you herself I will not be so cruel as to deprive her of such a treat.

In 1816 Tom was ordained deacon, and in 1817 became a priest. For two years he was curate in the Cotswold villages of Windrush and Sherborne, and seems to have settled there very happily. In March 1817 John reported to Coleridge that Tom had

> ...gone to his Curacy. His is very comfortable there, and begs you to remember that he has a spare bed and some honey wine for anybody named Coleridge, and that the Cheltenham coach will land anyone from Oxford at half past one, and take them back at eleven the next morning. His great man, old Lord Sherborne, is quite a character for Smollett... He wears a black cap to church, invites the parson always to dinner, scratches his head and says "I'll tell ye what, Mr. Keble. Nobody likes a good sermon better than I do, and nobody likes a long one worse". Tom's energies are a little cramped by the nearness of this great personage, but on the whole it is very well, as the Ladies of the family are most exemplary in their charity and religious duties.

Tom's work does not seem to have been confined to the church, for later that year he apologised to John for being unable to dine with him because he was "just going to Stow in the capacity of manager to the Bank".

John became a Tutor at Oriel in 1818 and Tom a Tutor at Corpus Christi the year after. The brothers arranged to take services at Eastleach on alternate Sundays; their father would take occasional services during the week and do most of the visiting. Life at Eastleach, though, was not without its problems. In 1818 John told Coleridge

> We go on here pretty much as usual, except that our friends the Independents build every now and then a new meeting house and catch up some of our stray sheep with privy paw; and now and then some favourite lamb, of whom we had good hopes, grows up dishonest and increases the population unlawfully. Such things reconcile a man to quitting a congregation which else would cost him a sharp pull or two, after they have had a good three years in which to wind themselves around him.

For a while the brothers continued to tend their flocks - teaching at Oxford during the week and riding to Eastleach, or sometimes to help their father at Coln St. Aldwyn at weekends. But John was restless; the pull of the Church was strong. On April 14th 1820 he wrote to Mrs. Margaret Pruen at Fladbury near Evesham. The Kebles were close friends of the Pruens and visited Fladbury on a number of occasions. Writing from Oriel, he told her:

> Do not suppose that I am uncomfortable here. I should be ungrateful indeed if I were, with such friends about me and such opportunities of improvement, and my brother living next door to me; now, I thank God, become quite a stout man - indeed, it makes me quite ashamed to think that I should be complaining about anything: and I do not mean to do so - but I hardly think there is any harm in looking forward to being a mere Curate again one of these days, instead of the half and half kind of animal into which I now seem to be transmogrified.

In the following year his letter to Mrs. Pruen was more resolute: "I know very well it is not the life for me, and I always feel more at home in my parish in two hours than in my College in two weeks".

In 1823 John accepted the living of Coleby in Lincolnshire, and wrote of it to Coleridge with enthusiasm; ten days later, though, he changed his mind in favour of Southrop, a mile south of Eastleach. He explained his decision to Coleridge:

> ...I have however rather violent misgivings at the notion of leaving... the two poor little parishes in the Cotswolds... : sometimes I think I will go and represent their case to the Rector, and get him to put the house in repair and let me reside in it. I had thought of hinting to our Bishop at the last visitation that it was almost necessary to do so; the poor places especially Burthorpe are in a most pitiable condition, the farmer quarrelling, the labourer oppressed and starved, and typhus fever prevalent among them: a resident curate could not expect to do much, but it would at least be giving them one chance more of partial reformation...

1823 was an eventful year in the lives of John and Tom: their mother died in May, Elizabeth was ill and Tom became engaged. His bride-to-be was Elizabeth Jane Clarke, daughter of a former Fellow of Corpus Christi who became Rector of Maisey Hampton, two miles west of Fairford. The Clarkes were family friends of the Kebles, and 'Bessie' (so called to avoid confusion with Elizabeth Keble) and her sister Charlotte had grown up with the Keble children. John was now a full time curate at £100 a year in the three villages of Southrop, Eastleach and Burthrop (E. Turville and E. Martin), on the banks of the Leach stream. A stone footbridge connects the latter two places. (Plate VIII); it is known as Keble's Bridge, but the name, according to Pevsner, commemorates earlier generations of the family who held the manor of Eastleach Turville.

On June 10th John told Coleridge:

...I have taken the curacy of Southrop, which, as perhaps you may remember, lies very convenient for my former preferment, and there I am now living - with a deaf handmaid, a little girl, and a clerk and gardener and groom etc. etc. by no means dumb. The house is twice as large as I wanted, the garden about thrice. The population may be 320 or 330 - so that with the other two I have the care of about 1000 souls... Tom is even now gone over to Cirencester to look for a lodging there, as he has just undertaken the curacy - it is only 8 miles from home and is so far desirable: but we are a little afraid the church may prove too large for him, as he is not very strong in the chest. So you see between us we are likely to have some work, though I must confess he will have more than his share - his population will be between 4 and 5000.

In spite of his duties John was able to find time to do some gardening. That September he told Coleridge:

...the house is in the middle of the village, too large by half for me (plate 15); the garden ditto, and sadly overlooked, but with good capabilities, if I had but a sixpennyworth of taste to avail myself of them; however, I cannot well lay it out worse than it is, and therefore I am going to plant away this October with all my might, intending, if I live and stay here so long, to make a grand revolution in the course of next year.

15. Southrop Old Vicarage.

John invited his friends and Oxford pupils to Southrop: it was here that the first discussions took place which led to the foundation of the Oxford Movement. Important visitors included Hurrell Froude, Isaac Williams and Robert Wilberforce (son of William Wilberforce, the campaigner against slavery). The matters they discussed at these 'reading parties' would find expression in the 'Tracts for the Times', begun by John Henry Newman in 1833, (from which the alternative name for the Movement - 'Tractarian' - would be derived). Pevsner remarks that "Southrop should be a place of pilgrimage for all devout Anglo-Catholics".

Isaac Williams left us his impressions of John at this time:

Although Oxford had made Keble so formidable, as a don and tutor usually is, yet we found ourselves with him as if he were the youngest, so that John Parker - a rude countryman who acted as clerk, gardener, and groom - used to say, "Master is the greatest boy of the lot". It was to me quite strange and wonderful that one so distinguished should always ask one's opinion, as if he was younger than myself. And one so overflowing with real genuine love in thought, word and action, was quite new to me, I could scarcely understand it.

Tom Keble was now settled at Cirencester, and Coleridge, who had taken a Law degree at Oxford, was now a judge and busy about his business in the West Country. On March 2nd 1824 John sent him an invitation:

...Will you come and see me on your way from Circuit? ...if you will stay three days you shall go over to Cirencester on one of them, and visit both the Parson and the Clarke, (as a fellow of a college and a country parson I have a double right to make bad puns[2]). But when you come, I shall want you for one whole day to myself, having divers matters to talk over with you of highest consequence to Church and State. And Southrop, as I have now had some experience, is not a bad place for cosy conversations.

John and his friends were anxious to do all they could to help their Church to assert its independence from the State, and Coleridge might have been able to advise on the constitutional aspects of their case.

Coleridge records that early in 1825 John began seriously to contemplate the publication of the collection of his hymn-verses "The Christian Year", which he had begun in 1819. His original plan was to defer publication until he had completed the entire series and leave it "to come out when I shall be fairly out of the way", but in the event "The Christian Year" was published anonymously in 1827. The arrangement of the poems is based on the festivals and services of The Book of Common Prayer. Its success and influence were considerable: by 1866, the year of John Keble's death, the number of editions had reached ninety five. In these verses, as in many of his other poems, John showed his love of the countryside. Walking around his Cotswold parishes, or riding to see his ageing father and his sisters, he observed the plants and animals of the fields and hedges and streams, and found inspiration for his poetry. John was an admirer of Wordsworth, whom he had met at Oxford just after his ordination. Edward Pusey, a leading figure in the Oxford Movement, recorded that Wordsworth "proposed to the author that they should go over the work together with a view to correcting the English". Nevertheless, John's English was good enough for him to be elected non-resident Professor of Poetry at Oxford in 1831.

Could John have been thinking of the Leach when he penned his 'Hymn for First Sunday after Epiphany'?

... See the soft green willow springing
Where the waters gently pass,
Every way her free arms flinging
O'er the moist and reedy grass.

Long ere winter blasts are fled,
See her tipp'd with vernal red,
And her kindly flower display'd
Ere her leaf can cast a shade.

Though the rudest hand assail her,
Patiently she droops awhile,
But when showers and breezes hail her,
Wears again her willing smile.

Thus I learn contentment's power
From the slighted willow bower,
Ready to give thanks and live
On the least that heaven may give.

In March 1825 John received a letter from Sir William Heathcote, one of his former Oriel pupils. Heathcote had succeeded to his uncle's estate at Hursley, near Winchester. Heathcote needed a curate at Hursley, and offered the post to his friend and mentor. John was reluctant to move away from his father and sisters, neither was his brother very strong. He felt, though, that the move was right and proper, and it was agreed that he would leave the Cotswolds at the end of September. Tom would take over the curacy at Southrop following his marriage and would be on hand to help at Fairford. He and Elizabeth Clarke were married at Cirencester by John on June 14th 1825.

In his remaining months at Eastleach John continued with his plans for the church. On August 1st he wrote to Tom:

...Another doleful event is that we were going to construct such a pretty new roof for the aisle at Eastleach, ofwith Froude had drawn a plan, and the rogues of Churchwardens last week, during my absence, had the timbers all shortened with a view to lowering the roof, so it will all be spoiled and I have given it up for a bad job. But this comes of gadding about...

Late in 1826, when John was apparently settled in Hursley, things at Fairford changed for the worse. The youngest of the Keble children, Mary Anne, died aged twenty seven. Keble's biographer Walter Lock described her as "John's 'sweetheart', the bright, fresh, merry-hearted one, who wanted every one to live in sunshine, to whom he was accustomed to talk more freely than to anyone else..." Poor lame Elizabeth was left alone to care for her eighty year old father. It was inevitable that John, whose filial duty was absolute, would return to Fairford, which he did in December 1826 after spending little more than a year at Hursley. He was happy to be home, though, as a poem he wrote the following year shows:

FAIRFORD AGAIN

The road-side airs are sweet that breathe of home,
When from their hedgerow nooks the merry flowers
Greet our return, much wondering they should roam
Who might have stayed within these pleasant bowers.
For wonders seen by ocean or by land,
For treasures won in some far orient clime,
No ear have they, but leaves by breezes fann'd
Awake them soon, and showers at morning prime...

In 1827 Tom became vicar of Bisley, a large and scattered parish in the hills near Stroud, where he was to stay for the rest of his life. The suffering which Cobbett had noted the previous year (p.6) was everywhere to be seen. On July 1st John (whose dislike of Puritanism was as intense as ever) told Coleridge that Tom had "from 5 to 6000 people, many of them half-starving Clothiers, and a good many Dissenters". On September 24th he wrote:

Tom has had the care of the Church on him for 2 or 3 Sundays, and on Saturday his wife and child were to join him, having been kept a little longer here, for the small babe to be fit for travelling after vaccination. They are going on very jollily, only I think old Tom finds the charge of so large a place a little heavy, and I dare say he will be obliged to have a Curate before long... My father is very comfortable, tho' he says he feels himself more feeble than he was. He lets me do all his duty now, and will I dare say all the winter.

(It is interesting to read the reference to vaccination; it was less than thirty years since Edward Jenner had made the discovery at nearby Berkeley, and protected young John Phipps from smallpox.)

Despite the many challenges facing Tom at Bisley, he and Bessie seem to have settled down well. Their young son (also called Thomas) was a source of amusement, and on May 23rd 1828 John told Mrs. Pruen that "Master Thomas makes divers remarks which are accounted very wise and knowing by his poor infatuated Grandpapa and Aunt at Fairford".

"Granpapa", at eighty years of age, was still fairly spry; on September 29th 1828 John wrote to Coleridge at length:

> ...just after your letter came, my father said all of a sudden one fine Friday, I think, "Bessy, we must go to Bisley on Monday, so write to tell them". No sooner said than done: the whole party consisting of our three selves, Eliz. Tucker and 2 servants started the 25th August, and the next day I left them all a most jolly party at Tom's, to convey Mrs. Clarke and her daughter to Lyme... and I was not sorry myself for a bit of an excuse to smell, taste, see and hear my dear friend the sea.

John was still concerned about his brother's workload. His letter went on

> (Tom's parish) is a very trying one, not only in respect of mere labour, of which of course there is plenty, but still more on account of the hold which Puritanism in various forms has got of almost all the people's minds: there is so much tender ground to tread on, that an anxious person like Tom could really find it I think too much for his health, if he had not got such a cheerful and sensible and zealous coadjutrix: as it is, I never saw him so well or so comfortable: but it is in the way of hard work, harder I fear than I should ever like...

This "hard work" was to include a great deal of building and rebuilding. Bisley stands on a plateau 784 feet above sea level, so the tall spire of its church was a landmark. By 1829 Tom found it necessary to have the spire repaired; this was to be the first of many building works which he would undertake. The list is extensive: a new vicarage for Tom and his family in 1832; Oakridge church, 1837; Chalford school, 1842; Bussage church, 1846; Bussage school, 1848; France Lynch church, 1857; Eastcombe chapel, school and school house, 1868; France Lynch school, 1871. In addition, Bisley church itself underwent a thorough restoration. Tom restored Bisley Wells, the water supply in the centre of the village, and increased the number of spouts from five to seven. This commemorated the marriage of the Prince and Princess of Wales in 1863.

Tom also established an annual Well-dressing, when on Ascension Day local schoolchildren would decorate the Wells with flowers. One innovation, though, has had a lasting effect on the whole Church of England: Tom revived the practice of a daily service in his church, both morning and evening. His friend Isaac Williams took up the idea, and it spread throughout the country.

At Fairford John continued to carry out his father's duties. An 1831 letter to Tom gives one insight into a clergyman's life outside his church. A lady had walked over from Maisey Hampton to see him:

> ...What she wanted with me was to try and get her old friend Thos. Tidmarsh out of prison - i.e. Northleach, where he is committed for poaching; however, on consultation with (the magistrate) who committed him it was agreed that he should stay a week or two more: so I rode over to Northleach and saw him...

Busy as John was with caring for his remaining family and with deputising for his father, he nevertheless followed with care and concern the political events threatening his Church. The passing of the Reform Bill in 1832 spurred him to action, and on July 14th 1833 he preached the sermon on "National Apostasy" in the University Church in Oxford which is taken to mark the beginning of the Oxford Movement. Dissenters continued to trouble him; on February 28th 1834 he told Tom

> ...We hear most doleful accounts of Mr. Peters, who is regularly joining himself to the Baptists, and has had public notice given in the meeting that he shall probably be baptized in a few weeks; he... talks of building a meeting at Quenington.

Farm labourers continued to live on the brink of starvation. Keble's remedy was emigration to the colonies - a policy soon to be encouraged at Bisley by the churchwardens there, who would organise and pay for families to go to Australia. Keble did what he could to help the poor workers, but it could never be enough. There was always the dreaded workhouse, of course, but for those who refused to be separated from their families the outlook was grim.

In January 1835 Keble senior finally gave up the ghost at the age of eighty nine. John continued for the time being to minister to Coln St. Aldwyn and to visit Tom and his family at Bisley. On January 29th he wrote to Mrs Pruen at Fladbury. Fearing the kind of person who would replace his father as vicar, he referred to "this wretched Puritanism which is doing so much more and more mischief". He thanked her for her donation to the Oakridge Chapel Fund (one of Tom's ventures) and told her "the subscription gets on slowly, but I hope surely".

For some time a relationship had been developing between John and Charlotte Clarke, Tom's sister-in-law. John's duty to his father was over, and he was free to make his own way in the world. Charlotte was an attractive and cultured lady, though weak in constitution; she would need some degree of care for all of her life. Could John support her financially? When William Heathcote wrote to him again in April 1835, offering John the living of Hursley, he knew that he could.

On October 10th 1835 John and Charlotte were married by Tom in Bisley church in the presence of Elizabeth Keble and Tom's wife (who signed herself "Eliz. Clarke"). Soon after, John, Charlotte and Elizabeth Keble left the Cotswolds for good and settled

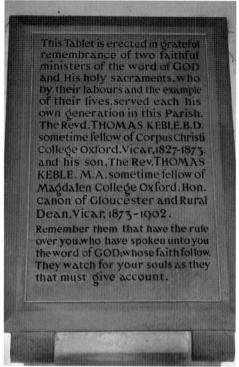

This Tablet is erected in grateful remembrance of two faithful ministers of the word of GOD and His holy sacraments, who by their labours and the example of their lives, served each his own generation in this Parish. The Revd. THOMAS KEBLE. B.D. sometime fellow of Corpus Christi College Oxford. Vicar, 1827-1873. and his son, The Rev. THOMAS KEBLE. M.A. sometime fellow of Magdalen College Oxford. Hon. Canon of Gloucester and Rural Dean. Vicar, 1873-1902.

Remember them that have the rule over you, who have spoken unto you the word of GOD; whose faith follow. They watch for your souls as they that must give account.

16. John Keble (posthumous portrait by George Richmond 1876).

17. Tablet in Bisley Church recording tenure of Bisley living by Thomas Keble and son.

at Hursley. John remained a leader of the Oxford Movement, however: of the ninety "Tracts for the Times" published between 1833 and 1845 John wrote nine, Tom wrote four, and Newman twenty four. Hurrell Froude died in 1836; in 1845 Newman converted to Roman Catholicism and around 1850 a few others, including Robert Wilberforce, also joined the Church of Rome. John Keble and Edward Pusey remained leaders of the Oxford Movement all their lives.

Elizabeth Keble died in 1860. John took his wife, whose health was declining, to resorts on the south coast of England. It was during one such visit, to Bournemouth, that John died after a short illness on 29th March 1866. (The portrait shown in plate 16 was painted posthumously and presumably shows him towards the end of his life.) He was buried in Hursley churchyard near the grave of Elizabeth. Charlotte lived for only six weeks after John's death, and was buried at his side. Tom died on 5th September 1875 and was succeeded by his son, also called Thomas. Their combined tenure of the Bisley living amounted to 75 years and is commemorated by a tablet in Bisley church (plate 17).

The principles of the Oxford Movement spread throughout the Anglican Church, and there is a sense in which every High Church service today is an act of commemoration: it is largely because of the devotion and efforts of John and his friends that the teachings and practices of the early undivided 'catholic' church were retained.

Although John Keble lies in a Hampshire churchyard, the part of the Cotswolds from Bisley to Eastleach is assuredly 'Keble country'.

Chapter 6 - FURTHER READING

Battiscombe, Georgina: *John Keble - a Study in Limitations*. Constable (1963).
Keble, John: *The Christian Year*. Everyman Library (1914).
Lock, Walter: *Biography of John Keble*. (1893).
Rowell, Geoffrey: *The Vision Glorious*. Oxford University Press (1983).

[1] Subsequently Sir John Coleridge (1790-1870): judge and nephew of the poet.
[2] Presumably an allusion to Chaucer's *Canterbury Tales*. - Ed.

7. ARTS AND CRAFTS IN THE COTSWOLDS
(i) William Morris

In the late nineteenth and early twentieth centuries the Cotswolds became the home of several craftsmen, founders of the Arts and Crafts movement. William Morris was the first in 1871, to be followed some twenty years later by Ernest Gimson and Ernest and Sidney Barnsley, whose decision to make the Cotswolds their home was almost certainly influenced by Morris. The tradition continued when, in 1902, C.R. Ashbee moved his Guild of Handicraft from the East End of London to Chipping Campden. It is now possible, in towns and villages all over the Cotswolds, to find craftsmen and craftswomen producing hand made goods of high quality in much the same way, and according to the same principles, as these Arts and Crafts pioneers.

KELMSCOTT: William Morris (1834-1896)

"A house that I love with a reasonable love I think..."

Kelmscott is, literally, a backwater. The sleepy hamlet (sleepy, that is, except when the manor opens to the public) lies at the end of a lane, on a river bank in the flat country of the upper Thames, just a few miles east of Lechlade.

William Morris claimed that he dreamed of Kelmscott Manor before he saw it. Whatever the truth of this, twenty years after becoming Kelmscott's tenant he set in it the closing scenes of his dream-fantasy "News from Nowhere".

William Morris, poet, artist, craftsman and socialist, was born in March 1834 at Walthamstow, London ("...once a pleasant place enough, but now terribly cocknified and choked up by the jerry-builder", he reminisced). Morris "lived in the ordinary bourgeoise style of comfort" and was brought up in "what I should call rich establishment puritanism; a religion which even as a boy I never took to". He was educated at Marlborough School ("a new and very rough shod school"). Its influence, according to Morris, was negligible ("I may fairly say I learned next to nothing there, for indeed next to nothing was taught"), but the surroundings were to have a profound effect on Morris's whole attitude to the world around him:

...the place is in very beautiful country, thickly scattered over with prehistoric monuments, and I set myself eagerly to studying these and everything else that had any history in it, and so perhaps learned a good deal...

In June 1852 Morris went up to Exeter College, Oxford ("I took very ill to the studies of the place, but fell to very vigorously on history and especially medieval history..."). He fell under the influence of the Oxford Movement, but "this latter phase did not last me long, as it was corrected by the works of John Ruskin, which were at the time a sort of revelation to me"; at the same time ("much to my own amazement") he discovered that he could write poetry.

It was at Oxford that Morris met Edward Burne-Jones, who would remain his close friend for the rest of his days. Through Burne-Jones Morris met other friends, including Charles Faulkner of Pembroke College with whom he would later work. The group called themselves 'The Brotherhood', and Morris was known to them as 'Topsy', on account of his uncut mass of red hair and his bushy beard. The American novelist Henry James described him some years later as "short, burly, corpulent, very careless and unfinished in his dress... He has a loud voice and a nervous restless manner and a perfectly unaffected and businesslike address. His talk indeed is wonderfully to the point and remarkable for clear good sense. He is an extraordinary example, in short, of a delicate sensitive genius and taste, saved by a perfectly healthy body and temper".

When he left Oxford, Morris ("I who had originally been intended for the Church!!!") resolved "to take to art in some form". Edward Burne-Jones recalled the moment vividly. In July 1855 he and Morris had been visiting the magnificent Norman churches of Northern France:

> ...it was while walking on the quay at Havre at night that we resolved definitely that we would begin a life of art, and put off our decision no longer - he should be an architect and I a painter. It was a resolve only needing final conclusion; we were bent on that road for the whole past year, and after that night's talk we never hesitated more. That was the most memorable night of my life.

Burne-Jones's admiration for his friend was almost total:

> Morris has a deal of my time. He is one of the cleverest fellows I know, and to me far more congenial in his thoughts and likings than anyone it has been my good fortune to meet with... . He is full of enthusiasm for things holy and beautiful and true, and, what is rarest, of the most exquisite perception and judgement in them... If it were not for his boisterous mad outbursts and freaks, which break the romance he sheds around him - at least to me - he would be a perfect hero.

Morris's enthusiasm for English Gothic architecture which he had gained from his mentor John Ruskin led him to the offices of the eminent architect G.E. Street, whose headquarters at that time were in Oxford. In January 1856 Morris articled himself to this leading proponent of the revived English Gothic style. He met there the senior clerk Philip Webb, who was to become another close and lifelong friend. (Burne-Jones and Webb would, forty years later, visit Morris on his deathbed).

In the autumn of 1856 Street moved his office to London, and here Burne-Jones introduced Morris to the painter Dante Gabriel Rossetti. Rossetti had been the acknowledged leader of the Pre-Raphaelites, a group of painters who urged a return to the simple naturalism of Italian painters before Raphael (d. 1520), claiming that after Raphael art had declined to an academic, purposeless state. Rossetti urged Morris to take up art; "If a man has any poetry in him, he should paint, for it has all been said, and they have scarcely begun to paint it". Morris, though, confessed that he "studied the art in but a very desultory way for some time".

In 1857, when he was twenty three, Morris fell in love with the seventeen year old Jane Burden (plate 18), whom Rossetti was using as a model. In 1859 the couple were married, and moved into the Red House which had been designed for them by Philip Webb in the (then still undeveloped) countryside of Bexley Heath in Kent. Webb, Burne-Jones and Morris himself designed most of the contents.

18. Jane Morris as La Belle Iseult,
painted by William Morris in 1858.

Though two children were born (Jenny in 1861 and May in 1862), the marriage did not mature. It is significant that in an autobiographical letter written in 1883 Morris relegated his family to a brief final sentence, though he did describe his daughters as "very sympathetic with me as to my aims in life" - implying, probably correctly, that his wife was not.

In 1861 Morris, "with the conceited courage of a young man", set up the firm of Morris, Marshall, Faulkner & Co. The members, apart from Morris, included Burne-Jones, Rossetti, Webb and the Pre-Raphaelite artist Ford Madox Brown. Peter Marshall was a surveyor and engineer, and, like his close friend Ford Madox Brown, a painter and designer. Charles Faulkner, Morris's Oxford friend, was the accountant. Morris modestly described the Company as "a sort of firm for producing decorative articles", but the goods which "The Firm" produced - furniture, metalwork, stained glass (Plate IX), wallpaper, jewellery, carpets, tapestries etc. - were of high quality.

Morris had a clear view of the proper role of machinery. He recognised that to achieve his aim of making his products accessible to everyone, machinery was essential. A machine, though, was a tool in the hands of a craftsman, there to serve his purpose in "working soundly and without haste at making goods that we could be proud of". He hated the squalid conditions in which men were forced to work, at the mercy of machines which were mass-producing cheap and "nasty" goods to put even more money in the pockets of the "idle rich". In his 1885 lecture "Useful Work versus Useless Toil" Morris distinguished "good" work from "bad".

> ...one has hope in it, the other has not. It is manly to do the one kind of work, and manly also to refuse the other.
>
> What is the nature of the hope which, when it is present in work, makes it worth doing?
>
> It is threefold, I think - hope of rest, hope of product, hope of pleasure in the work itself; and hope of these in some abundance and of good quality; rest enough and good enough to be worth having; product worth having by one who is neither a fool nor an ascetic; pleasure enough for all of us to be conscious of it while we are at work...

In this passage Morris encapsulated the philosophy of the Arts and Crafts movement in which he and his friends would play a leading part. In an earlier lecture, "The Lesser Arts" (1878), Morris had conceded that

> Nevertheless there is dull work to be done, and a weary business it is setting men about such work, and seeing them through it, and I would rather do the work twice over with my own hands than have such a job: but now only let the arts which we are talking of beautify our labour, and be widely spread, intelligent, well understood both by the maker and the user, let them grow in one word popular, and there will be pretty much an end of dull work and its wearing slavery, and no man will any longer have an excuse for talking about the curse of labour, no man will any longer have an excuse for evading the blessing of labour.

Morris believed that true craftsmen were not specialists, but could turn their hands to any essential task, be it weaving, dyeing, carpentry or metalwork. He himself was more than willing to tackle any job however menial, placing himself not one degree above his fellow man. Thus he would turn in an instant to a loom, a vat of dye or a printing press, as the occasion demanded.

In 1865, through ill health, Morris moved with his family to premises in Queen Square, Bloomsbury, and transferred his workshops there also. "An antiquated, ex-fashionable region, smelling strongly of the last century" wrote Henry James, who was much impressed by Morris.

> ...everything he does is superb and beautiful. But more curious than anything is himself. He designs with his own head and hands all the figures and patterns used in his glass and tapestry, and furthermore works the latter stitch by stitch with his own fingers - aided by those of his wife and little girls.

His poetry had almost been neglected while he had lived at the Red House, but the move to London seems to have motivated him; between 1868 and 1870 he wrote a massive collection of narrative poems, 'The Earthly Paradise', which were published in three volumes. It was at this time that Morris "made the acquaintance of an Icelandic gentleman, Mr. E. Magnusson, of whom I learned to read the language of the North, and with whom I studied most of the works of that literature ...their utter unconventionality took my heart by storm". Some of Morris's translations of the Icelandic Sagas were published in 1870.

On May 17th 1871 Morris wrote to Charles Faulkner:

I have been looking about for a house for the wife and kids, and whither do you guess my eye is turned now? Kelmscott, a little village about two miles above Radcot Bridge - a heaven on earth; an old stone Elizabethan house like Water Eaton, and such a garden! close down on the river, a boat house and all things handy. I am going there again on Saturday with Rossetti and my wife: Rossetti because he thinks of sharing it with us if the thing looks likely...

Philip Webb cast his professional eye over the property, and Faulkner went too. Thereupon Morris and Rossetti agreed to rent Kelmscott manor (Plate XI) for £60 a year. Kelmscott Manor would be Morris's country house for the rest of his life, and his final resting place would be in the nearby churchyard.

In November 1895, one year before his death, Morris described Kelmscott Manor in an article which he wrote for "The Quest", the magazine of the Birmingham Guild of Handicrafts

Through a door in the high unpointed stone wall you go up a flagged path through the front garden to the porch. The house from this side is a lowish three storied one with mullioned windows, and at right angles to this another block whose bigger lower windows and pedimented gable-lights indicate a later date. The house is built of well-laid rubble stone of the district, the wall of the latter part being buttered over, so as to say, with thin plaster which has now weathered to the same colour as the stone of the walls; the roofs are covered with the beautiful stone slates of the district, the most lovely covering which a roof can have, especially when, as here and in all the traditional old houses of the countryside, they are "sized down"; the smaller ones to the top and the bigger towards the eaves, which gives one the same sort of pleasure in their orderly beauty as a fish's scales or a bird's feathers.

Morris went on to describe the garden and the rooms. Writing of the parlour, he recalled "many a memory of hot summer mornings passed in its coolness amidst the green reflections of the garden". He described the view from the tapestry room.

...through its south window you can not only catch a glimpse of the Thames clover meadows and the pretty little elm-crowned hill over in Berkshire, but if you sit in the proper place, you can see not only the barn with its beautiful sharp gable, the grey stone sheds, and the dove-cot, but also the flank of the earlier house ...

Morris also confessed that it was

a house that I love with a reasonable love I think: for though my words may give you no idea of any special charm about it, yet I assure you that the charm is there.

Rossetti's occupancy of Kelmscott turned out to be a mistake. He was bored by the village, describing it as the "doziest dump of old grey beehives". He was a sick man, and suffered from insomnia and bouts of paranoia, dosing himself with chloral and laudanum, and taking walks in the meadows around the house, often in the company of Jane Morris. He fell in love with Jane, and when Morris visited Iceland in July 1871, accompanied by Eiríkr Magnússon, Rossetti spent much of his time drawing and painting her.

During Rossetti's stay at Kelmscott Morris had perforce to live in London to manage his firm. He yearned for his country house, though, and on February 13th 1872 he wrote to Georgiana ('Georgie'), Burne-Jones's wife:

I have come down here for a fortnight to see spring beginning, a sight I have seen little of for years, and am writing among the gables and rook-haunted trees, with a sense of the place being almost too beautiful to live in...

In the summer of 1872 Rossetti, in a serious state of decline, went on a long visit to Scotland, which did him much good. By the end of the year he was again at Kelmscott, much to Morris's annoyance. In a letter to his friend Mrs. Aglaia Coronio, Morris expressed his exasperation:

Rossetti has set himself down at Kelmscott as if he never meant to go away, and not only does he keep me from that harbour of refuge (because it is really a farce our meeting when we can help it) but also he has all sorts of ways so unsympathetic with the sweet simple old place, that I feel his presence there as a kind of slur on it: this is very unreasonable though, when one thinks why one took the place, and how this year it has really answered that purpose; nor do I think I should feel this about it had he not been so unromantically discontented with it and the whole thing, which made me very angry and disappointed.

Rossetti's continued presence at Kelmscott, and Morris's commitments in London, made it difficult for him to take a break. On March 26th 1874 he wrote to Mrs. Louisa Baldwin (mother of Stanley Baldwin, the future Prime Minister):

...I very much long to have a spell of the country this spring, but I suppose I hardly shall. I have so many things to do in London. Monday was a day here to set one longing to get away: as warm as June: yet the air heavy as it often is in England: though town looks rather shocking on such days, and then instead of the sweet scents one gets an extra smell of dirt...

Morris seems to have accepted the affair between his wife and Rossetti, but it can have done nothing to help matters. However, in 1949 George Bernard Shaw, who knew Morris, reviewed a biography of Morris by Lloyd Eric Grey.

...Mr. Grey, in one passage, suggests that he was lonely and affection-starved at Lechlade because Mrs. Morris neglected him for Rossetti, who never tired of painting her. This is a mistake... His wife was beautiful, and knew that to be so was part of her household business. His was to do all the talking. Their harmony seemed to me to be perfect. In his set, beauty in women was a cult: Morris had no more reason to be jealous of Rossetti than Mrs. Morris of... Lady Burne-Jones, whose memoir of her husband shows that Morris was her hero.

Whether or not Morris was jealous of Rossetti, the latter's disruptive behaviour made it inevitable that he would have to leave Kelmscott. "In the summer of 1874", writes Morris's biographer J.W. Mackail, "he finally left it; not a little to Morris's relief for many reasons. The manor-house soon resumed its quietness and simplicity...".

The firm of Morris, Marshall, Faulkner & Co. was wound up in 1875, amid rancour among the partners over claims for compensation. Reasons for the dissolution were several, and Morris, with scarcely a break in his work, established in the following year the firm of Morris & Co., with himself as the sole proprietor. In a letter of September 1883 he regarded the new firm with satisfaction:

Through all this time I have been working hard at my business, in which I have had a considerable success even from the commercial side; I believe that if I had yielded on a few points of principle I might have become a positively rich man; but even as it is I have nothing to complain of, although the last few years have been slack in business. Almost all the designs we use for surface decoration, wallpapers, textiles, and the like, I design myself. I have had to learn the theory and to some extent the practice of weaving, dyeing and textile printing: all of which I must admit has given me and still gives me a great deal of enjoyment.

One of the first commissions for stained glass which Morris & Co. received was for G.F. Bodley's new church at Selsley, on the Cotswold scarp above Stroud. As well as Morris there is work by Burne-Jones, Rossetti and Ford Madox Brown; lovers of the Pre-Raphaelites should not miss this church.

Morris managed to get away to Kelmscott whenever he could spare the time, travelling on the recently opened East Gloucestershire Railway to Lechlade and from there by horse and trap. On November 8th 1875 he wrote to Jane:

It began to rain again before I got to Lechlade at first to my infinite disappointment: however when I got here and had had my lunch and, as it were, made myself free of the river by an insane attempt to fish, I began to feel very comfortable, and took out my work and looked at it. The floods are already very high, and as it is certainly going to rain for the next 24 hours I expect to see something curious...

On September 4th 1876 Morris and a group of friends travelled to Broadway to visit Cormell Price. "Crom" Price had been a school friend of Burne-Jones in Birmingham and a member of the Brotherhood at Oxford. After he and Morris graduated they remained close friends. Price had taken a lease on Broadway Tower, and in 1867 had had it repaired and restored. Friends from his Oxford days were encouraged to come and stay. ("I am at Crom Price's Tower among the wind and the clouds", Morris told Aglaia Coronio). Stopping at Burford for a meal en route to his friend, Morris was angered by the drastic work being done at the church. It was yet another example of the "restoration" which was being done to parish churches and cathedrals all over the country. Morris and his friends had already made their views known, in 1874, by adding their names to a letter complaining about the demolition and rebuilding of part of Hampstead church. It was ironic that one of the signatories to that letter was the eminent architect Sir Gilbert Scott; it was Scott's radical alterations to Tewkesbury Abbey which spurred Morris to write his famous letter to 'The Athenaeum', which appeared on March 10th 1877.

...Would it not be of some use once for all, and with the least delay possible, to set on foot an association for the purpose of watching over and protecting these relics, which, scanty as they are now become, are still wonderful treasures, all the more priceless in this age of the world, when the newly invented study of living history is the chief joy of so many of our lives?

Your paper has so steadily and courageously opposed itself to those acts of barbarism which the modern architect, parson, and squire call 'restoration', that it would be waste of words to enlarge here on the ruin that has been wrought by their hands; ...there are many thoughtful people who would be glad to sacrifice time, money and comfort in defence of these ancient monuments ... What I would wish for, therefore, is that an association should be set on foot to keep a watch on old monuments, to protest against all 'restoration' that means more than keeping out wind and weather, and, by all means, literary and other, to awaken a feeling that our ancient buildings are not mere ecclesiastical toys, but sacred monuments of the nation's growth and hope.

Morris's proposal was, he told Rossetti in a letter, (April 3rd 1877), "...an attempt to put a spoke in the wheel of the 'restorers' of ancient buildings who have so grieved my soul. I think there is some chance of it being of use at last". Morris's hope, according to Mackail, was that "...if the destruction done by the restorers could not be stopped, (the Society) might at all events make it clear that it was destruction and not preservation". It was at this time that Morris & Co. stopped accepting commissions for stained-glass windows in ancient churches.

Morris's letter to 'The Athenaeum', and another on April 4th 1877, resulted in the formation of the Society for the Protection of Ancient Buildings, with Morris as its first Honorary Secretary. Morris dubbed it 'Anti Scrape' after its campaign against the Victorian practice of wholesale removal of plasterwork in churches to expose the bare stone walls. Morris visited churches scheduled for "restoration" and doubtless made his feelings plain to clergy and architects alike. But Philip Henderson, in his biography, voiced the opinion that "...had it not been for Scott and his like, disastrous as their efforts often were, there would have been little enough medieval architecture left in England for Morris and his Society ...to protect."

In the year that the Society for the Protection of Ancient Buildings was founded Morris refused nomination for the Chair of Poetry at Oxford, and instead started a series of lectures to working men on 'Art and Society'. By instinct Morris was a socialist if not, in theory at least, a revolutionary. He defined Socialism in an article in the magazine 'Justice' in 1894.

> ...what I mean by Socialism is a condition of society in which there should be neither rich nor poor, neither master nor master's man, neither idle nor overworked, neither brain-sick brain workers nor heart-sick hand workers, in a word, in which all men would be living in equality of condition, and would manage their affairs unwastefully, and with the full consciousness that harm to one would mean harm to all - the realization at last of the meaning of the word COMMONWEALTH.

John Mackail, in his biography of Morris, seems to have blamed Shaw for Morris's political views. Shaw retorted "Mackail regarded his [Morris's] socialism as a deplorable aberration, and even in my presence was unable to quite conceal his opinion of me as Morris's most undesirable associate. From his point of view Morris took to Socialism as Poe took to drink."

Later in the 'Justice' article Morris refers to the debt he owed to John Ruskin:

> The latter, before my days of practical Socialism, was my master towards the ideal aforesaid, and, looking backward, I cannot help saying how deadly dull the world would have been twenty years ago but for Ruskin! It was through him that I learned to give form to my discontent, which I must say was not by any means vague. Apart from the desire to produce beautiful things, the leading passion of my life has been and is hatred of modern civilization.

In the biography of her father which May Morris wrote in 1936 she acknowledged his debt to Ruskin:

> My father's affection for Ruskin never altered as the years passed, and I can recall many allusions to him that expressed it. He had a great admiration, too, of Ruskin's fine rhetoric, and I have heard him say, of the passage in the chapter on 'The Nature of Gothic' where the countries of the South and the North are spread out before our eyes and contrasted, that it was some of the finest writing in the English language.

In 1878, Morris and his family, in need of more space in London, purchased 'The Retreat', Upper Mall, Hammersmith, which he renamed 'Kelmscott House'. The opening chapters of 'News from Nowhere' were set at this house, and the final chapters at Kelmscott itself. Mackail remarked that Morris was consoled "to think that the water which ran under his windows at Hammersmith had passed the meadows and grey gables of Kelmscott".

In August 1880 Morris hired a houseboat, and at 3 p.m. on August 10th he and his family, accompanied by 'Crom' Price, the Hon. Richard Grosvenor ("Dick"), William de Morgan and two servant-girls, set off on a journey from Hammersmith up river to Kelmscott. At Oxford Jane Morris went ahead by train to Lechlade while the others continued on the river. Morris described the journey in a long letter to Georgie Burne-Jones:

> Night fell on us before we got to Radcot, and we fastened a lantern to the prow of our boat, after we had with much difficulty got our boats through Radcot Bridge. Charles was waiting for us with a lantern at our bridge by the corner at 10 p.m., and presently the ancient house had me in its arms again: Jane had lighted up all brilliantly, and sweet it all looked you may be sure.

The time was 10.30 p.m. on August 16th. Ten years later Morris used this journey as the basis of the concluding chapters of 'News from Nowhere':

> Presently we saw before us a bank of elm-trees, which told us of a house amidst them, though I looked in vain for the grey walls that I expected to see there. As we went, the folk on the bank talked indeed, mingling their kind voices with the cuckoo's song, the sweet strong whistle of the blackbirds, and the ceaseless note of the corncrake as he crept through the long grass of the mowing-field; whence came waves of fragrance from the flowering clover amidst of the ripe grass.
>
> In a few minutes we had passed through a deep eddying pool into the sharp stream that ran from the ford, and beached our craft on a tiny strand of limestone gravel, and stepped ashore into the arms of our up-river friends, our journey done.

Morris was probably inspired to write 'News from Nowhere' by the publication in 1888 of Edward Bellamy's 'Looking Backward'. It was a reaction against Bellamy's kind of Utopia, in which machinery was held in high esteem. In Morris's book, a man awakes in the year 2012 in a Marxist state. It is a pastoral idyll where handicrafts have been revived, money and laws have been dispensed with, pollution has been eliminated and machinery has at last been put properly to the service of man. 'Old Hammond' explains that

> The wares which we make are made because they are needed: men make for their neighbours' use as if they were making for themselves, not for a vague market of which they know nothing and over which they have no control: as there is no buying and selling, it would be mere insanity to make goods on the chance of their being wanted; for there is no longer anyone who can be compelled to buy them. So that whatever is made is good, and thoroughly fit for its purpose...

(Philip Henderson comments that "it would be an insult to Morris's intelligence to suppose that he really believed in the possibility of such a society, where the only work that appears to be going on is a little haymaking at Kelmscott ... In reality it is an Arts and Crafts Utopia with very little relation to anything we know as communism.")

At Kelmscott House in Hammersmith Morris was busy with fresh interests. In his bedroom he placed a tapestry loom, and he moved a carpet loom from Queen Square to the coach-house. He proceeded to weave fine tapestries and pile carpets, some of the latter rivalling in design the best that Persia and India produced. Tapestry weaving, though, could not be fully developed at Hammersmith; there was insufficient space. Morris & Co. were finding the Queen Square premises cramped, too; their cotton-printing and dyeing activities were expanding, and a move had become imperative. On a visit to see his friend Cormell Price at Broadway, he and 'Crom' had driven to Blockley, near Chipping Campden, to look at the Silk Mill. Morris would dearly have loved to move his works there, but the place was remote from both London and Kelmscott, and he was forced by his associates to accept that his new premises would have to be nearer the capital. In 1881 Morris & Co. took over an old factory at Merton Abbey in South London. The buildings had been a silk-weaving factory in the early eighteenth century, and were later used for printing fabrics. The move was, of course, an upheaval, and in November Morris confessed "I am in an agony of muddle, I now blame myself severely for not having my way and settling at Blockley. I knew I was right; but cowardice prevailed". The tapestry shown in Plate X dates from the Merton Abbey period. Bernard Shaw visited the Merton works, and in 1949 recalled that "When I went through Morris's Merton factory with him, I dared to say 'You should get a machine to do that'. He replied 'I've ordered one'."

In spite of the demands of his work, nothing could keep Morris from Kelmscott for ever. In September 1881 he wrote, again from Kelmscott,

We went a most formal expedition on Saturday, by water to Lechlade: then took a trap there and drove to Cirencester, which turned out to be a pleasant country town, and to us country folk rather splendid and full of shops. There is a grand church there, mostly late Gothic, of the very biggest type of parish church, romantic to the last extent, with its many aisles and chapels: wall-painting there and stained glass and brasses also: and tacked on to it an elaborate house, now the town hall, but built doubtless for lodging the priests who served the many altars in the church. I could have spent a long day there; however, after mooning about the town a bit, we drove off again along the long stretches of the Foss-way (Roman) over a regular down country, the foot-hills of the Cotswolds, pleasant enough, till we came to the valley which the tiny Coln cuts through, where we set ourselves to seeking the Roman villa: said valley very beautiful, the meadows so sweet and wholesome... The Roman villa was very interesting...

Later that month, as whole families around Kelmscott laboured with the harvest, Morris described the scene to Georgie.

It has been a great pleasure to see man and maid so hard at work carrying at last. Hobbs[1] began at it on Wednesday morning, and by the next morning the thatchers were putting on the bright straw cap to the new rick: yesterday they were carrying the wheat in the field along our causeway and stacking it in our yard: pretty as one sat in the tapestry room to see the loads coming on between the stone walls - that was for the other rick though, just beyond the little three-cornered close in front of the house.

By this date Morris was giving lectures the length and breadth of Britain. He had begun in December 1877 at the Trades' Guild of Learning in central London. The lecture was entitled 'The Decorative Arts: Their Relation to Modern Life and Progress'. In these lectures Morris's themes were avowedly socialist; he criticized the "philistinism of modern society", and asserted that "art cannot have a real life and growth under the present system of commercialism and profit mongering". Describing one of his lectures on 'Art and Socialism' in Leicester in January 1884, Sydney Gimson (brother of Ernest Gimson, see Chapter 8) commented "He was not a good lecturer. His lectures were always read, and not too well read, but they were wonderful in substance and full of arresting thoughts and apt illustrations. In their phrasing and general form they were beautiful."

In 1883 Morris was made an Honorary Fellow of Exeter College, Oxford. The same year he joined the Social Democratic Federation (formerly the Democratic Federation). Its Hammersmith branch had a choir, which rehearsed at Kelmscott House under the baton of Gustav Holst (Chapter 13). At the end of 1884 Morris resigned from the Federation in bitter protest over the quality of its leadership, and helped to form the Socialist League, of whose journal, 'The Commonweal', he became the editor. 'News from Nowhere' appeared in instalments in 'The Commonweal' before it was published in book form in 1891.

In those years Morris was kept busy with lectures, political rallies and much writing, but his thoughts were never far from his country house. In September 1887 (the year of the portrait in plate 19) he was able to report to Georgie

I had three very good days at Kelmscott: once or twice I had that delightful quickening of perception by which everything gets emphasized and brightened, and the commonest landscape looks lovely: anxieties and worries, though remembered, yet no weight on one's spirits - Heaven in short.

and it may have been to Georgie that he wrote in August 1888

We have had all the birds here again. The herons have been stalking about the field in the gravest manner; and I have seen the kingfishers very busy. One ducked down into the water before me and came out again with a little fish.

Through the Society for the Preservation of Ancient Buildings Morris was doing what he could for local churches. Thus in 1887 in an Appeal for the Preservation of Inglesham Church, near Lechlade he wrote

...It is a very remarkable example of early Gothic architecture, seldom equalled, and never surpassed among buildings of its size and refinement and beauty of design... It has never been 'restored' and thus has escaped the process which has obliterated so much of the history of our ancient Churches...

Two years later, though, in 1889, he found it necessary to give a more urgent warning.

...it is much to be feared that if something is not done the Church will become ruinous... we may say that it is a singularly beautiful and gracious specimen of a thirteenth century building, with a few later insertions. Its two bells are hung in a very pretty bell-cot, one of the prettiest among several examples in the neighbourhood. It is situated in a piece

19. William Morris (photograph by Frederick Hollyer 1887).

of country full of interest and character at the present end of the Thames navigation, and its elegant bell-cot and west end cannot be missed by anyone going up the Thames to Kempsford (it is close to the water's edge) or going along the Thames and Severn canal, which joins the Thames at this spot.

Years later, May Morris recalled her father's

pleasure of 'real' holiday-visits to Kelmscott, where nothing jarred, and the house, and the birds and flowers, and the river, all were welcoming in their serenity. Cockerell[2] writes about one of the later of these visits, where they went walking, but the morning was so lovely, that before long they sat under a tree and watched the cloudless sky, and the flocks of starlings and pigeons. And the magic of the day and the place was yet on them in the afternoon, when they just 'lolled about' and picked nuts and plums and lay on the grass chatting.

At the first Arts and Crafts Exhibition in November 1888 Morris lectured on tapestry-weaving, and attended a lecture by Emery Walker[3] on printed manuscripts. This stirred Morris's interest in printing. Predictably, on his return to Hammersmith he was soon immersed in designing letters and typeface. His belief that good books had to be works of art, irrespective of their contents, brought into being the Kelmscott Press. The first book to be printed was his 'The Story of the Glittering Plain' in May 1891, to be followed that October by 'Poems by the Way'.

Morris became ill that year with gout and a kidney complaint; this was an additional burden, as he was worried about the condition of his daughter Jenny, who had long been an epileptic. Father and daughter took a holiday in Folkestone, and then France, to rest and recuperate.

At Christmas 1892 Morris's daughter May and her husband Henry Sparling took George Bernard Shaw with them to visit Morris and Jenny at Kelmscott. Sparling reported that Shaw amused himself by "pasting into a scrapbook all the notices of his play... Morris has just gone off to try for a pike, having vainly endeavoured to get either Shaw or myself to share his fishing enthusiasm... He is extremely well and hearty".

In 1892 the Kelmscott Press brought out its own edition of 'News from Nowhere'. The title page, (plate 20), depicts the east face of Kelmscott Manor, and the typeface is Morris's 'Golden Type'. For all the books printed by the Kelmscott Press Morris used a paper specially made in Kent which resembled a medieval paper. He even went to supervise its manufacture, and made a sheet of it personally. The Press printed many books, but outstanding among them was 'The Works of Geoffrey Chaucer'. Henderson describes the 'Kelmscott Chaucer' as undoubtedly "one of the great books of the world, a superb production, from the beautiful design on the white pigskin binding with the silver clasps... to each double-page spread, with its sturdy Gothic type, splendid Morris borders and the 87 Burne-Jones pictures... Morris has impressed his personality on this great folio so powerfully that its impact almost knocks one down."

20. Title Page - 'News from Nowhere', with drawing of Kelmscott Manor.

The limited edition of 438 copies was completed in May 1896, much to the relief of Burne-Jones, who a few months earlier had confessed "I am getting worried about Morris and about the Chaucer. He has not done the title page yet, which will be such a rich page of ornament with all the large lettering. I wish he would not leave it any longer".

In July 1896 Morris, at his doctor's suggestion, travelled by sea to Norway. He found the journey wearying and the fjords depressing. Back in England in mid-August he wrote to Webb from Hammersmith, "Somewhat better, but hated the voyage; so glad to be home". He told Jenny

Dearest own child,

I am so distressed that I cannot get down to Kelmscott on Saturday; but I am not well, & the doctors will not let me; please my own dear forgive me, for I long to see you with all my heart. I hope to get down early next week, darling. I send you my very best love & am

Your loving father
W.M.

William Morris died at Kelmscott House, Hammersmith, on October 3rd 1896. His wife, daughter May and Georgiana Burne-Jones were among those present at the end.

On October 6th Morris was taken to Kelmscott for the last time. The coffin was met at Lechlade station by four farm workers. In stormy weather a group of mourners followed the cortege along the lanes to Kelmscott Church. E.P. Thompson described the day:

> The coffin was borne to the church in an open haycart, festooned with willow-boughs, alder and bullrushes. Among the small group of mourners were his close friends, like Ned Burne-Jones, workmen from Merton Abbey, the villagers from Kelmscott, and members of the Art Workers Guild.

Here Thompson quotes Cunninghame Gordon, an old political friend of Morris: "Inside, the church was decorated for a harvest festival, the lamps all wreathed with ears of oats and barley, whilst round the font... lay pumpkins, carrots and sheaves of corn."

Morris's gravestone was designed by Webb, who also designed the commemorative Morris Cottages built in the village in 1902 at Jane Morris's expense. On the front is a stone plaque depicting 'Morris in the Home Mead', It was carved by George Jack, Webb's pupil and Morris & Co.'s furniture designer, from a sketch by Webb.

Jane Morris and May continued to weave and embroider for Morris & Co. in London. Jane sold Kelmscott House in Hammersmith, and in 1913 bought Kelmscott Manor. She lived there intermittently for the rest of her life. Jane, Jenny and May all now lie in the Morris grave at Kelmscott.

In a lecture on August 6th 1907 John Mackail paid tribute to his friend:

> ...There was hardly one of the productive arts that he did not touch; there was none he touched into which he did not put fresh life, which he did not bring in some way or another into new vital connexion with its finest traditions, and which he did not reinstate as an art combining imagination with craftmanship - an art to be a joy to the maker and the user.

In the words of George Bernard Shaw:

> With such wisdom as my years have left me I note that as he [Morris] has drawn further and further away from the hurly burly of our personal contacts into the impersonal perspective of history, he towers greater and greater above the horizon beneath which his best advertised contemporaries have disappeared.

Chapter 7 - FURTHER READING

Bradley, Ian: *William Morris and his World*. Thames & Hudson (1978).
Cumming, Elizabeth and Kaplan, Wendy: *The Arts and Crafts Movement*. Thames & Hudson (1991).
Henderson, Philip: *William Morris - His Life, Work and Friends*. Thames & Hudson (1967).
MacCarthy, Fiona: *William Morris: A Life for Our Time*. Faber & Faber (1994).
Morris, William: *'News from Nowhere' and Selected Writings and Designs*. Penguin Classics (1986).
Thompson, E.P.: *William Morris - Romantic to Revolutionary*. Lawrence & Wishart (1955).

[1] The Hobbs family lived at nearby Manor Farm. Charles Hobbs inherited Kelmscott Manor in 1883.
[2] Sydney Cockerell, who became Morris's private secretary and a close family friend.
[3] The Emery Walker Library of Kelmscott Press books is preserved at Cheltenham Art Gallery and Museum.

8. ARTS AND CRAFTS IN THE COTSWOLDS
(ii) Sapperton: Gimson and the Barnsleys

When William Morris lectured at Leicester in January 1884, he stayed with Josiah Gimson, the head of a local engineering firm. Josiah's son Sydney recalled that, after the lecture,

> Morris, my sister Sarah, [my brother] Ernest and I ...had a delightful talk which I can never forget. Sarah left us after about an hour but the other three of us sat talking until nearly 2 o'clock.
>
> I am sure that one reason for this long sitting was that Morris was particularly interested in Ernest, then 19 years old and articled to the Leicester architect, Isaac Barradale, and saw something of the possibilities in him. At any rate when Ernest was anxious to have some experience in a London architect's office, some two years later, he, after much hesitation for fear of intrusion, wrote to ask Morris's advice and perhaps a letter of introduction to a suitable architect. At once Morris sent him three letters of introduction. Delighted and excited, Ernest took the three letters up to London, but he only had to present one, to J.D. Sedding, who at once took him into his office, where Ernest stayed for two years... Ernest went far and was recognised as one of the great craftsmen of his generation. I know that he always felt he owed his great opportunity to the visits of William Morris to Leicester.

When Gimson went to Sedding's office (next door to Morris, Marshall, Faulkner & Co.'s showrooms in Oxford Street), Gimson met Ernest Barnsley, and through him his brother Sidney. The Barnsleys, who were also training to be architects, were two of the five children of a Birmingham builder, one Edward Barnsley, and were much the same age as Gimson (Ernest was born in 1863, Gimson in 1864 and Sidney in 1865). Ernest Barnsley joined Sedding's office in about 1885; Sidney moved to the capital soon after, and became articled to Norman Shaw, who had by now set up his own practice. Sidney Barnsley's colleagues included the architect W.R. Lethaby, who five years later would be a co-founder of the firm of Kenton & Co., furniture designers.

Gimson was unhappy with his life in London. His friend, the ceramic decorator Alfred Powell, described Gimson's mood at this time:

> I remember him once speaking of the sheer inability of business wisdom among the commercially successful to understand good word and believe in it. On the other hand it would readily accept the 'make-believe' and push and establish that with avidity. Keeping aloof from this commercialism he looked upon as 'our success, not

our failure, as some seem to think.' He desired commercialism might leave handiwork and the arts alone and make use of its own wits and its own machinery. Let machinery be honest, he said, and make its own machine-buildings and its own machine-furniture if it likes: why not? ...So professional architecture did not interest him. He wanted architecture full to the brim, and found this empty...

Gimson left Sedding's office in 1888, in the same year that Sidney Barnsley left Norman Shaw's. The two men had completed their training, and were free to make their own way in the world. For two years they travelled separately - Barnsley touring the Byzantine churches of Greece and Gimson travelling in England, France and Italy, gaining experience mainly of domestic architecture.

On returning to London, Gimson settled happily for a while and joined several Societies and Committees with which William Morris was associated, including the Society for the Protection of Ancient Buildings. In the summer of 1890 Gimson wrote to a friend in Australia:

I have joined the Anti-Scrape Society. Morris was good enough to propose me as a member. I attend Committee Meetings every Thursday afternoon. Morris, Philip Webb and many interesting people are always there. After the meeting we all adjourn to Gatti's for tea and have an hour's talk of which Morris is of course the life and soul. He is a splendid fellow. I admire him more every day. He and Burne-Jones have just been doing a fine piece of tapestry which has been on public view at the shop.

W.R. Lethaby, who knew Gimson well, remarked that:

...Gimson became a keen and understanding member of the Committee, regularly attending the weekly meetings and visiting buildings in the Society's interest. Morris, as artist, made the profoundest impression on Gimson and the Society was itself a remarkable teaching body.

By this time, Gimson and his friends had developed a very keen interest in furniture design, and in 1890 Gimson, Sidney Barnsley, Lethaby and two others set up the firm of Kenton & Co., named from Kenton St., near the partners' workshops in Bloomsbury. They employed craftsmen to turn their designs into saleable furniture. It was not the first time that architects had banded together in this way; the pattern had been established in 1861 by the formation of Morris, Marshall, Faulkner & Co.

Kenton & Co. survived for less than two years before it ran out of capital, but for Gimson and Sidney Barnsley it was a crucial period; the firm provided them with the opportunity to observe directly the craft of furniture-making, and led them further to consider the real possibility of a life away from central London and the discipline of architecture. Gimson had discovered, too, an aptitude for plasterwork. In 1890 he wrote to a friend:

I have taken to furniture designing and plasterwork. I spend 4 or 5 hours a day working in a little plasterer's shed modelling friezes and ribbed ceilings. I get on capitally and shall soon be able to undertake work on my own account. I shall have one or two things in the next 'Arts and Crafts Exhibition' I hope, and some pieces of furniture as well.

Following the collapse of Kenton & Co. the urge was strong in Gimson and Sidney Barnsley to leave the big city and live as honest craftsmen in the country. Sidney's brother Ernest was persuaded to join their scheme, which was a radical one: Gimson had already bought a plot of land and built a house on the south side of Leicester, with the intention of moving there. Ernest Barnsley had moved to Birmingham in 1887 and set up his own architectural practice; he had married and started a family. He now brought them temporarily to Gray's Inn in London, and Sidney Barnsley and Gimson took rooms nearby. Alfred Powell visited Gimson there:

Here his ideal began to show itself, and it was wonderful in old smoky London to find yourself in those fresh clean rooms, furnished with good oak furniture and a trestle table that at seasonable hours surrendered its drawing-boards to a good English meal, in which figured, if I remember right, at least on guest nights, a great stone jar of the best ale.

William Morris would certainly have approved of, and quite possibly encouraged, a move to the country; living for some of his time in the Cotswolds he may even have influenced their final choice of destination. It was not, though, before "much scouring of the country from Yorkshire to the South Downs", as Powell put it, that the Cotswolds were chosen.

In 1893 Gimson and the Barnsleys moved to the hamlet of Ewen, near Cirencester, but this was only to be a temporary base while they found a permanent location. After a year they made their home at Pinbury Park on the edge of the Frome Valley near Sapperton. In Alfred Powell's words:

The Cotswolds have become common knowledge since then; at that time they were a mystery land of difficult hills and deeply wooded valleys dividing the romantic Vale of White Horse from the Severn and the Welsh borderland. Pinbury lay some five miles to the west of the old market town of Cirencester, and practically the whole of that distance was, as it is still, covered with loveliest woodlands.

Having rented Pinbury from Lord Bathurst, the house, which was in a state of disrepair, was renovated by Ernest Barnsley for himself and his family, while his brother and Gimson occupied adjacent cottages (plate 21). One of the buildings at Pinbury was made into a workshop, and here the three men designed and made good solid Arts and

21. Gimson's living room in his cottage at Pinbury. (Drawn by A.H. Powell.)

Crafts furniture in the best traditions of William Morris. No attempt was made to disguise dowels, joints or dovetails, but these were even made a feature of the finished piece, while the simplicity of construction and the lack of ornamentation made the purpose of the article obvious.

In about 1895 Ernest Gimson's cousin Miss Lucy Morley came to Pinbury from Lincolnshire to keep house for Gimson and Sidney Barnsley, and it was not long before she and Sidney Barnsley were married. The group photograph (plate 22) was taken outside Gimson's cottage, about 1895.

The arrival of Gimson and the Barnsleys would have been the subject of conversation in the village shop and Bell Inn at Sapperton. Most villages at that time had their carpenters, blacksmiths and wheelwrights, but here were men making furniture for sale which they had designed themselves. Their success went a long way toward reviving traditional crafts in the Cotswolds, and a way of life which had been in decline.

The three men seem to have been very content with their lives at Pinbury. Like William Morris along the upper Thames, they explored the area around their home on foot, and much of the inspiration for their wood carvings and Gimson's plaster work must have come from their keen observations of the plants and animals in the fields and woods around Sapperton. David Verey remarked that

22. Group photograph outside Gimson's cottage at Pinbury, about 1895, (left to right: Sidney Barnsley, Miss Lucy Morley (later Mrs. S. Barnsley), Ernest Gimson, Mrs E. Barnsley and Ernest Barnsley with their two daughters).

The country was a necessity to Gimson. He absorbed everything in nature around him. Socially he was all the time 'drawing together and invigorating whatever threads of true village life were still discernible.'

In this, Verey was echoing Alfred Powell:

It is to be remembered that throughout this time [Gimson] was quite alive to the entire necessity to himself and his work of the country and of this Gloucestershire country in particular. Without it he could not have had half the power. He watched and he wondered - absorbing everything around him. If you showed him any notable flower, or tree, or bird, or beast, he knew it well, and it opened his mouth to speak what was in him. So with books also. Wordsworth, for whom he was always ready, brought a brightness into his eyes, and opened the way for him to say things about nature and humanity - things he had spent his life considering. Wordsworth spoke to the child in him, and, as a friend who knew him long says, 'he always came out wonderfully to children.'

In 1900 Gimson married a Yorkshire girl, Miss Emily Thompson, whom he had met on one of his visits to that region in the 1880s. The couple had much in common, sharing a love of nature and also of traditional English folk music. The marriage was a happy one, and Emily Gimson lived at Sapperton until her death in 1940.

On June 30th 1901 Sidney Barnsley wrote from Pinbury to Philip Webb:

> The gardens are looking most beautiful now after the rains, with roses in masses, hanging over grey stone walls and climbing up in the cottages, but fruit we have none, save gooseberries and currants. Still we have the comforting feeling of 1000 gallons of cider in the cellar to tide us over this barren year but we shall miss the apples for pies during the winter months... as to our work, furniture is still being made and sold and things look quite cheerful, the difficulty now being to complete the orders we get, and so we are launching out as business men.

The increasing number of orders necessitated the employment of three cabinet makers, and a workshop was rented at the Fleece Hotel in Cirencester.

It was in this year that Lord Bathurst, who was returning from army service abroad, began to look for a suitable home for himself and his family. Ernest Barnsley suggested to him that the lease of Pinbury could be given up in exchange for permission to build three cottages, and the conversion to workshops of farm buildings at Daneway, by the side of the Thames and Severn Canal below Sapperton. An agreement on these lines was reached in 1902, and Gimson and Ernest Barnsley became partners in the new venture; meanwhile at Pinbury Lord Bathurst commissioned Ernest Barnsley to rebuild a wing at the rear of the property, and Gimson designed and executed plaster work for the ground floor ceiling.

On July 6th 1902 Sidney Barnsley wrote to Philip Webb:

> My brother and Gimson have already started workshops at Daneway having 4 or 5 cabinet makers and boys so far, with the hopes of chairmakers and modellers in the near future. I am an outsider from this movement - still going on making furniture by myself and handing over to them any orders I cannot undertake, and orders seem to come in too quickly now as we are getting more known.[1]

In 1902 the three men each built a cottage in Sapperton. Sidney Barnsley built Beechanger and his brother Upper Dorval House. Gimson's cottage was The Leasowes, and - a strange choice in this region of stone and tile - it was thatched. This thatch was destroyed in a fire in 1941 and replaced by tiles.

At Pinbury Gimson had devoted much of his effort to plaster work, and it was not until the move to the Daneway workshops that he turned his attention seriously to designing furniture. The three men continued to exhibit work at the important Exhibitions of the Arts and Crafts Society, and these, together with the displays at the

23. Daneway House, where Ernest Gimson had his showrooms. (Drawn by F.L. Griggs).

Daneway House showrooms (plate 23) brought Gimson and Ernest Barnsley more orders than they could handle. The Dutchman Peter Waals, from the Cirencester workshop, was made foreman and cabinet-maker at Daneway.

Waals' contribution to the work at Daneway was considerable; Sir George Trevelyan, who became Waals' pupil at Chalford, wrote of him:

> Gimson would be the first to acknowledge the immense debt he owed to him as colleague. Though Gimson was, of course, the inspiration and genius, he used Waals from the outset in close co-operation. The association of these two men was an essential factor in the evolving of the Cotswold tradition.

At Daneway Gimson's pole-lathe proved an insufficient means of supplying the demand for chairs, and the water-wheel was used to provide the driving-power. Gimson employed a young man, Edward Gardiner, to learn the craft; in later years Gardiner recalled his 'apprenticeship':

...After making but a few chairs in plain turning, Mr. Gimson brought down his first design in bead turning for chairs, soon followed by a design for a beaded settee. I was much disquieted by this as being only a beginner Mr. Gimson was treating me like an experienced craftsman and I was not at all sure I could rise to it... Anyway Mr. Gimson was pleased with my work and the Daneway men never criticised it.

In the yard of Richard Harrison, the wheelwright at Sapperton, Gimson set up a smithy. On Alfred Powell's recommendation a young man from nearby Tunley, Alfred Bucknell, was engaged; as the work developed the number of men increased to four. The smithy produced high quality metal work, such as handles and locks for the furniture, firedogs, tongs and other fireplace fittings, candlesticks and altar crosses.

In the memorial volume of 1924 Alfred Powell, who was a frequent visitor to Daneway, recalled his visits to Gimson.

Much insight into his inner life was to be had at Daneway House among all his furniture. At the first glance all was of an extraordinary interest. Then one saw the beauty of the work: the substance, the development of the various woods, of the ivory, the silver, the brass, of inlays of coloured woods and shells... I think his greatest pleasure was to know, as he did, that he had convinced so many of the real pre-eminence of good handiwork.

Gimson's attitude to machinery allowed no compromise. He would use no power machinery in his workshops. On April 18th he wrote to W.R. Lethaby.

I suppose all designers with workshops of their own have in unprosperous times been faced with the problem of machinery. It has faced me often - sometimes seemed to be a question of machinery or no shop at all and I have wavered about it but always ended by knowing that of the two alternatives I would rather have no shop at all.

The furniture coming out of Daneway at this time was described by Annette Carruthers:

Most of the furniture was made of native English woods such as oak and walnut, of solid construction with much use of exposed dovetailed joints and tenons. Octagonal panelling on doors was a characteristic feature, probably deriving from Waals' experience of the Dutch tradition... Many pieces were decorated with simple inlays of ebony or ivory, at which Waals excelled, and more exotic pieces, such as cabinets and small boxes decorated with flower and leaf designs inlaid in ivory and silver, were created for a richer market. One of Gimson's ideals was that the simpler pieces of oak furniture should be cheap enough for cottagers to afford, but his cabinet-makers' standards were so high that this proved impossible.

24. Oak Dining Table by Sidney Barnsley; top consisting of three boards held together with double dovetails.

While Gimson and Ernest Barnsley supervised the work in the Daneway workshops, up the hill at Sapperton Sidney Barnsley was both designing and making his own furniture. Eric Sharpe compared the work of Sidney Barnsley and Gimson:

> The former was a designer of furniture of a very high order, probably more practical-minded and possibly more original. He made his own furniture himself without assistants, and in that way... many discoveries may be made (plate 24). Gimson's mind was more receptive and capable of assimilating suggestions and ideas from work of the past, or of contemporaries, pulling it all together and making it his own (plate 26).

Gimson and Sidney Barnsley continued (perhaps in a spirit of friendly rivalry?) to display work at exhibitions of the Arts and Crafts Society, but Ernest Barnsley was concentrating on architectural work, and by 1905 his partnership with Gimson had come to an end.

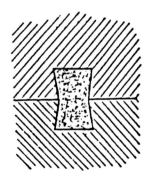

25. Double dovetail joint, as used in table shown in plate 24.

26. Walnut sideboard with plate-stand and feet in ebony. Designed by Gimson and made at Daneway workshops around 1910.

In August 1907 a certain Norman Jewson "stepped out of the train at Cirencester." He was to stay for sixty-eight years. Born in Norwich, Jewson graduated from Cambridge before spending three years in an architect's office in London, "which I disliked as a place to live in permanently the longer I stayed there, though I recognised its advantages in other ways." Having completed his apprenticeship, Jewson took a holiday in the Cotswolds, armed with a tent and a sketch book.

In 'By Chance I Did Rove', Jewson left reminiscences of Gimson and the Barnsleys which paint a vivid picture of life at Sapperton in the early years of the century. "In Gloucestershire", he wrote, "as I found out afterwards, many old customs and ways of life that had long been given up elsewhere still lingered on and were to do so for nearly another decade." After wandering by horse and trap as far afield as Stow-on-the-Wold and Chipping Campden he made his way back to Cirencester, as he had been strongly recommended to visit Sapperton and see Ernest Gimson's workshops at Daneway House.

At Daneway Jewson was met by Peter Waals and taken to the showrooms:

Such furniture as Gimson's I have never seen before, which was no wonder, for although it was traditional to the extent of the use of the best craftsmanship in construction and finish, it was entirely original in design and had an assured distinction which only a master mind could have evolved. In its design, grace of form was combined with extreme simplicity to emphasise the beauty of the wood. Oak, mahogany, burr-elm and ebony were used in different places, each of which had its special treatment to bring out the beauty of the material, while instead of hiding the construction, the perfectly made dovetails were allowed to make a natural pattern where they occurred. It was a completely new style, but one that had nothing tentative about it. Indeed, it had the assured mastery which only genius could have achieved.

From Daneway Jewson made his way to Sapperton. Eventually, "summoning up my courage, for I was painfully shy of meeting the great man", he made his way to Gimson's cottage. He described Gimson as "a tall, well-built man with a slight stoop, a large rather heavy face, except when he smiled, a brown moustache and wide-open contemplative eyes. His expression was that of a man entirely at peace with himself and all the world."

Norman Jewson was taken on as an 'improver' (unpaid assistant) on a month's trial. The venture was evidently successful, for Jewson became a close friend of Gimson, and an important member of the Daneway team of craftsmen until Gimson's death twelve years later.

Jewson took lodgings at Frampton Mansell, a mile away, as there was no suitable place for him in Sapperton village. Later he found a cottage at Oakridge Lynch on the hill opposite ("...a tiny little place with one sitting room and a long narrow room where a loom for wool weaving had been fixed"). Jewson lived at Oakridge for a year before a cottage became vacant at Sapperton - actually two cottages, joined by a door on the ground floor. Jewson lived in one of these until his marriage in 1911 to Mary Barnsley, eldest daughter of Ernest Barnsley, when the couple moved into the larger adjacent dwelling. To this they in due course annexed two small nearby cottages. These three cottages together were known as 'Bachelor's Court' ("...though our advent made the name a misnomer we kept it").

Ernest and Emily Gimson's love of traditional music brought two important visitors to Sapperton. Gimson's friend Arnold Dolmetsch, who had revived recorder-playing in England, often stayed at Pinbury, and Cecil Sharp, the collector of folk-music, visited the Gimsons after they had moved to Sapperton village. Gimson, and Ernest Barnsley too, took an active part in the life of their adopted village, and F.L. Griggs commented that "in all the village pastimes he (Gimson) was the leader, and the youngest; no merry-making or dance went half so well without him... With his wife he taught Sapperton to enjoy itself." ('Fred' Griggs was an architect and engraver of etchings who lived at Dover's House in Chipping Campden. He was a friend of Gimson and Jewson, and towards the end of Gimson's life worked with him on several commissions. Most of the drawings in the Gimson memorial volume, plate 23 for example, are his.)

According to Jewson, Gimson had planned to found a 'craft village' on the lines of William Morris's 'Utopia', where there would be "healthy employment for all in making useful and beautiful things or [in] productive agriculture, giving everyone an intelligent interest in their work, time to do it as well as might be, with reasonable leisure for other interests." The population would be "...largely self-supporting with their farms, mills, wheelwrights, carpenters, masons and other tradesmen.". It seems that Gimson had bought the land, about two miles from Sapperton, and made sure of a water supply. Unfortunately the war intervened, and Gimson's early death in 1919 put an end to the project. What, one wonders, might have come of this?

Gimson and Ernest Barnsley continued to act as advisers for the Society for the Protection of Ancient Buildings, but Barnsley ("a big, handsome, jolly type of man, fond of good company, good food and good cheer of every sort", according to Jewson), was busy now with his own architectural commissions. His alterations and renovations at Pinbury and Daneway, and the extensions to the cottage at Sapperton which formed the basis for his own Upper Dorval House, would have earned him a local reputation. Perhaps it was Lord Bathurst who recommended him to the Hon. Claud Biddulph and his wife, though Ernest Barnsley's previous association with William Morris, whose work interested the Biddulphs, may have helped. The Biddulphs had inherited the estate at Rodmarton, three miles south of Sapperton, and needed a house, as the mediaeval manor house had been demolished in the eighteenth century. Ernest Barnsley was asked to design a small country dwelling at Rodmarton. He began work in 1909 assisted by Norman Jewson; progress was interrupted by the First World War and resumed in 1918.

After Ernest Barnsley's death in 1926, the work was completed by Jewson. Rodmarton Manor has been described as 'the last great manor house built in England.' It was certainly bigger than Claud Biddulph had anticipated and is Ernest Barnsley's finest achievement. The stone and tiles were quarried locally and oak for the roof-joists, panelling and floors was obtained from trees on the estate. Labour too was local: carpenters, joiners, estate workers and the local blacksmith all found employment. The Barnsleys, Peter Waals and, in due course, Sidney Barnsley's son Edward all designed furniture for the house; the gardens, laid out as a series of 'rooms' surrounded by hedges of holly, beech and yew, provide a perfect setting. Work by the Sapperton craftsmen can be seen elsewhere in the Cotswolds (Verey gives details) but there can be no finer memorial to them than Rodmarton Manor.

Gimson, too, remained active as an architect. Soon after the war had started, he was commissioned by May Morris to build a pair of cottages at Kelmscott. He also designed Kelmscott village hall, though this was not built until 1933. In September 1918 Gimson wrote from Sapperton to his friend Sydney Cockerell (p.77,80):

> ...I was there [at Kelmscott] on Saturday meeting a stupid Viscountess who wanted some cottages built with fronts like mine and behinds like Webb's. "You see I want them for carefully selected respectable artisans and I wish them to be a standing example to the underpaid farm labourers in their wretched hovels of what they too

might have become had they been sober and industrious!" Did you know there were such women? I didn't![2]

Gimson's most important architectural work was at Bedales School in Hampshire, and though a number of other working drawings survive which show originality of thought, few of these projects were ever built. Perhaps his other consuming interests prevented him from becoming a great architect, but there can be no doubt that Gimson was a leading figure in the twentieth century Arts and Crafts movement in Britain.

Ernest Gimson died in August 1919, aged fifty five, and lies buried in Sapperton churchyard; Emily Gimson lived on at Sapperton until her death in 1940. In the Gimson memorial volume F.L. Griggs paid a long tribute to Gimson which could easily have been written of William Morris.

> ...Art for art's sake or for luxury, or any art that did not minister to some human need, did not concern him - he found more to like in such as the make of an old lantern. It followed that in his affections old rural and domestic uses were as much linked with the craft as the craftsman himself ...He would say that not for nothing there lingered some repute for sound craftsmanship, even in our factories. He saw no good in the flight of the younger country people to the big towns - it was only one more proof that England was suffering as from a disease which had marred her once lovely face, and was attacking her heart.

Following Gimson's death Sidney Barnsley supervised the remaining work at Daneway, and he completed Gimson's work at Bedales. When the Daneway workshops closed in 1920 Gimson's foreman, Peter Waals, took over a derelict mill at Chalford. Many of the craftsmen who had been employed at Daneway joined him there, where he continued to produce high quality furniture until his death in 1937. It is interesting that there was rather more machinery at Chalford than there had been at Daneway; Waals did not consider that the craftsmen were therefore less directly involved in the business of making furniture, nor that the products were necessarily of an inferior standard. In Cheltenham Art Gallery hangs a painting by Sir William Rothenstein which depicts five of the Chalford craftsmen. Rothenstein lived at Iles Farm, Oakridge, on the hill above Chalford. When he bought Iles Farm, Rothenstein employed Norman Jewson as architect for repairs and alterations.

In 1926 Norman Jewson bought Owlpen Manor, in a secluded Cotswold valley to the east of Dursley, though he confessed that he "could not afford to live in it." The house had been uninhabited since 1850 and a considerable amount of renovation was necessary. In Jewson's autobiography there is a copy of the fine etching of Owlpen Manor by F.L. Griggs. Norman and Mary Jewson continued to live at Sapperton, and he worked in his architect's practice in Cirencester till his retirement. When Sapperton church was repaired in 1933 and later, Jewson's advice ensured that the work was done with the greatest of care. Norman Jewson died at Sapperton in 1975 at the advanced age of 91.

Ernest and Sidney Barnsley both died in 1926 and were buried in Sapperton churchyard, as was Ernest Gimson before them. By the sides of the path leading to the church door, three slabs of Edgeworth limestone mark the graves of the men who brought the Arts and Crafts movement to this part of the Cotswolds.

Chapter 8 - FURTHER READING

Burrough, B.G.: *Three Disciples of William Morris*. The Connoisseur Magazine: Part 1, Vol. 171, Part 2, Vol. 172, (1969).
Greensted, Mary, *Gimson and the Barnsleys*. Alan Sutton (1991).
Jewson, Norman: *By Chance I Did Rove*. Gryffon Publications (1986).
Lethaby, W.R., Powell, A.H., and Griggs, F.L.: *Ernest Gimson, His Life and Works*. Shakespeare Head Press and Basil Blackwell (1924).
Verey, David: *The Buildings of England-Gloucestershire: The Cotswolds* (ed. Pevsner). Penguin (1979).

[1] Unpublished letter. Cheltenham Museum and Art Gallery
[2] Unpublished letter. Leicestershire Museums Service

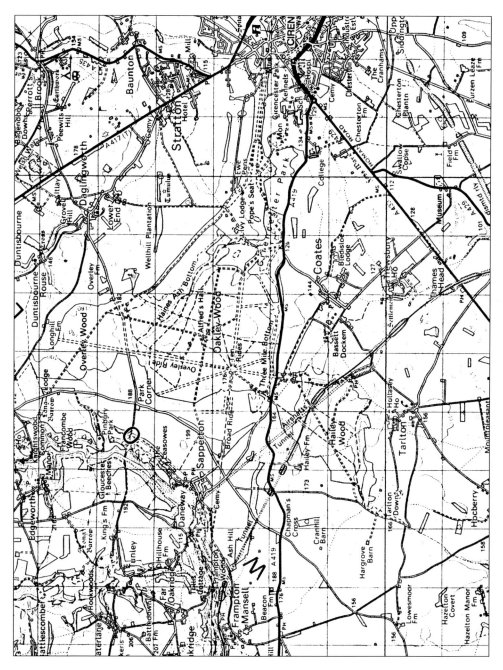

Map II. Oakridge - Sapperton - Cirencester Park. By permission of the Controller of Her Majesty's Stationery Office © Crown Copyright. 100037129.

I. Cotswold Sheep, showing the white face and prominent forelock typical of the breed.

II. View of Wallbridge and the Stroudwater Canal, showing red cloth drying on 'tenter-racks' on the hillside. The canal is no longer in use.

III. View of Cirencester House looking west from the Church Tower and showing the yew hedge. The broad avenue beyond the house is Queen Anne's View Ride.

IV. The Hexagon.

V. Pope's Seat

VI. Warren Hastings' birthplace at Churchill.

VII. Monument to Warren Hastings in Daylesford churchyard. The monument was moved to its present position when the 'new' church of 1860 was built.

VIII. The 'Keble Bridge', connecting the villages of Eastleach Turville and Eastleach Martin.

IX. Window in memory of Mary Hartley, Bradford Cathedral. Designed by William Morris and made by Morris, Marshall, Faulkner & Co.

X. Detail from the 'Woodpecker' tapestry, designed by Morris about 1885, and inspired by the legend of King Picus, who was turned into a woodpecker by the sorceress Circe.

XI. Kelmscott Manor.

*XII. The manor house 'Burnt Norton', which inspired
Eliot to write the poem of that name.*

9. ARTS AND CRAFTS IN THE COTSWOLDS
(iii) Chipping Campden: C.R. Ashbee
and the Guild of Handicraft

In the year that Gimson and Ernest Barnsley established their workshop at Daneway, a parallel venture began in Chipping Campden. 1902 saw the sleepy north Cotswold town startled by the arrival of 150 strangers from the East End of London - members of the Guild of Handicraft and their families, led by Charles Robert Ashbee. Ashbee had formed the Guild in 1888, when he was 25, at Whitechapel, in the East End of London. Ashbee was, like Gimson and the Barnsleys, an architect by training. As an undergraduate at Cambridge he had met Edward Carpenter, twenty years his senior, a charismatic figure who had forsaken his prosperous family background for a working-class existence as a market gardener near Sheffield. Carpenter was a prominent figure in the 'Back to the Land' and 'Simple Life' movements which had arisen out of the teachings of John Ruskin and, later, of William Morris. In 1886 Ashbee heard Carpenter lecture on "Private Property" at the Hammersmith branch of the Socialist League (founded by William Morris the year before). After the lecture Ashbee was invited to join Morris's group for supper, where they discussed the principles of Socialism.

Carpenter's beliefs were based on friendship - the friendship of man, which demanded the breaking-down of class barriers. He praised the working man, deplored his working conditions and longed for a return to self-sufficiency in a rural environment. Carpenter's philosophy must have influenced Ashbee; on leaving Cambridge he felt compelled to settle among working men, and moved to Whitechapel. While training as an architect he lived at Toynbee Hall, and lectured on Ruskin in the surrounding area.

While at Toynbee Hall, Ashbee started a reading class to study Ruskin's work; it was this reading class which led directly to the formation of the Guild of Handicraft. Guilds of various sizes and degrees of professionalism were appearing all over the country at this time, but Ashbee's was to become one of the largest and socially most significant. From his class at Toynbee Hall arose a group of young men who studied both the theory and the practice of design. They developed their skills with plaster, paint and gold leaf, and in their work Ashbee saw the opportunity, in the slums of Whitechapel, to realise the aspirations of Ruskin, Morris and his own idol Edward Carpenter. The Pre-Raphaelites Holman Hunt and Edward Burne-Jones were encouraging of Ashbee's efforts, but William Morris was not, believing by then that the Utopia of which he had (literally) dreamed could not be attained by anything short of politically radical methods. "One well-known cleric", Ashbee recalled, "- an ecclesiastic who shall be nameless - wrote in response to my request for sympathy 'I wish you would start your venture anywhere else but in Hell' ". (The cleric in question was Canon Rawnsley of Crosthwaite near Keswick, who in 1895 became a co-founder of the National Trust).

The Guild of Handicraft was inaugurated in 1888. From the outset it had a training school, teaching boys the principles of art and design, so that there was rarely a shortage of young men ready and able to join the Guild.

In 1891 the Guild of Handicraft moved from Toynbee Hall to its own premises at Essex House in the Mile End Road. Here it was able to extend its activities by making jewellery, furniture and articles in base and precious metals. The business expanded rapidly now, and commissions started arriving from many quarters - architect friends of Ashbee, artists and supporters of the Arts and Crafts Movement in general and of the Guild in particular. In November 1897 Ashbee joined the Art Workers' Guild, and remained a member for the rest of his life.

From about 1896 Ashbee's architectural training was taking place in the office of the eminent architect G.F. Bodley, a choice no doubt influenced by Bodley's Gothic Revival architecture at Cambridge. Once qualified, Ashbee set up his own practice in Chelsea and much of his work was effected by the Guild of Handicraft.

In 1898 three significant events occurred. Ashbee married Janet Forbes, aged nineteen. From the start Janet Ashbee was in full sympathy with the aims of the Guild and shared with her husband its crises and its successes. In that year too Ashbee acquired some of the Kelmscott presses, two years after William Morris's death. Ashbee transferred them to Mile End Road, along with a number of Morris's printers, and established the Essex House Press. 1898 also saw the Guild of Handicraft become a Limited Company. The new Guild published a book of rules, a copy of which was given to each newly elected Guildsman. It began:

> The Guild of Handicraft is a body of men of different trades, crafts and occupations, united together on such a basis as shall better promote both the goodness of the work produced and the revival of Art and Craft, and to apply these in such manner as changing circumstances permit or as shall be most helpful to its individual members.

Among its other objectives the Guild aimed

> ...to promote that other side of life, which whether in time of holiday or work, whether in sports, by music, by drama, or any form of Art brings men together and helps them to live in fellowship.

Ashbee's Guild was nothing if not democratic in its organisation. Policy decisions were made by a group of Guildsmen, sixteen in number, elected from the members. These Guildsmen were also responsible for discipline, and each of them made a small contribution from his wages as an investment in the Guild. Unlike William Morris or Gimson and Ernest Barnsley, Ashbee (or "C.R.A." as he preferred to be known) encouraged his workers to design their own pieces of work; he saw the making of good articles as the means by which the men would develop intellectually and spiritually. In "Craftmanship in Competitive Industry" Ashbee wrote:

> What I seek to show is that this Arts and Crafts movement, which began with the earnestness of the Pre-Raphaelite painters, the prophetic enthusiasm of Ruskin and the titanic energy of Morris, is not what the public has thought it to be, or is seeking to make it: a nursery for luxuries, a hothouse for the production of mere trivialities and useless things for the rich. It is a movement for the stamping out of such things by sound production on the one hand, and the inevitable regulation of machine production and cheap labour on the other... The Arts and Crafts movement, then, if it means anything, means Standard, whether of work or of life, the protection of Standard, whether in the product or in the producer, and it means that these two things must be taken together...

Now that Ashbee had gathered his workmen together, he could not regard the East End of London as a suitable environment in which to put his plans into effect; Ruskin had taught that good craftsmanship needed good health in clean surroundings. During the years at Essex House Ashbee took Guild members to stay in country cottages in Middlesex, Essex, Buckinghamshire, Oxfordshire and Gloucestershire. They visited the old silk mill at Blockley, which William Morris had rejected as being too far from London, and went to Chipping Campden, just a few miles further on. Ashbee needed to look no further. In the autumn of 1901, soon before the lease on Essex House was due to expire, Ashbee proposed to the Guild that they should move from the grime of Whitechapel and start a new life in the Cotswolds. He did, though, acknowledge the debt which he owed to London. Recalling Canon Rawnsley's admonishment about 'starting his venture in Hell', he wrote:

> ...The life of a great modern city is not, nor can it ever be, congenial to the work the Guild sets out to do - good honest craftsmanship with or without the aid of the machine. Good honest craftsmanship is better done the nearer people get into touch with the elemental things in life. It is the complexities of modern life that make the approach so difficult...

The decision to move from Mile End Road was, of course, not to be made without full discussion by the workmen. Some, for various reasons, could not go. Others, mainly older men, preferred 'the devil known' to a strange town in what could have been a foreign land. Even among those prepared to go it is doubtful if many felt much confidence or enthusiasm. Two weeks were allowed for decisions to be made before the move to Campden was put to the vote. In the event, out of 33 Guildsmen able to vote 22 indicated themselves to be in favour. The townsfolk of Campden were due for a shock. The year was 1902.

The task of transporting the Guild - workshops, tools and about 40 craftsmen with their families - was a major undertaking, but gradually it was achieved. The new base was the old Silk Mill in Sheep Street (plate 27), which had been reconstructed by Ashbee; ("...the character of the old work has been preserved, and there can still be seen the green twinkle of the lattice windows of the old silk weavers..."). The ground floor became a showroom, offices and rooms for the Essex House Press. On the floor above were installed the silversmiths, jewellers and enamellers, and the second floor was given over to cabinet making, wood carving (plate 28) and french polishing. The smithy, because of the noise which it generated, required a separate building nearby. Woolstaplers' Hall, the fourteenth century building in Campden High Street which was until recently a museum, became the Ashbees' new home.

From its inception Ashbee had intended that the Guild should represent much more than a means of earning a living by producing high-quality articles. It was to mean a whole way of life. Thus, the nucleus of a good library which Ashbee had brought from London was considerably expanded to include the major English poets, playwrights and novelists, as well as 'politically correct' works by William Morris and Edward Carpenter. There was a Guild Museum, a School of Arts and Crafts at Elm Tree House ("where we have a loan of exhibits from the Board of Education"), a workingmen's club at Island House, a Sports Club ("a necessary feature in the life of the whole"), and, at Braithwaite House, a guest house ("or hall of residence, where twelve of the unmarried men live, and where guests can be housed"). Physical education classes were organised at the School of Arts and Crafts for the men (plate 29), and cookery classes for the women (plate 30). Guildsmen joined the local Cricket and Football Clubs. Plays were annually performed in public for the good both of the actors and the community; "...the other day", Ashbee wrote, "we acted a Ben Jonson play, of which the proceeds go to the making of a bathing lake." This was made from the pool at Westington Upper Mill, and here the local schoolchildren were taught to swim. Among the visitors for the play was the poet John Masefield (chapter 12), who loved Campden and wanted to settle there.[1] Masefield's association with the Arts and Crafts movement was not only as Ashbee's friend but also as a tenant for some years of Pinbury Park, the former home of Gimson and the Barnsleys (p.83).

When the Guild of Handicraft arrived in Campden the town, not much more than a large village in 1902, was rather a run-down sort of place, still perhaps coming to terms with the decline of the wool industry which had once given it prosperity. Toward the end of the nineteenth century it was visited by Algernon Gissing, brother of the novelist George Gissing. In 1924 he recalled the visit as one of great pleasure. He remembered

...the grey wool town of Chipping Campden, slumbering so peacefully in its hollow. This is such a dreamlike spot that since I cannot say here a great deal about it, possibly I should pass it by altogether. But this I positively cannot do. Once more I must in fancy stand at that truly Gloucestershire stile and drop down through the fields into the long silent street which has never lost for me that spell of enchantment under which it

27. *The Old Silk Mill, Chipping Campden.*

28. *The Carving Shop, Guild of Handicraft.*

seemed to lie when I first entered it as a boy. No imagination was needed. Here was the old world itself, touched by a magic wand centuries ago and still remaining spellbound. After hours of sunlight on these lonely hills with the skylarks and the plovers, late in the afternoon I saw below me this wide secluded basin, made as it seemed simply to catch the sun, and basking there in the radiance was the little grey town with a majestic church tower shining at one end of it... Between the church tower and the sun lay the antique town in one graceful curve of what seemed infinite detail and variety yet of matchless harmony.

When the Guild arrived, Campden was still ruled by the local landowners and clergy, and the working man "knew his place." In 1903 Ashbee wrote:

One of the things that, coming into the country, our people feel most - and perhaps it is right they should - is the extraordinary disregard for time that the folk in the country seem to have. The old proverb, "Time is money", seems never to come home to them … they will haggle for months over five shillings when the delay may mean the loss to them of as many pounds.

But the shopkeepers of Campden were quick enough to seize an opportunity when it presented itself; the "newcomers" found themselves being charged more for goods than the local people. Things gradually settled down, though, as Campden got used to the ways of the Guild workers.

Another new face in Campden about this time was that of the architect and artist F.L. Griggs (p.91), who first set foot in the town in 1903 when he was making drawings for the "Highways and Byways" series of guide books; in 1904 he came back to live there for the rest of his life. It was by his efforts that public subscription enabled the National Trust to purchase Dover's Hill in 1929. For most of his life in Campden Griggs lived at Dover's House in the High Street, where he was visited by Norman Jewson, (p.90). Griggs loved Campden passionately, and became much involved in the life of the town, performing in Ashbee's plays with members of the Guild. With Norman Jewson and others Griggs founded the Campden Trust in 1929, and designed some of the wrought iron signs still visible above the shops and inns. A number of the properties in Campden High Street were bought and restored by the Trust, and the War Memorial near the Town Hall is Griggs' design.

At the Silk Mill there was no shortage of work for the Guild. Everyone was busy; responsibility for designing products was shared, but Shirley Bury notes that

Unlike the collaborative design process between designer and craftsman which Ashbee had initiated in relation to silver, metalwork and jewellery, he alone was responsible for designing for the woodworking shop up to 1900 and there is no evidence to suggest any closer involvement by the craftsmen at a later stage.

29. *The Physical Training Class, Guild of Handicraft.*

30. *The Cookery Class, Guild of Handicraft.*

As for Ashbee's work as a furniture designer, she said that:

> ...though interesting in the context of the Guild of Handicraft, [it] is not very
> original or typical of the movement of which he was avowedly a member. In most
> cases his designs had more in common with the best trade furniture of the period
> than with the innovatory work of contemporaries such as C.F. Voysey, William
> Lethaby, Ernest Gimson and Sidney Barnsley.

The first year for the Guild in Campden could be judged a success socially as well as
commercially. Members of the Guild worked hard to be accepted into the community,
and local people made an effort too. The swimming pool was soon to open, a Whit
Monday fete had been very successful, the Brass Band had been revived and Campden
generally, and the Guild in particular, had become a big attraction for visitors. In these
early years the 'great and the good' were frequently to be seen at the Woolstaplers' Hall
or the Silk Mill, or strolling in Campden High Street. The social historians Sidney and
Beatrice Webb came over from their summer residence at Aston Magna, near Moreton-
in-Marsh; the actress Mrs. Patrick Campbell visited from Stanway, where she was
staying with Lady Elcho, and John Masefield would come to dream of making
Campden his home.

Ashbee was well pleased with the region of England to which he had brought the
Guild. In 1905 he felt able to write:

> It is one of the privileges that the Cotswolds to this day enjoy that they have, more
> fortunately than other parts of England, escaped the defilement of the Industrial
> Revolution.
>
> And thus it comes that we have preserved for us still in a fairly healthy state in
> and around Campden such crafts as walling, stone dressing, lead glazing, thatching,
> slatting and wattling - crafts often handed down from father to son,... with some
> quality of traditional design felt by the craftsman as being part of the craft, and not
> relegated to an eclectic architect or a landlord building 'en amateur' as a matter with
> which the workman has no concern or of which he has no understanding. No one
> with any sentiment of beauty or fitness can to this day pass down Campden High
> Street, perhaps the loveliest thing of its kind in England, without a sense that on the
> whole the local craftsman, even into our own time, has felt this too.

Ashbee spent part of each week at his architect's practice in Cheyne Walk, Chelsea.
Along the street was the house, designed by himself and paid for by Janet's father as a
wedding present, in which he and Janet had lived after their marriage. (It was
subsequently let to the painter J.M. Whistler). At Campden, too, Ashbee was building -
in this case cottages for poor families. His conservationist views were in accord with
those of William Morris's Society for the Protection of Ancient Buildings ('Anti Scrape')
and he had been a member of the National Trust since its early days. Describing

Campden, he was pleased to note that "our medieval and Elizabethan forefathers had some instinctive gift for placing their dwellings", and he was distressed by the insensitive development which he saw taking place around him:

> There is scarce a house that does not speak of some tradition, some beauty. But architecture, like the rest of the arts, must be alive to be genuine. For the most part the residents value their beautiful heritage for the association, not for the beauty. They cut out the mouldings of the stone work, replace the lattices by plateglass and zinc bars, thus destroying the proportion of the whole house front; they have (fortunately in only one or two cases) put in some appalling shop windows, and latterly the local builders have been speculating in cheap brick villas - the red disease that has ruined Stratford-on-Avon - with a view to meeting the housing difficulty. It is ignorance that does these things for the most part...

Ashbee could not doubt that his life, and those of his workers, in this old and beautiful Cotswold town was as near as he could hope to get to his image of Morris's socialist Utopia. Indeed, he could have claimed to have moved further away from capitalism than Morris or Ernest Gimson. For better or worse theirs was a system of employer and employee, of 'hire and fire.' Ashbee, on the other hand, allowed the Guild to organise itself as a democratic brotherhood; they made many of the decisions, elected the Guildsmen and, increasingly, designed the products of their workshops themselves. Ashbee, as 'director', saw his role as keeping Guild affairs running smoothly, actively encouraging the special talents of the men, and above all maintaining high standards of craftsmanship. He was as much at ease in the company of the Guild workers, while still always 'the master', as he was with his intellectual friends. Fiona MacCarthy writes:

> The life of the Guild, as it became established in its peaceful rural setting, formed the most thoroughgoing expression of the radical beliefs of the Arts and Crafts movement. Although many craftsmen (and artists) of the period put forward these same theories and, to a greater or lesser extent, practised them, no one but Ashbee had attempted to develop the ideas of William Morris on so many fronts and in so ambitious a manner. No one else had had the courage (and is it so surprising?) to push forward to its logical conclusion the idea that men are responsible for what they make and that workers should all, if possible, be artists...

Ashbee was at this time a tall handsome man with a rather large moustache and a small tuft on the chin which did not claim to be a beard (plate 31). Extremely affable with those he liked, he could be very discourteous to those he did not.

Janet, 24 when the Guild arrived in the Cotswolds, and younger by fifteen years than her husband, was a lively, friendly, intelligent and attractive young woman. She had immersed herself in Campden life, and took a particular interest in the town's children, spending much time with them and being loved in return. Having had a musical training she helped compile the "Essex House Songbook", a collection which included folksongs, carols, humorous verses and marching songs that Guildsmen had accumulated since the Guild had started. John Masefield and the playwright Laurence Housman (another of the Ashbees' friends) contributed words for some of the songs (plate 32), Janet and her husband wrote some others, and the whole was a kind of 'scrapbook' of the Guild from its Whitechapel days to the present. It was intended to portray the comradeship and craftsmanship on which the whole organisation depended. Janet Ashbee was its editor, and at the Silk Mill Morris's old Kelmscott machines printed it in her husband's own 'Endeavour' type.

Although Janet was no older than many of the workmen, she seems to have assumed a maternal responsibility for them; her daughter Felicity recalled in 1988 that:

31. C.R. Ashbee. (Portrait by the American architect Frank Lloyd Wright.

> ...perhaps the Londoners were a bit quick off the mark, especially with their courtship methods (my mother had to have one of the boys on the mat within the first week for what she described as "...Whitechapeling frightfully with the local damsels...").

Life at Woolstaplers' Hall was plain, simple and comfortable; the house was very 'Arts and Crafts' in its décor and very welcoming. It was a centre for the Guild's social life and there was much to-ing and fro-ing. Friends would arrive for a sing-song, a poetry reading or just a chat, and on a Friday night Guild members would join the Ashbees for their musical entertainment.

At the Silk Mill new designs of jewellery were appearing, the silversmiths were handling commissions for cups, tableware and church silver (plate 33), the woodworkers were busy and the Essex House presses were rolling. Financially, though, all was not well and some of the Guildsmen were aware of it. Like the Blockley Silk Mill which William Morris had rejected, the one at Campden was proving to be too far from the London markets. The Guild's Brook Street and Dering Yard showrooms were increasingly expensive to maintain, many of the Guild's loyal patrons were themselves short of money, larger London firms were plagiarising some of Ashbee's designs and producing cheap copies, and sales of Essex House books were disappointing, especially in the crucial

HONEST DOVER'S FANCY.

Words by John Masefield. 1904.
Air: "Greenwich Park." 1698.

Campden town
Is quiet after London riot;
Campden street
Is kindly to the feet;
Campden wold,
So bonny to behold,
Is merry with the blowing wind & glad with growing wheat.

Campden fields
Are covered up with buttercup,
And bluebells slight
That tremble with delight;
Cuckoos come
When blossom's on the plum
And blossom's on the apple trees in petals red and white.

Campden woods
Are ringing with the blackbirds singing
Thrill! thrill! thrill!
O merry orange bill!
Sweet! sweet! sweet!
Says the chaffinch in the wheat;
All the pretty birds that are do delicately trill!

Dover's Hill
Has bramble bushes full of thrushes;
Tall green trees
That set a heart at ease;
Soft green grass
Where little rabbits pass
To nibble yellow buttercups amid the honey bees.

32. Page from the Essex House Songbook.

American market. The Song Book had not proved as popular as had been hoped, and the new Bible for use in churches failed to attract sufficient subscribers. The Guild's Minutes record that 1904 was a bad year for trade; the number of men was reduced and some of those who remained were on short time. The Annual Report for 1905 noted the Directors' regret "that for the first time in the history of the Company a loss, and that a heavy one, has been made on the year's working." A loss was reported again in 1906 (two thousand pounds, according to Ashbee).

Part of the problem was general to the Arts and Crafts movement. It had beset Gimson and the Barnsleys. How could high quality goods be produced cheaply enough for most people to afford? Even simpler pieces took time to make if they were to meet the Guild's standard, and time was money.

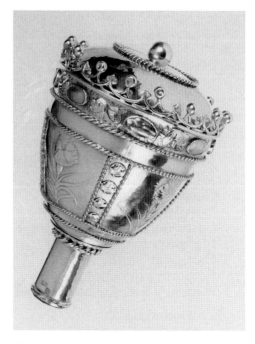

33. Mace-head by C.R. Ashbee.

The first workshop to be affected was the Essex House Press, which closed in 1906. Since it began, sixty books had been produced - twenty in London and forty in Campden, of high quality. It was hoped that the Press would restart operation when the economic climate improved, but it never did.

Despite such difficulties the Guild went on as best it could, while realising that it would have to do some fundamental reappraisal of its organisation.

Ashbee accepted a commission to restore the Norman Chapel at Broad Campden for Dr. Ananda and Mrs. Ethel Coomaraswamy. Mrs. Coomaraswamy was the sister of Fred Partridge, who had worked for the Guild as a jeweller. Her husband was a geologist, philosopher and an expert on Indian Arts and Crafts. Born in Ceylon, his mother was English and he had received all his education in England. Very soon he and his wife would be returning to England, and would contribute to the intellectual life of Campden.

Restoration of the Norman Chapel began in 1905 and was completed in 1907. Ashbee retained as much of the original building as he could - the north and south doorways, the chancel arch and much of the nave walls, together with two Perpendicular windows. Internally the house held a curious mixture of Eastern and English objets d'art. As well as William Morris tapestries and a copy of the Kelmscott Chaucer there was a Kelmscott press, bought from the Guild by Coomaraswamy to print his large tome on Sinhalese art. (The Coomaraswamys became shareholders of the Guild and gave it much needed business).

At Campden the Guildsmen were considering their financial plight. They had been forced to accept that their comfortable Arts and Crafts world was no longer viable. No longer would they be able to take as long as they wanted to make things in the way that they wanted (resulting in a stockpile of expensive articles which they could not sell); they would have to start making what the public wanted at a price it could afford. In 1906 and 1907 Clearance Sales were held in the London showrooms and a lot of stock was sold. The 1907 catalogue announced that the Guild were "prepared to dispose of their large stock of hand made silverware, jewellery, etc., at special sale prices." The catalogue bore colour pictures of silver and enamel brooches and pendants, and details of a wide range of articles in "silver and other metals."

Following its reorganisation the Guild was barely recognisable. No stock was made unless it was cheap and could find a ready market. Saturday working ceased and weekday hours were reduced. Ashbee's cherished principles were having to be set aside. Appeals to shareholders for more financial support were largely unsuccessful (though expressions of goodwill were given easily enough) and by August 1907 a third of the Guild's craftsmen had left to look for more secure work. The silversmiths and jewellers were almost idle, Ashbee's own architectural work was diminishing and only in the woodwork shop was there significant activity. In spite of Ashbee's insistence that better days would return, toward the end of 1907 the decision was made: the Guild would have to go into voluntary liquidation.

Ashbee could not conceal the bitterness he felt at the collapse of his dream. Toward the end of "Craftmanship in Competitive Industry" he wrote:

> The object of these pages has been to show that the carrying through of the experiment of the Guild in the country in the manner its promoters had hoped was premature; that the thing can be done, but not yet; that we must wait until the public thought and the public conscience are a little more with us. The Arts and Crafts, it would seem, cannot be permanently carried on, on any large scale, where the community's first concern is to exploit them for profit. The realization of this fact is a matter of time... As for the immediate and practical side of the experiment with which we have here dealt, it is no good knocking your head against a brick wall...

Some of the Guildsmen did indeed stay in Campden to "practise their Arts and Crafts." They included George Hart (designer of the altar set in Campden church) and his brother, the woodcarver Will Hart, loyal craftsmen from the Whitechapel days. Alec Miller stayed, who had come to Campden in 1903 from Glasgow. Jim Pyment stayed - the woodshop foreman who had revived the Town Band - and so did a handful of others. In 1909 the Guild formed a much looser federation of private businesses run by men who for one reason or another would not return to city life. Some, perhaps, really believed in Ashbee's vision of the 'Simple Life.' Others probably preferred a rural existence to life in the town, and a few of the older men may have thought employment elsewhere unlikely. Whatever the reasons, for the time being a core of Guildsmen remained in Campden.

When the Coomaraswamys' marriage failed, the couple separated and vacated the Norman Chapel at Broad Campden, and in 1911 the Ashbees left Woolstaplers' Hall and moved into the Norman Chapel in their place. They continued to be involved in Campden life, Ashbee working at the still thriving School of Arts and Crafts at Elm House until, just before the First World War, Gloucestershire County Council reorganised its system of education and the School was closed.

Ashbee continued with his architectural work, and in October 1914 he visited Rodmarton Manor (p.92). Afterward he wrote in his Journal:

> I've seen no modern work equal to it, nothing I know of Lutyens or Baker comes up to it. And when I ask why, I find the answer in the system, the method rather than the man. It is a house built on the basis not of contract but of confidence and Barnsley has been allowed a free hand to put all his personal knowledge and technique into the work. The Eng. Arts and Crafts Movement at its best is here - so are the vanishing traditions of the Cotswolds.

It is, perhaps, curious that Ashbee had so little to do with Gimson and the Barnsleys. The Guild was, of course, a much larger body than existed at Sapperton, and the two groups were organised in quite different ways, but the spirit of Ruskin and Morris moved in both and in each others' work they should have found more to admire than to criticise.

When World War I broke out Ashbee pleaded that he be allowed to 'take the King's shilling' but was not allowed to do so. In 1915 and 1916 he toured America (as he had done several times before) and lectured on the Arts and Crafts Movement. He also gave talks aimed at persuading the United States to join its Allies in their European struggle. In December 1916 Ashbee saw an advertisement inviting people "over call-up age" to teach English in Cairo so that younger men could be released for War service. Ashbee went to Egypt in January 1917, but he was moved in 1918 to Jerusalem to advise the military government on the redevelopment of the city. (Ashbee was not without experience in the field of town planning; five years earlier he had been working on the new plans for Dublin). Janet joined him there, with their family of four little girls, in April 1919.

The Ashbees left Jerasulem for England in 1923, and settled at Janet's old home, Godden Green near Sevenoaks in Kent. Here Ashbee added more books, including several whimsical ones and a biography of his mother, to the large number on craftsmanship and its social implications which he had written throughout his adult life. He also edited his journals, of which there were 44 volumes, and undertook the task of reducing these to seven shorter ones.

"C.R.A." died at Godden Green on May 23rd 1942, aged seventy nine. Following his death Janet moved to Lancashire, but exchanged letters with old Guildsmen and their families until she died at the age of 83.

The Guild of Handicraft is still remembered at Campden. Ashbee's swimming pool at Westington has long gone, but in the Silk Mill the Hart family are still silversmiths, and Jim Pyment's family have a building firm. At Woolstapler's Hall a stained glass window designed by Ashbee is a pun on his name, and a plaque is displayed which was the work of Will Hart, the woodcarver who had been in charge of Braithwaite House. Among the many craftsmen who have settled in this part of the Cotswolds the Arts and Crafts tradition which transformed the life of Campden lives on.

Was the venture worthwhile? Although the Guild of Handicraft was ultimately a financial failure it was in other ways a success. It brought employment and contentment to many people, though it also brought disillusion. Ashbee did not achieve his Utopia, but his ability and his determination brought him nearer to it than most men could hope to achieve. Whether the Guild conferred any lasting benefit on Campden is debatable. Felicity Ashbee summarised the arguments when she and her sister Mary unveiled the commemorative plaque at the old Silk Mill in 1988:

> There seem to be two quite distinct schools of thought about the coming of C.R.A. and the Guild of Handicraft to Campden.
>
> One - and this, naturally, was the one I and my sisters were brought up in - was that when the 160 or so East Enders of the Guild descended upon the rural beauty of Campden, they shook it out of a stagnant sleep, and while themselves admittedly gaining from the beauty and the quiet, they none the less opened new windows onto the world for its unsophisticated inhabitants.
>
> The other school of thought is that the advent of C.R.A. and his Guild, and the Guildsmen's families, was a regrettable intrusion into a perfectly functioning rural community, whose pace of life, ancient traditions and values were thus irretrievably damaged. Rather like what is happening today in the rain-forests of Brazil!
>
> In fact the truth *must* lie somewhere in between.

Chapter 9 - FURTHER READING

Ashbee, C.R.: *Craftsmanship in Competitive Industry*. Essex House Press (1908).
Ashbee, C.R.: *The Last Records of a Cotswold Community*. Essex House Press (1905).
Crawford, Alan: *C.R. Ashbee: Architect, Designer, and Romantic Socialist*. Yale University Press (1985).
Gissing, Algernon: *The Footpath Way in Gloucestershire*. Dent (1924).
MacCarthy, Fiona: *The Simple Life-C.R. Ashbee in the Cotswolds*. Lund Humphries (1981).
Massé, H.J.L.: *The Art Workers' Guild 1884-1934*. Shakespeare Head Press (1935).
Skipwith, Peyton: *Ashbee and the Guild of Handicraft*. The Connoisseur Magazine, April 1989.

[1] Masefield probably knew Campden through his visits as a boy to Woolas Hall, on the slopes of Bredon Hill (see p.140).

10. BROADWAY - FURNITURE FOR TODAY:
Gordon Russell (1892-1980)

Soon after the Guild of Handicraft arrived in Chipping Campden a boy started at the nearby Grammar School who would later become a leading figure in furniture design and manufacture. Gordon Russell, the son of a bank employee, was born at Cricklewood, London, on May 20th 1892. The family moved to Tooting, then to Repton, and finally to the Cotswolds when his father bought the Lygon Arms at Broadway. Gordon Russell and his brother Don became boarders at Chipping Campden Grammar School ("a pleasant, sunny, unhurried period", he recalled). On Saturday mornings Gordon and Don would walk the four and a half miles over Fish Hill

> to the tune of 'The Blue Bells of Scotland' from the Church tower, and we were met by mother driving the pony cart. We seldom got very far - there were so many things to investigate on the way, such as men at work on various interesting jobs, birds' nests, cider making, or even smoking an occasional Woodbine, then five for a penny. It was a notable expedition, however often it was repeated.

When Russell left school at the end of 1907 he worked for three months as purser on the SS Veronese, and travelled to South America. On his return he took charge of a workshop in Broadway where a group of men repaired antique furniture, most of it for his father's hotel. Here he acquired skills which he would put to good use. He also became aware of the Arts and Crafts movement.

Russell's father went to Campden to see the work of the Guild of Handicraft. He visited Ernest Gimson in his workshop at Daneway and Gimson and Sidney Cockerell came to Broadway. (In later years Harry Gardiner, who had worked at Gimson's smithy, took charge of the metal-working shop at Broadway, making fittings for Russell's furniture). At Campden Russell joined a small life-class, and among the craftsmen he met there were Will Hart the woodcarver, his brother George the silversmith and Fred Griggs the architect and artist. ("This meeting of workers in so many different crafts was very important to me, for it freed my imagination to try my hand at designing various things", he wrote).

At Broadway Russell started experimenting:

> ...I was trying to solve a problem, finding out the snags for myself and endeavouring to resolve them... My knowledge of design had grown from looking at good old things, always a sound background. But I looked at them for inspiration, not in

order to imitate... I was always going off at a tangent and designing the most improbable things, with the complete assurance of youth.

At the outbreak of war Russell enlisted in the Worcestershire Regiment, and in 1915 saw active service in France. In 1917 he became an officer, and early in the final year of the hostilities was awarded the Military Cross for his gallantry in organising a counter-attack. The story is told in his autobiography 'Designer's Trade.'

When the war was over Russell returned to the Cotswolds and, like many men back from the trenches, found himself facing an uncertain future. He recalled how, at the age of 27, he sat in the Lygon Arms and wondered what he was going to do; he had no qualifications other than a sound knowledge of old furniture and its construction. The age of machinery had long arrived, and he decided to explore its use in furniture manufacture. He knew that his family would help him; they could and would give financial backing for schemes in which they believed.

Don Russell came home soon after Gordon, and it was decided that the brothers and their parents would set up the firm of "S.B. Russell & Sons". A younger brother, Dick, joined the firm when he left school in 1920.

On May 20th 1920 (Gordon Russell's birthday), Toni Denning came from London for interview for the post of Gordon's assistant, and on June 21st (her own birthday), she started work at Broadway. After just five months Gordon Russell and Toni Denning were engaged, and in August 1921 they were married in London.

At Broadway Russell continued with his experimental furniture designs and financed his work by developing the antiques side of the family business. His parents liked the new pieces, but his brother Don was less sure, feeling that it would be difficult to sell expensive, modern furniture. Gordon reluctantly agreed. "People bought antiques if they could afford them," he said, "reproductions if they could not, and there was to them nothing else."

The firm persevered, however, and in 1922 S.B. Russell & Sons exhibited at the Art Gallery in Cheltenham. A direct result was an invitation to show some work at the exhibition of the British Institute of Industrial Art in the Victoria and Albert Museum the following year. (Heal's, the other firm selected, was one of the few firms still developing ideas based on the Arts and Crafts tradition). S.B. Russell & Sons was now producing high quality furniture in their Broadway workshops, and in 1924 they exhibited a cabinet in the British Empire Exhibition at Wembley. It was bought by Lord Dunsany for the then high sum of two hundred pounds.

At Broadway new showrooms had been opened: public reaction was mixed.

There was no doubt at all that people found our showrooms an interesting place to visit, although many seemed to think we were crazy. They simply could not understand, for instance, why we refused to stain our furniture, as at that time almost all furniture was finished a 'rich Jacobean colour', or, in the trade, 'Jaco' for short. We followed the example set by Gimson and other designers of showing the natural wood, just because it was a lovely material, but the bare idea of any departure from established conventions seemed ridiculous to some people.

Russell's view of the Arts and Crafts tradition was not iconoclastic (he admired much of the work which it had produced), but was realistic. Although William Morris saw a role for machines in releasing craftsmen from dull, repetitive tasks in order to do more creative work, and at Sapperton Gimson and the Barnsleys used circular saws and other machinery for particular purposes, an insistence on hand-crafted production wherever possible was the movement's downfall. Their pieces could only be made in small numbers, and were therefore expensive. Russell saw the irony. "Arts and Crafts goods", he said, "could only be bought by people whose incomes came from the use of machinery". Russell's view was nearer to that of Ashbee, who wrote in his Journal "Machinery is necessary in modern production, so also is human individuality. Machinery in so far as it destroys human individuality is bad, in so far as it develops it is good."

After a lifetime of machine-based design and production Russell was able to reconcile the two disciplines. In his autobiography he recognised the worth of the best handwork, bringing as it did the craftsman into a much more intimate relationship with his material than machinery ever could.

In 1978, two years before his death, Russell spoke on "Skill" to the Royal Society of Arts and the Faculty of Royal Designers for Industry, where he reminded his audience

> Do not forget that hand and machine are complementary - an improvement in one leads in time to an improvement in the other and, as William Morris noted nearly a hundred years ago, any improvement in the work men do leads rapidly and inevitably to an improvement in the men who do it.

Russell recalled that it was the Great War which had initiated the mechanizing of the wood-working industry. He regretted that mass production of furniture had begun when few, if any, designers had had experience of machine manufacture. Both manufacturer and public were, he said, exploited by the production of cheap, poor quality articles. Designers capable of original thought were not valued highly, and instead "almost everyone in the trade was busy imitating someone or something". Repairing antiques was one thing, he said, but copying them or imitating them was quite another. Because antiques were expensive, many were buying reproductions, and for them good contemporary furniture simply did not exist . The 'arts and crafts' work of Morris, Gimson and the Barnsleys, Ashbee and others was known only to a tiny group of people; good craftsmen were wasting their time making second-rate furniture or withdrawing from public life altogether and supplying just a few wealthy customers.

Russell saw his future in designing furniture of and for his own time and producing it to a high standard. In about 1923 he visited John Gloag in London and showed him photographs of contemporary furniture which was being made at Broadway. Gloag was an authority on architectural history and, at that time, the assistant editor of "The

Cabinet Maker". Gloag was impressed by the photographs and visited Broadway. He later observed that

> the influence and aims of the Russell Workshops at Broadway, Worcestershire, go far beyond the designing and making of furniture. The development of these workshops must have vivid interest for every one who cares for the future of craftsmanship, for Gordon Russell is creating something in Broadway that foreshadows an enlightened alliance between handicraft and machine-craft. He has never surrounded his work with a glittering integument of vague aspirations. Good workmanship and fitness have been the first concerns, and in the cabinet-making shops and the smiths' shop they form the basic principles of all production.

Gloag published some of Russell's photographs in "The Cabinet Maker" and in the yearbooks of the Design and Industries Association. He admired the work of the building department at the Russell workshops, which had been created originally to undertake the restoration and enlargement of the Lygon Arms. "When this work was completed", he wrote,

> and the gracious old building had modern additions in good Cotswold stone, cut and shaped easily and naturally in the old tradition of the Cotswolds, it was found that a singularly fine instrument had been created: a staff of men animated by the spirit that ran through the Russell Workshops, invigorated by the same ideas of good workmanship, having the same informed respect for tradition; a staff that made it possible for Gordon Russell to consider a practical extension of his conception of real modern craftsmanship in stone.

Russell himself had already expressed his admiration of the building techniques of Gimson, the Barnsleys, Norman Jewson and Fred Griggs, and this must have influenced the standard of building work done at Broadway.

Perhaps Gordon Russell's greatest contribution to twentieth century furniture-making in Britain was to emphasise the importance of integrating design and machine manufacture. He saw, as had his Arts and Crafts predecessors, that "design affects the whole pattern of life, and good design was an essential part of the good life", but he pointed out that designing for the machine would require a very different training from designing for hand production if the product were not to be inferior in quality. The point had already been made in Germany by Walter Gropius, who founded the Staatliches Bauhaus at Weimar in 1919 to teach methods of designing for machine production, but it needed a craftsman of Russell's conviction to drive it home in England.

Gordon and Toni Russell were living in Spencer Cottage, next to the Lygon Arms, when their first child, Michael, was born in 1922. Their thoughts began to turn to the idea of a larger house, and when their second child, Oliver, was born in 1924 a move became urgent. Failing to find a suitable house they decided to have one built to their own design.

That summer they found a site at Kingcombe, just below Dover's Hill and overlooking Campden. On Boxing Day 1924 the first sod was cut by Russell himself, and building soon began. They moved into the house in May 1926.

The Russells were finding life full: as if caring for two young children and supervising the building of their new home were not enough, they were busy at Broadway preparing for the 1925 Paris Exhibition, where in due course they were to win a gold and two silver medals. The print cabinet on a stand shown in plate 34 dates from this period.

Pondering the fact that most of the men who had designed good furniture in the tradition of William Morris had been architects, it seemed to Russell that the ability to think in three dimensions, obviously essential in an architect, was of equal importance in a designer of

34. Print Cabinet by Gordon Russell. (1925).

furniture. He urged that the two disciplines should be as one - that architects should "reach into the rooms and details of a house" to ensure that the houses could contain well designed articles available from stock.

Gordon and his younger brother Dick persuaded their father that Dick should train for four years at the Architectural Association School. ("None of us regretted this step, though it threw a great deal of his work back on me", Gordon Russell recalled). The Broadway workshops had by now taken on several kinds of job. They were, for example, producing for schools, libraries and other institutions large numbers of turned chairs with rush seats, the design of which could be derived from the chairs which Ernest Gimson had been taught to make by Philip Clisset, the chair-bodger at Bosbury near Ledbury. As well as the turned chairs many larger pieces left the Broadway workshops, either for the mass market or in ones or twos for special orders. "There was no doubt about it", Russell proclaimed, "our standards of workmanship were getting pretty good...". The late twenties were Russell's most prolific years as a designer; he created literally thousands of designs, not only for furniture (plate 35) but also for pieces in metal and in glass.

When Dick returned from the Architectural School, the effect of his training in designing for machine manufacture was soon apparent, and as the Broadway workshops became more and more mechanised the furniture coming out of them was increasingly of Dick's design. In 1929 it was decided necessary to open a showroom in London. A

35. Sideboard by Gordon Russell. (1926).

shop was therefore rented in Wigmore Street, which offered for sale not only Russell furniture but also glass items (some designed by Gordon Russell) and textiles.

The years of the late twenties, then, were the time when S. B. Russell & Sons changed direction, and radically. No longer would the firm adhere to the style (and largely the methods) of the Arts and Crafts movement; no longer would they concentrate on elaborate single pieces made to special order though this was still possible; no longer would the designs be the work of one man, Gordon Russell. From now on simple, high quality furniture of twentieth century design would be produced to contract order. There would be a team of designers led by two men. One of these was Gordon Russell's brother Dick; the other was W. H. Russell (no relation), who had been sent by Percy Wells, the head of the cabinet-making section at Shoreditch Technical Institute, and who had worked his way up to the position of head designer. The design team could now offer complete rooms, made in batches of six - a move which finally integrated the previously distinct disciplines of furniture making and architecture. The Russell workshops had embraced the 'new' Modernism.

Company organisation, too, saw changes. On 4th November 1927 a new firm, The Russell Workshops Ltd., was formed, and following the stock market crash on Wall Street Gordon Russell Ltd. was founded on September 28th 1929.

In 1930 Russell received a telephone call from Frank Murphy. Murphy had just begun the manufacture of radio sets and wanted Russell's firm to design and make the wooden cabinets. Following the telephone call Murphy visited Broadway, Gordon and Dick Russell went to the Murphy factory at Welwyn Garden City,and a contract was signed: this would be mass production on a scale quite new to the Russell workshops. As a result Dick Russell joined Murphy's company but continued working for Gordon Russell Ltd. as a freelance designer and consultant. Frank Murphy obtained wooden radio cabinets of very high quality (plate 36), and the necessary increase in mechanisation and. the mass production of precisely engineered articles gave Gordon Russell Ltd. valuable experience at the time when it was most needed.

36. Radio Cabinet by R.D. Russell, as used by Murphy Radio Co. (1935).

After 1933 Gordon Russell himself did not attempt further designs for forty four years.

In 1935 Russell contacted Nikolaus Pevsner, best known today as Editor of the "Buildings of England" series. In 1934 the rise of Nazism had forced Pevsner to leave his job in the Dresden Art Gallery and emigrate to England. He obtained a temporary post at Birmingham University, from which base he toured the country, visiting firms and studying how goods were designed. He was invited by Russell to act as a buyer for Gordon Russell Ltd. and for several years advised on the selection and display of glass, textiles and rugs for the firm's showrooms. Following his departure in 1939 he became one of the foremost authorities on art and architecture in England. He remained a friend of Russell, and in his autobiography the latter recalled that, more than forty years after their friendship had begun, Pevsner and his daughter were staying with the Russells at Broadway when Pevsner received the news that he had been awarded the Royal Gold Medal by the Royal Institute of British Architects in recognition of his work as an architectural historian. It was at Broadway, too, that the publisher Allen Lane held a party to mark Pevsner's sixty-fifth birthday.

Gordon Russell Ltd. went from strength to strength. By 1934 the firm employed more than 400 workers; Dick Russell at Murphy's was busy designing radio cabinets and the Broadway workshop could not cope with the demand for them. Pevsner recalled that "it was not only obviously inadequate, but the radio work - a hundred per cent machine work as it had to be - was bad for the mentality of Broadway. Furthermore, the growth of a large factory would be bad for the amenities of Broadway". It was decided to build a factory on the Guinness estate at Park Royal in London, and the firm moved there in July 1935.

The years before the outbreak of the Second World War were a time of achievement and prosperity for Gordon Russell Ltd. Pevsner had no doubt who was responsible.

The factory prospered, the contract work prospered, and the showrooms were doing well. Everybody worked with pleasure - because everybody worked for Gordon Russell personally. He went round the workshops and knew all the cabinet-makers, all the upholsterers, the smiths and of course the draughtsmen. He went round the showrooms, sympathetic and amused. He criticised constructively and kept policy in his hands, and his wisdom shone warmly through everything he said and did.

In the middle of all this activity, on January 28th 1938 S. B. Russell died. It was his wife's birthday and exactly thirty four years after taking over the Lygon Arms. He was buried at Chipping Campden, and Gordon Russell carved his father's tombstone.

Russell saw that if he was to further his aim of bringing good design to the general public he would have to expand the outlets available. He formed the Good Furnishing Group, and for nearly a year Russell furniture was sold in selected stores all over England.

In 1939 the company's ambitions were put firmly to one side. The London showrooms were closed, the Park Royal factory was taken over by the Admiralty, and at Broadway the workshops turned their attention to making Mosquito wing nosings, ammunition boxes, wind-tunnel models, instrument cases and model aircraft for recognition-training. In October 1940 much of the furniture and textiles which it had been assumed would be in safer keeping at Broadway than in London, were destroyed when a German incendiary bomb ignited the thatched barn.

From this point Gordon Russell's commitment to the firm decreased in favour of his other activities. On October 19th 1940 he resigned his managing directorship, one R. H. Bee being appointed in his place, though Russell remained on the board of the company. In that year he was elected Royal Designer for Industry.

Through the war years and after, Gordon Russell sat on numerous bodies advising on design and manufacture. They included the Utility Furniture Advisory Committee (1942), set up by Hugh Dalton, President of the Board of Trade; the Council for Industrial Design (later the Design Council), which he joined in 1943, becoming chairman in 1947, and the Board of Trade Design Panel (1943-47) with its organising committees for the 1946 'Britain Can Make It' Exhibition at the Victoria and Albert Museum and the 1951 Festival of Britain on the South Bank.

In 1947 Russell was made a Companion of the British Empire. In 1952 he became an Honorary Designer at the Royal College of Art, where his brother Dick, who had become a successful London architect, was now Professor of Furniture Design. Seven years later Gordon Russell became a Senior Fellow of the College. In 1955 he was knighted. The Design Centre in the Haymarket, which Sir Gordon Russell had helped to found, was opened by him in April 1956.

At Broadway the workshops were busy making contemporary furniture. A notable contract which they were given was to supply two thousand chairs for the nave of the new Coventry Cathedral.

From 1960 Sir Gordon Russell spent more of his time at his beloved Kingcombe. Work there had not ceased with the building of the house; extensions became necessary, and these had to be planned and their construction supervised. The sloping gardens needed a staircase, and when Campden railway station closed a supply of stone became available. The development of the house and garden is lovingly described in 'Designer's Trade'.

For Russell, retirement was not an option. He had too much to offer and wanted to offer. The list of committees, Councils, governing bodies, Associations, Societies, Institutes etc. which were given

37. Sir Gordon Russell.

the benefit of his experience is long. (He even gave advice on the designs of British postage stamps and bank notes). Wherever he went, this tall, large man with grey hair and a clipped moustache had a military bearing which gave him an air of authority. Honours were bestowed on him by Birmingham University, the Royal College of Art, the Royal Institute of British Architects and the Institute of Landscape Architects.

In 1968 Pevsner reviewed Russell's professional life:

Making the best furniture by hand, making the best modern furniture by hand, selling the best modern fabrics and other furnishings with it, making the best-designed modern furniture by machine, selling it through others, designing modern furniture on a national scale, and so in the end directing the whole national movement towards good modern design - no personal development could be more logical and more satisfying.

In 1978 Sir Gordon Russell was told that he had motor neurone disease, a progressive wasting of the muscles. Undeterred, he gave his address on "Skill" at the Royal Society of Arts in November that year. On July 11th 1980 he was awarded an Honorary Doctorate of the Royal College of Art at a Convocation ceremony at Kingcombe. Three months later he died, and was buried at the parish church in Campden.

During Russell's lifetime the Arts and Crafts movement gave way to a machine-based furniture manufacturing industry. In designing specifically for machine production Russell demonstrated that the transition from handcraft to mass production need not, and in the Russell workshops would not, mean a fall in standards. He showed that high quality furniture could at last be accessible to "ordinary people" (a favourite phrase of his).

In 1977, just three years before he died, Sir Gordon returned to designing furniture - for Kingcombe. He enlisted the help of Adriaan Hermsen, who had recently retired from his job as Works Manager at Gordon Russell Ltd. after nearly fifty years with the company and its predecessor. The pieces which were made for Kingcombe included a remarkable and beautiful dining table with a yew top and laburnum base. "When the pieces were made", wrote Jeremy Myerson, "they revealed a strong affinity with the Arts and Crafts movement of his boyhood; it was as if fifty years of Modernism had passed without really touching him".

Chapter 10 - FURTHER READING

Payne, C.M.: *Gordon Russell's Furniture*, Antique Collecting Magazine, Vol.14 No.4, (1979).
Pevsner, Nikolaus: *Patient Progress Two: Gordon Russell.* Studies in Art, Architecture, and Design Vol. 2: Victorian and After. Thames & Hudson (1968).
Russell, Sir Gordon: *Designer's Trade (an autobiography)*. Allen & Unwin (1968).
Russell, Gordon: *Furniture*. 'Things We See' series, Penguin (1953).
Russell, Sir Gordon: *Looking at Furniture*. Lund Humphries (1964).

11. POETRY FROM THE COTSWOLDS

PERCY BYSSHE SHELLEY (1792-1822)

In the year 1814 the poet Percy Bysshe Shelley was desperately unhappy. His marriage of but three years to Harriet Westwood was in crisis. His wife, barely twenty years of age, was growing away from her husband as she matured, and a separation seemed inevitable. The poet pleaded with Harriet for reconciliation, and indeed on March 23rd 1814 their marriage, which had been solemnized under Scots law, took place again in the Church of England. But Harriet, despite being pregnant with their second child, was not to be persuaded, and in June she moved to her father's house in Bath, taking their first daughter Ianthe with her. Shelley sought solace in the company of Mary Godwin, and at the end of July travelled with Mary to Switzerland, during which journey Shelley even wrote to Harriet urging her to join them, a request that unsurprisingly was rejected. Six weeks after leaving England Shelley and Mary returned to an atmosphere of hostility: relations between the families of Shelley, Harriet, and Mary were bad, and the poet was in some financial difficulty. Early in 1815 Shelley's grandfather, Sir Bysshe Shelley, died, and the poet received a settlement from his father, which he shared with Harriet.

That summer began for Shelley with a spell of poor health, and he came under the care of the eminent London surgeon Sir William Lawrence. Shelley's condition gradually improved, and he decided to rent a house near his friend the poet Thomas Love Peacock at Bishopsgate, near Windsor Great Park, where Mary joined him in August that year.

The following month, at Peacock's instigation a boating expedition was organised, in which Shelley and Mary, accompanied by Peacock and their friends Charles and Mary Clairmont, would travel up the Thames as far as conditions would allow, in an attempt reach the river's source. The project turned out to be a very enjoyable holiday; it certainly had a beneficial effect on Shelley, as Peacock recorded:

…We started from, and returned to, Old Windsor, and our excursion occupied about ten days. This was, I think, the origin of Shelley's taste for boating, which he retained to the end of his life. On our way up, at Oxford, he was so much out of order that he feared being obliged to return. He had been living chiefly on tea and bread and butter, drinking occasionally a sort of spurious lemonade, made out of some powder in a box, which, as he was reading at the time the *Tale of a Tub*[1] he called the powder of *pimperlimp*. He consulted a doctor, who may have done him some good, but it was not apparent. I told him, "If he would allow me to prescribe for him, I would set him to rights." He asked "What would be your prescription?" I said "Three mutton chops, well peppered." He said " Do you really think so?" I said " I am sure of it." He took the prescription; the success was obvious and immediate. He lived in my way for the rest of our expedition, rowed vigorously, was cheerful, merry, overflowing with thorough enjoyment of life.

Shelley's mood was indeed uplifted. Charles Clairmont told his sister Clara that their original intention had been to proceed along a canal which connected the Thames to the Severn, and so follow that river to its source. However, this was not to be. Charles later wrote to Clara:

... all this airy scheme was soon laid aside, for the Commissioners would

38. Shelley (portrait by Amelia Curran, 1819).

not let us pass the Severn Canal under £20. This was out of the question; so, having satisfied ourselves on these points, we determined at least to draw our boat up to the very spring of the Thames before we returned. We made a most bold endeavour at this last project; but, by the time we got three miles above Lechlade, the weeds became so enormously thick and high, that all three of us tugging could not move the boat an inch; the water also, a little further on was so shallow that it barely covered the hoofs of some cows standing in the middle to drink.

The party returned to Lechlade, where they stayed two nights at the local tavern. In the nearby churchyard Shelley was moved to verse. The poem which he wrote there has an atmosphere which is tranquil and reassuring, and even the moment of unease near the poem's end is quickly set aside.

A SUMMER EVENING CHURCHYARD
Lechlade, Gloucestershire

The wind has swept from the wide atmosphere
Each vapour that obscured the sunset's ray;
And pallid Evening twines its beaming hair
In duskier braids around the languid eyes of Day:
Silence and Twilight unbeloved of men,
Creep hand in hand from yon obscurest glen.

They breathe their spells towards the departing day,
Encompassing the earth, air, stars and sea;
Light, sound and motion own the potent sway,
Responding to the charm with its own mystery.
The winds are still, or the dry church-tower grass
Knows not their gentle motions as they pass.

Thou too, aerial Pile! whose pinnacles
Point from one shrine like pyramids of fire,
Obeyest in silence their sweet solemn spells,
Clothing in hues of heaven thy dim and distant spire,
Around whose lessening and invisible height
Gather among the stars the clouds of night.

The dead are sleeping in their sepulchres:
And, mouldering as they sleep, a thrilling sound,
Half sense, half thought, among the darkness stirs,
Breathed from their wormy beds all living things around,
And mingling with the still night and mute sky
Its awful hush is felt inaudibly.

Thus solemnized and softened, death is mild
And terrorless as this serenest night:
Here could I hope, like some inquiring child
Sporting on graves, that death did hide from human sight
Sweet secrets, or beside its breathless sleep
That loveliest dreams perpetual watch did keep.

On returning to Bishopsgate Shelley's spirits were so raised that he was able to write to Thomas Jefferson Hogg.

My dear friend,
Your letter has lain by me for the last week, reproaching me every day. I found it on my return from a water excursion on the Thames... The exercise and dissipation of mind attached to such an expedition have produced so favourable an effect on my health, that my habitual dejection and irritability have almost deserted me, and I can devote six hours in the day to study without difficulty...

One might speculate on how much more inspiration Shelley might have found for verse, had he journeyed further into the quiet backwaters of the Cotswolds!

EDWARD THOMAS (1878-1917)

Edward Thomas's much loved poem 'Adlestrop' owes its origin to a visit he made to the village of Dymock, tucked away in the north west corner of Gloucestershire, many miles from the Cotswolds. Keith Clark has told the story of the poets who made Dymock their home, in 'The Muse Colony'. These 'Dymock Poets' included Lascelles Abercrombie, Robert Frost and Wilfrid Gibson. In the years and months just before the First World War they brought to this remote area other writers - Rupert Brooke, John Drinkwater, W. H. Davies, the children's writer Eleanor Farjeon, and Edward Thomas.

Thomas was born in London in 1878. His father was Welsh, while on his mother's side were both Welsh and Spanish blood. He had long wished to become a writer, and his first published work, 'The Woodland Life', appeared in the year that he went to Oxford University. In it he already showed the love of nature and of the countryside which would be seen in much of his later work, including 'Adlestrop'.

In 1899 Edward Thomas married Helen Noble, and two years later they settled in Kent. In 1906 they moved to Steep, near Petersfield in Hampshire, where Thomas worked at reviews and literary criticism. His abiding passion for things rural led him to walk and cycle extensively in southern England. His biography of Richard Jefferies (1909), for example, describes vividly the countryside and people of rural Wiltshire, while 'The South Country' of the same year is a broader picture of pastoral England at that time.

In February 1913 Thomas met the American poet Robert Frost, four years his senior, at the Sussex home of the poet Vivian Locke-Ellis, and began a friendship which lasted until Thomas's death four years later. Helen Thomas recalled that

> To Edward he was an inspiration, and he and Robert could hardly have been more devoted. They had been drawn together by Edward's recognition of Robert's genius, when Robert had failed to make any mark in America. Edward's reviews of his early volumes of poetry published in England laid the foundation for Robert's success here and later in his own country. And Robert in his turn encouraged Edward - who had not then written any poetry - to think of himself as a potential poet, and thus in the last two years of his life to give Edward his deepest intellectual satisfaction and pleasure.

Thomas's first published poem was written in December 1914.

Robert Frost was persuaded by his friends Wilfrid Gibson and Lascelles Abercrombie to move with his family from Beaconsfield to Dymock, and did so in the spring of 1914, taking a cottage, 'Little Iddens', at Leddington near Ledbury. It was not long before Thomas began visiting the Frosts at their new home, and decided that the area would be very suitable for the family's holiday that year. At the beginning of August Thomas and his son Merfyn set out by cycle from Steep to Leddington, and on August 4th (after "a horrendous, dislocated journey", Myfanwy recalls) Helen arrived at Leddington accompanied by daughters Myfanwy and Bronwen, a Russian boy who had been lodging with the Thomases while on holiday from nearby Bedales School, and the family dog 'Rags'. (The 'horrendous' journey is described in Helen Thomas's 'Time and Again'). The whole family stayed for a month at the house of a fruit farmer, a field or two away from the Frosts.

During his visits to Dymock Thomas met Abercrombie and Gibson, and renewed his acquaintance with Rupert Brooke (soon to be a major War poet), who happened to be visiting Gibson. Another visitor to Dymock was John ('Jack') Haines, a relative of Abercrombie's wife Catherine. Haines was a solicitor who lived at Hucclecote near Gloucester; he was also an amateur botanist and a poet, and a friend of Edward Thomas, Robert Frost, W.H. Davies and the Gloucestershire poet and composer Ivor Gurney. Accompanied by Frost or Thomas, Haines went on botanical excursions in the Cotswolds, on

39. Edward Thomas.

May Hill near Gloucester or in the fields and lanes around Dymock. Frost visited Haines at Hucclecote, and Thomas often cycled there and stayed with Haines while journeying to Coventry.

The journey which seems to have inspired Edward Thomas to write 'Adlestrop' took place on Tuesday, June 23rd 1914, when he travelled from Paddington to Ledbury, and hence to Leddington, to stay with the Frosts. Thomas recorded the journey in his Field Notebook 75:

23 JUNE 1914. A glorious day from 4.20 a.m. and at 10 tiers above tiers of white cloud with dirtiest grey bars above the sea of slate and dull brick by Battersea Park. Then at Oxford tiers of pure white with loose longer masses above and gaps of dark clear blue above haymaking and elms.

Then we stopped at Adlestrop, through the willows could be heard a chain of blackbirds' songs at 12.45 and one thrush and no man seen, only a hiss of engine letting off steam.

Stopping outside Campden by banks of long grass, willowherb and meadowsweet, extraordinary silence between two periods of travel - looking out on grey dry stones between metals and the shining metals and over it all the elms willows and long grass - one man clears his throat - a greater than rustic silence. No house in view. Stop only for a minute till signal is up.

The railway timetable for this period shows that if Thomas caught the 10.20 train from Paddington (consistent with "at 10… by Battersea Park"), then the stop at Adlestrop was scheduled, and at almost the time he noted. Thomas may not have expected the train to pull up there, which might explain why he describes it as having stopped "unwontedly".

ADLESTROP

Yes, I remember Adlestrop -
The name, because one afternoon
Of heat the express train drew up there
Unwontedly. It was late June.

The steam hissed. Someone cleared his throat.
No one left and no one came
On the bare platform. What I saw
Was Adlestrop - only the name.

And willows, willow-herb, and grass
And meadow-sweet, and haycocks dry,
No whit less still and lonely fair
Than the high cloudlets in the sky.

And for that minute a blackbird sang
Close by, and round him, mistier,
Farther and farther, all the birds
Of Oxfordshire and Gloucestershire.

Thomas returned to London on June 26th or 27th. (Myfanwy Thomas has said that her father had arranged to accompany Eleanor Farjeon to the ballet to see Pavlova dance). Eleanor Farjeon was at this time a close friend of the Thomases, and remained so for fifty years. "She never ceased", wrote Helen Thomas, "to be the one who rejoiced with us on happy occasions or on whose sympathy and comfort we relied in sadness". In late August 1914 Eleanor Farjeon went to Herefordshire and joined the Thomases, who were already at Leddington, for a short holiday.

Edward Thomas enlisted in the army in July 1915. In 1917 he went to France, and on Monday, April 9th that year he was killed at Arras.

Thomas's poetry first appeared, under the pseudonym 'Edward Eastaway', in anthologies. One such was 'An Annual of New Poetry', which was reviewed by J.C. Squire, writing as 'Solomon Eagle'. The verses of Frost, Gibson and Drinkwater did not impress him, but he claimed to know who 'Eastaway' was, and was full of praise for what he read.

The one poet whose contributions make this work really worth having is Mr. Edward Eastaway. ... One's knowledge did not prepossess one in favour of his poetry; one did not think that a real gift for verse could remain so long unexploited without becoming atrophied. But the unlikely has happened; and his poems are better than his prose, good though some of this has been. ... he is worth fifty Frosts. His verse does not sing, and it never shouts; yet the absence of music in the words is compensated for by a sort of music of the mind...

In the Foreword to Thomas's 'Collected Poems' Walter de la Mare wrote

When ... Edward Thomas was killed in Flanders, a mirror of England was shattered of so pure and true a crystal that a clearer and tenderer reflection can be found no other where than in these poems... Loose-woven, monotonous, unrelieved, the verse, as verse, may appear to a careless reader accustomed to the customary. It must be read slowly as naturally as if it were talk, without emphasis; then it will surrender himself, his beautiful world, his compassionate and suffering heart, his fine, lucid, grave and sensitive mind. This is not a poetry that will drug or intoxicate, civicise [sic] or edify - in the usual meaning of the word, though it rebuilds reality, It enobles by simplication...

In 1963 Helen Thomas recalled the few years when her husband had been writing verse.

Robert [Frost] and his family returned to America, where he found himself famous, and Edward enlisted in the Artists Rifles and began to write poetry. But there was no enthusiastic reviewer to praise his poems. No publisher would take them and only a few of his intimate friends thought well of them. And Edward was killed at Arras before he knew that by his few poems his name would be remembered.

Adlestrop station was closed in 1966 (plate 40 is one of the last pictures taken). A nameboard and a bench were preserved, and placed in a bus shelter which was built at the end of the village street. The short poem, simple yet so vivid in its portrayal of a sleepy country railway station on a hot summer afternoon, appears on a metal plaque in the bus shelter. It brings thousands of visitors each year - poetry lovers and railway enthusiasts alike to this corner of the Cotswolds. Myfanwy Thomas wrote in 1992:

It is wonderful that, 75 years after my father was killed in action at the battle of Arras, his poetry should become more and more known; but I wish, in a way, that lovely as it is, 'Adlestrop' had not appeared quite so often as representative of his work when there are so many other fine and varied poems.

40. Adlestrop Station around 1963, shortly before its closure.

W. H. DAVIES (1871-1940)

In 1905 George Bernard Shaw received from a certain W.H. Davies a slim volume, 'The Soul's Destroyer and Other Poems', which had been printed privately in the East End of London. "...before I had read three lines", Shaw recalled,

> I perceived that the author was a real poet... Here, I saw, was a genuine innocent, writing odds and ends of verse about odds and ends of things, living quite out of the world in which such things are usually done, and knowing no better (or rather no worse) than to get his book made by the appropriate craftsman and hawk it round like any other ware.

Shaw arranged to meet the poet in a south London pub and resolved then and there to help him. Davies was recommended to send copies to various critics. One of these was Edward Thomas "and", wrote Helen Thomas,

> ... my husband was surprised and delighted to find that he was reading the work of a genius. He communicated his discovery to his friend Edward Garnett and together they went to see W.H. Davies at 'The Farmhouse' - a Common Lodging House. This meeting and the enthusiastic review Edward [Thomas] had written of the poem established a friendship between himself and Davies which resulted in his coming to stay with us at our real farmhouse in Kent.

Following favourable reviews the book was taken up by a literary agent and the first edition was sold out.

William Henry Davies was born at his grandfather's public house in Newport, Monmouthshire (now Gwent) on April 20th 1871. His father died when the boy was young, and when Davies's mother remarried he was adopted by his grandparents together with his brother and sister. As a schoolboy he was a frequent truant and often fighting. ("If I took off my coat to battle in the streets, the shirt itself came off in the lanes and fields"). Davies was a good athlete and, rather less expectedly, "not a bad scholar... I passed all my standards with ease".

When he was 22 years old Davies went to New York on a cargo ship, and for five years he travelled by whatever means were available across the American states, sometimes working, ("here and there as the inclination seized me"), more often begging, occasionally returning briefly to England as a cattle-man, and all the time gaining the wealth of experience which he would later describe in his autobiography. At the end of this period Davies returned to England for what he assumed would be the last time, but he could not settle, and a newspaper article on the Gold Rush turned his thoughts to the Klondyke. He was soon on his way to St. John's, Newfoundland, from where he intended to make his way across Canada ("... without using a cent for travelling"). The accident which put an end to his plans (and almost to his life) happened at Renfrew, Ontario. When attempting to board a moving freight train Davies fell, and his right foot was severed at the ankle. ("I bore this accident with an outward fortitude that was far from the true state of my feelings"). In the hospital it was decided that the leg would have to be amputated at the knee, and this was done. Such was Davies's stamina and the standard of nursing care that five weeks later he was back in Britain. ("...all the wildness had been taken out of me, and my adventures after this were not of my own seeking, but the result of circumstances"). Davies went first to his home town of Newport, but did not stay long; he was soon in London, living in lodging-houses and writing verse. This he submitted regularly to publishers, who with equal regularity returned it. It was not until Shaw read 'The Soul's Destroyer', and Edward Thomas reviewed it, that he met with success, and began the career that established him as a major literary figure.

Davies ("...a short, stocky, dark man, rather Jewish-looking but with a strong Welsh accent" recalled Helen Thomas) went to live with the Thomases at their farmhouse near Sevenoaks in Kent on January 23rd 1906. His wooden leg fascinated Merfyn and Bronwen, who adored him and called him 'Sweet William'. In spite of his background Davies was a most untramplike person, being gentle and sensitive in his manner and fastidious in his dress and personal cleanliness. In the evenings ("...over a pipe and a pint of beer...") he told the Thomases of his early life and of his experiences in America. It was at Edward Thomas's instigation that Davies began to set down his narrative in the form of a book. On August 29th 1906 Thomas wrote to his friend Edward Garnett, who had some influence in the world of publishing:

Dear Garnett,

      I am sorry about the Poet's life. But I think I have succeeded in setting him to work to increase it - as far as possible in the way you suggest. I agree about the details and I think he can do them pretty well. All the additions he has planned are elaborations of episodes hardly touched on before, e.g. on tramp in the States and peddling in England...

Thomas and Garnett suggested that George Bernard Shaw be asked to write a preface. Shaw, having read the book "through from beginning to end" proposed the title 'Autobiography of a Supertramp' (prompted, no doubt, by his own recent title 'Man and Superman'). "Mr. Shaw", wrote Davies in the Author's Note, "in spite of his busy life, came forward with fine sympathy and kindness, and with his Preface the immediate popularity of the book was assured". In fact, the book was not "immediately popular", but sales increased and it was always in demand.

    Near the Thomas's farmhouse Edward rented a small cottage, and used one of the rooms as a study. Davies moved into the rest of the house, and lived there on the ten shillings a week which had been left him by his grandfather, and on such income as he earned from his poetry. In December 1906 the Thomases moved to Steep, near Petersfield in Hampshire, and Davies took a flat in London, at 12 Great Russell Street near the British Museum. The 'Autobiography', and Davies's poetry, here brought him the friendship of a number of literary men, as well as of sculptors and painters. Perhaps he was happiest when he visited these friends in their week-end homes in rural areas; it was the countryside which gave him much of his inspiration, and to which he responded most easily in his poetry. He shared this love with many of his contemporaries, including the Dymock Poets. Davies was a keen and careful observer of nature and in his verses expressed what he saw in an original and powerful way. His love-poetry, ranks him as one of the finest poets of his day. Some of these love-poems are so sensual that it is easy to believe that the poet was writing from his own experiences.

    In 1912 appeared the first volume of an anthology including poems by Lascelles Abercrombie, Rupert Brooke, G.K. Chesterton, W.H. Davies, John Drinkwater, Wilfrid Gibson, D.H. Lawrence, Walter de la Mare and others. The group became known as the 'Georgian Poets' to suggest the opening of a new poetic era with the accession of George V in 1910.

    The War scarcely affected Davies. Prevented by age and his disability from taking an active part, he continued writing poetry. Osbert Sitwell first met Davies in 1917, and remained his friend for the rest of Davies's life. In his introduction to 'The Complete Poems' Sitwell recalled the poet:

His cast of face was rather long and aquiline, but with broad, high cheek bones, and all of it, chin, mouth, long upper lip, nose and high forehead, was finely sculptured and full of character. Features and hair both exhibited a naturally proud, backward slant or tilt, though there was no natural arrogance in him. His eyes were dark: and gleaming, like those of a blackbird, and his skin possessed an almost nautical tinge. He was broad-shouldered and vigorous-looking, but of less than middle height. Having lost a leg he wore - for he could not afford the expense of a new metal limb - a heavy wooden stump, which made a wooden sound as he walked, and gave him a slow and very personal gait, making him raise and lower his shoulders as he moved...

In 1918 Davies spent a holiday with his friend the artist William Rothenstein at Iles Farm, Far Oakridge, a Cotswold hamlet high above the Golden Valley and facing Sapperton on the opposite hill. The visit may have influenced his later decision to move to the Cotswolds.

41. W. H. Davies (portrait by Augustus John, 1918).

On February 5th 1923, at the age of 51, Davies married the 23 year old Helen Payne, daughter of a Sussex farmer. The marriage was a happy one and brought Davies the companionship and domesticity which till then he had lacked. The couple lived first at East Grinstead, but later moved to Sevenoaks and then to Oxted in Surrey.

In 1926 the University of Wales conferred on Davies the honorary degree of Litt.D. In his citation Professor W.D. Thomas described Davies as

...a lover of life, accepting it and glorying in it. He affirms values that were falling into neglect, and in an age that is mercenary reminds us that we have the capacity for spiritual enjoyment. And so I present him to you, that the University of a people that loves beauty and homeliness may do honour to one that has interpreted its spirit to the wider world, and has revealed it to itself.

On March 14th 1928 Davies wrote from Oxted to John Haines saying that he and Helen were contemplating a move to Gloucestershire. They moved to Nailsworth in 1930; for the remainder of Davies's life this would be his home, though he and Helen would move four times in the town during that period.

Following the move to Nailsworth the first of Davies's books to appear was 'Ambition, and Other Poems'.

AMBITION

I had Ambition, by which sin
The angels fell;
I climbed and step by step O Lord,
Ascended into Hell.

Returning now to peace and quiet,
And made more wise,
Let my descent and fall, O Lord,
Be into Paradise.

Then followed 'Jewels of Song', an anthology from the whole range of English poetry which Davies compiled, and the poet's own 'Poems, 1931-32'. Happy in his Cotswold home and happy in his marriage, Davies produced in 1933 the prose works 'My Birds' and 'My Garden', as well as 'The Lover's Song Book', a collection of thirty romantic poems. When this was reprinted in 1935 as 'Love Poems' the number had increased to fifty.

NAILSWORTH HILL

The Moon, that peeped as she came up,
Is clear on top, with all her light;
She rests her chin on Nailsworth Hill,
And, where she looks, the World is white.

White with her light - or is it Frost,
Or is it Snow her eyes have seen;
Or is it Cherry blossom there,
Where no such trees have ever been?

1936 saw the publication of 'The Birth of Song', a slim volume of twenty four poems:

THE BIRTH OF SONG

I am as certain of my song,
When first it warms my brain,
As woman of her unborn child,
Or wind that carries rain.
The child and rain are born at last,
Though now concealed from sight -
'So let my song, unshaped and crude,
Come perfect to the light.

Although Davies was now living in semi-retirement his writing was compulsive. His eye for detail was as sharp as ever and his word-pictures vivid and lyrical.

Davies and his wife were at Newport on September 22nd 1938 for the unveiling of a plaque at his birthplace, Church House in Portland Street. John Masefield was there, and spoke the eulogy at the luncheon which followed. Davies responded:

"These things are usually done for people dead a hundred years or mere, and so I stand a living witness to my own glorification.

Davies's last work: was 'The Loneliest Mountain and Other Poems'. published in 1939.

THE LONELIEST MOUNTAIN

The loneliest mountain, with no house or tree,
Still has its little flower so sweet and wild;
While I, a dreamer, strange and but half known,
Can find no equal till I meet a child.

Davies died at his home, 'Glendower', on September 26th 1940. Osbert Sitwell, who had visited him earlier that year when his health was failing, wrote in his preface to 'The Complete Poems':

No-one who knew him will, or ever could, forget him, even had he never written so many lovely poems, fresh and exquisite as flowers, to keep his memory alive; and no-one who knew him will ever be able to recall him without a smile of pleasure and regret, without tenderness, and without gratitude for a character that was no less remarkable in itself than in the genius it supported and nourished, and of which even the little blemishes and flaws were singularly endearing.

JOHN DRINKWATER (1882-1937)

In 1918 the Cotswold village of Far Oakridge, near Sapperton, became the home for three years of John Drinkwater, friend of the Dymock poets Gibson, Frost and Abercrombie.

By the time, just before the First World War, that he had contributed poems to the anthologies 'Georgian Poetry 1911-1912' and 'New Numbers', Drinkwater had already begun to make a name both as a poet and as an actor. He was born in Leytonstone, Essex. Drinkwater's father was a teacher, and then an actor and general manager in several London theatres. The younger Drinkwater left school at 15 and for a time was a clerk in Nottingham. He joined a repertory company which Barry Jackson had founded in Birmingham, and soon left his office job to work full-time in the theatre. As well as being an actor, Drinkwater became the first manager of the Birmingham Repertory Theatre, and as a playwright he was receiving popular acclaim.

Drinkwater made regular visits to Gloucestershire, visiting not only his poet-friends at Dymock but also the portrait-painter 'Will' (later Sir William) Rothenstein at Iles Farm, Far Oakridge, two years before W.H. Davies stayed there (p.130).

Rothenstein had bought the decayed farmhouse and 55 acres of land in 1912 for £1,200, and proceeded to have the house renovated; he employed Norman Jewson (p.90) as his architect. Near Iles Farm was Winston's Cottage, also belonging to Rothenstein, and from 1914 to 1918 this was the home of the critic and caricaturist Sir Max Beerbohm. In 1916 John Drinkwater visited Rothenstein at Far Oakridge and met Beerbohm. When Beerbohm left Winston's Cottage, Drinkwater, who had fallen in love with the Cotswolds, rented the cottage and moved in with his wife Kathleen.

42. John Drinkwater.

At Oakridge, Drinkwater was in his element. His upbringing had been urban (he wrote some vivid poems on urban themes) but, like Edward Thomas, he loved and was happiest in a rural environment, and delighted in his new home. In the Foreword to his 'Cotswold Characters' Drinkwater expressed his feelings:

> The Cotswold countryside is, I think, the most beautiful in England. Not that it is by nature more lovely than that which, perhaps, any county can show... But the Cotswolds, especially in the more secluded corners, have the added glory of an almost unbroken tradition of character and of building... I am myself the tenant of a small cottage on a byway that is passed by a stranger hardly once in a week.

At Winston's Cottage Drinkwater completed one of his most successful plays, 'Abraham Lincoln', which transferred from Birmingham to London and to New York, with Drinkwater himself in the cast.

The poetry which Drinkwater wrote at Oakridge captured both the character of Cotswold people and the ethos of the Cotswold landscape.

THE COTSWOLD FARMERS

Sometimes the ghosts forgotten go
Along the hill-top way,
And with long scythes of silver snow
Meadows of moonlit hay,
Until the cocks of Cotswold crow
The coming of the day.

There's Tony Turkletob who died
When he could drink no more,
And Uncle Heritage, the pride
Of eighteen twenty-four,
And Ebenezer Barleyside,
And others half a score.

They fold in phantom pens, and plough
Furrows without a share,
And one will milk a faery cow,
And one will stare and stare,
And whistle ghostly tunes that now
Are not sung anywhere.

The moon goes down on Oakridge lea,
The other world's astir,
The Cotswold farmers silently
Go back to sepulchre,
The sleeping watchdogs wake, and see
No ghostly harvester.

In spite of his apparent contentment at Oakridge, and the success he was achieving with his plays and poetry, Drinkwater's marriage had become unhappy. He and Kathleen left Winston's Cottage in 1921 and divorced in 1924. Drinkwater remarried later, and continued with his writing and with theatre work. He died in 1937 at the age of 55. In his Memoirs, Sir William Rothenstein recalled with affection the neighbours who had rented Winston's Cottage, amongst whom was John Drinkwater:

...John, the poet incarnate, generous, high-minded, enthusiastic over the work of other poets, delighting in the countryside, in his garden, in playing host to friends...

T.S. ELIOT (1888-1965)

The manor house and garden of Burnt Norton are set among woods on the Cotswold scarp above Aston-sub-Edge, near Chipping Campden. A seventeenth century farmhouse, Norton Farm, originally occupied the site. In the eighteenth century Sir William Keyte, Member of Parliament for Warwick, who had abandoned his wife and younger children for his wife's maid, brought the maid and his two elder sons to Norton farmhouse. He proceeded to spend much of his money building a mansion nearby and making gardens. Some years later he turned his attentions to a young milkmaid, whereupon his former mistress and his two sons left. After a week of heavy drinking he again found himself alone, and in a fit of anger and desperation set fire to the mansion and died in the flames. There is now no sign of Keyte's house and the farmhouse has been considerably altered (a brick wing was added in 1902). It has at various times been used as a family residence and as a private school.

The present building (Plate XII) is unremarkable and unobtrusive but 'Burnt Norton' was immortalised in T. S. Eliot's poem of that name, written in 1935 and later becoming one of his 'Four Quartets' (1944).

Thomas Stearns Eliot was born on September 26th 1888 in St. Louis, Missouri. His father was an industrialist and his mother an (occasional) author. Eliot was the youngest son in a family of seven children. He graduated from Harvard University in 1909 and a year later took an MA in philosophy at the Harvard Graduate School. His first important poem, 'The Love Song of J. Alfred Prufrock', appeared in 1910. Following a year at the Sorbonne in Paris, Eliot returned to Harvard and taught philosophy.

In February 1913 Eliot took part in a private entertainment at the home of his aunt in Massachusetts. Here (though it may not have been the first occasion) he met Emily Hale, an acquaintance of his cousin. The friendship and exchange of letters between Eliot and Emily Hale continued until he died in 1965.

T.S. Mathews, Helen Gardner and Eliot's second wife Valerie have all suggested that the poet was in love with Emily. Whether this was so (and much of their correspondence is still not in the public domain) their affection was strong enough to survive Eliot's two marriages and his prolonged absences. Over many years they met in several places in California, where Emily taught drama at Scripps College, in Massachusetts, and in England.

In 1914 Eliot obtained a travelling fellowship to go to the University of Marburg, Germany, but the outbreak of war in August made this impossible. Instead, he went to Oxford University, where, inevitably, he met the American poet Ezra Pound. Pound became an important influence on Eliot's life and work and it was to Pound that Eliot's poem 'The Waste Land' (1922) was dedicated.

In June 1915 Eliot married Vivien Haigh-Wood. It was not a happy marriage, and this may have affected the mood of much of Eliot's later work. He was, too, in some financial difficulty at this time and for over a year was a schoolteacher. In March 1917 Eliot joined the colonial and foreign department of Lloyds Bank in London. A month later the United States entered the war; Eliot was rejected for service on medical grounds and stayed with the bank until 1925.

During this period Eliot wrote essays, reviews and a large number of poems. The attempts to do a demanding and responsible job by day and to concentrate on his writing at night imposed a strain on Eliot which was exacerbated by the state of Vivien's health at this time. The three months leave which he was granted at the end of 1921 may have averted a nervous breakdown.

Following the completion of 'The Waste Land' in 1921 Eliot, while continuing with the bank, took work as an editor and publisher. In 1925 he left the bank and joined Faber & Gwyer (later Faber & Faber) as a director. The 'Criterion', a review which Eliot had founded in 1922, was taken over by Faber

43. T.S. Eliot (portrait by Walter Stoneman, 1948).

and continued until 1939. Eliot's influence on poetry writing at this time was considerable: he was himself an eminent poet, and poets seeking publication by Faber would need his approval.

In 1927 Eliot became a British subject and a member of the Church of England. Perhaps he had been moving toward Christianity for a long time, but now he was able to play an active role in the life of the Church.

The first half of 1933 saw Eliot in the United States again, lecturing at Harvard and the University of Virginia. He was able to tell Emily Hale that he was seeking a permanent separation from Vivien.

When he returned to London Eliot immersed himself in his work and in Church duties. (He became Vicar's Warden at St. Stephen's, Gloucester Road). Eliot had begun to write for the theatre, and collaborated in a Christian pageant play, The Rock, which was produced at Sadler's Wells in 1934. It was while he was thus occupied that the news came that Emily Hale would be visiting England that summer with her uncle, Dr. John Carroll Perkins, and her aunt. Dr. Perkins, a Doctor of Divinity, was Minister of the Unitarian King's Chapel in Boston, Massachusetts. He and Mrs. Perkins had rented Stanford House and the adjacent Stanley Cottage in Chipping Campden for a six month holiday. Eliot's visit to Campden in 1934 was the first of many; the cottages were taken again in 1935 and 1937. (In 1935 Eliot seems to have visited Campden on no less than five occasions),

It was probably on one of these visits that Eliot felt inspired to write 'Burnt Norton', which was published as the last poem in his 'Collected Poems 1909-1935'. It is not an easy poem to understand, though a number of authors, including Carl Bodelsen (1958), Harry Blamires (1969) and Helen Gardner (1978), have offered helpful interpretations. The poem was written quickly, between 'Murder in the Cathedral' and Eliot's next play, 'The Family Reunion'. It was not until 1940, when Eliot was writing his poem 'East Coker', that he realised that 'Burnt Norton', which he had thought would stand alone, was really the first of four related poems, his 'Four Quartets'. (The other two were 'The Dry Salvages' (1941) and 'Little Gidding' (1942).)

'Burnt Norton' is a long poem, and copyright restrictions imposed in Eliot's will do not allow the quotation of more than ten lines, but the following short extract conveys the general flavour of the poem:

> If all time is eternally present
> All time is unredeemable.
> What might have been is an abstraction
> Remaining a perpetual possibility
> Only in a world of speculation.
> What might have been and what has been
> Point to one end, which is always present.
> Footfalls echo in the memory
> Down the passage which we did not take
> Towards the door we never opened
> Into the rose-garden.

Nearing the end of a failed marriage and after spending sometime with a woman for whom his feelings may have been rather more than affectionate, Eliot may well in this poem have contemplated the directions his life had taken. There is much more to the poem than that, though; the message of 'Burnt Norton' can apply to any of us. "The passage we did not take / Towards the door we never opened / Into the rose-garden" is the choice we did not make. For a moment "what might have been" is as real as "what has been", though it is, says Eliot, "...an abstraction / Remaining a perpetual possibility / Only in a world of speculation". The garden could be anywhere, and it does not matter. (The rose-garden of the poem, though, was real.)

Following Dr. and Mrs. Perkins' last visit to Chipping Campden in 1937 there is no record of Eliot visiting the area again. He spent the war years in London and with friends near Guildford. Vivien Eliot died in 1947. In 1948 the poet was awarded the Nobel Prize for Literature and the Order of Merit. Eighteen honorary degrees were conferred on him and both Oxford and Cambridge Universities awarded him honorary fellowships. His plays were produced at the Edinburgh Festival, in the West End and on Broadway. In 1957 he married Valerie Fletcher and lived happily for the rest of his life.

Eliot died on January 4th 1965. His ashes were buried in the churchyard at East Coker, Somerset, the village from which his ancestor Andrew Eliot had emigrated to America in the seventeenth century.

In her 1958 'Sunday Times' interview Helen Gardner asked Eliot if he would agree that 'Four Quartets' were his greatest poems. He thought that he would. Whatever the truth, in 'Four Quartets' we are taken, haltingly, on a journey from the 'private world' each of us occupies to a real, comprehensible world which we can share. For Eliot the journey began in a garden in the Cotswolds.

Chapter 11 - FURTHER READING

SHELLEY
Dowden, Edward: *The Life of Percy Bysshe Shelley*. Kegan-Paul, Trench & Co.(1896).
Holmes, Richard: *Shelley, the Pursuit*. Weidenfeld & Nicolson (1974).
Shelley, Percy Bysshe: *The Complete Poetical Works* (ed. T. Hutchinson). Oxford University Press (1943, rep. 1961).
THOMAS
Clark, Keith: *The Muse Colony*. Redcliffe Press (1992).
Farjeon, Eleanor: *Edward Thomas - The Last Four Years*. Oxford University Press (1979).
Moore, John: *The Life and Letters of Edward Thomas*. Alan Sutton (1983).
Thomas, Edward: *Collected Poems*. Faber (1958).
Thomas, Helen: *Under Storm's Wing*. Carcanet Press (1988).
DAVIES
Davies, W. H.: *Autobiography of a Supertramp*. Jonathan Cape (1922).
Davies, W. H.: *The Complete Poems, with an Introduction by Osbert Sitwell* Jonathan Cape (1963).
Hockey, L.W. : *W H. Davies*. University of Wales Press (1971).
The Essential W H. Davies. Jonathan Cape (1951).
DRINKWATER
Drinkwater, John: *Tides*. Sidgwick and Jackson (1917).
Drinkwater, John: *Cotswold Characters*. Oxford University Press (1921).
Rothenstein, Sir William: *Men and Memories*. Chatto & Windus (1978).
ELIOT
Bodelson, Carl: *Commentary on Eliot's 'Four Quartets'*. Copenhagen University Press (1958).
Eliot, T.S.: *Selected Essays*. Faber & Faber (1934).
Eliot, T.S.: *Collected Poems*. Faber & Faber (1954).
Gardner, Helen : *The Art of T S. Eliot*. Cresset Press (1949).
Gardner, Helen: *The Composition of 'Four Quartets'*. Faber & Faber (1978).

[1]Either a comedy by Ben Jonson or a satire of the same name by Jonathan Swift.

12. COTSWOLD LAUREATE:
John Masefield (1878-1967)

When the Guild of Handicraft at Chipping Campden performed Ben Jonson's 'The New Inn' in January 1903, the poet John Masefield was in the audience. The play had a profound effect on him, and he there and then conceived the idea of a revival of English theatre. Twenty years later, with the support of his wife, he would be able to indulge his own wishes in this direction at their home near Oxford. As a result of his friendship with the Ashbees (p.98) and his visits to Campden, Masefield came to love the area, and wanted to settle in Campden. This was not to be, but for most of the 1930s the Masefield family did live in the Cotswolds, at Pinbury Park near Sapperton.

John Edward Masefield was born at The Knapp, Ledbury, on June 1st 1878, one of five children of George Edward Masefield, solicitor, and his wife Caroline. His early years at Ledbury were happy; he was, he later recalled, "living in paradise". Following the death of his mother in 1885 and of grandparents in the following year the family moved to The Priory on the Worcester Read near the town centre. For two years young Masefield boarded at Warwick School till, at the age of thirteen, he was sent to the training ship H.M.S. Conway, moored then in the Mersey. It was here that he began to gain the knowledge of seamanship evident in his later writings.

In 1894 Masefield joined a sailing-ship company as an apprentice, but on his first voyage (to Chile via Cape Horn) he was violently ill and had to be sent home from Chile by steamship. Masefield knew that he could not be a sailor. Following a chance reading of Chaucer's poems he realised that his real desire was to be a writer. Aunt Kate, his father's sister-in-law, who had taken charge of the family following the death of George Masefield in 1891, had other ideas however; Masefield was put aboard a steamship bound for New York, where it was intended that he would join the sailing ship Bidston Hill.

In New York Masefield broke free. His determination to be a writer, and his aversion to the sea, were too strong. Before the Bidston Hill was due to sail he deserted, and for a few months lived the life of a tramp (as W. H. Davies was doing elsewhere in the States at the same time). When Masefield returned to New York, he spent some time serving in a bar before eventually taking a job in a carpet mill in Yonkers, where he stayed for two years. During this time he read Chaucer, and fell in love with the poetry of Keats. Shelley, Milton and Shakespeare followed, and before he was nineteen Masefield was himself writing sonnets and other kinds of poetry. These early forays into verse did not receive critical acclaim (he should not have expected them to), and Masefield's thoughts turned to home and to journalism. In July 1897 he worked his passage on a steamer bound for Liverpool.

He arrived at Liverpool in a condition of penury and, failing to find work, he made his way to London, though he was ill with tuberculosis. He found cheap lodgings in Fulham and obtained a job in a City bank as a junior clerk. For a few years he moved around boarding-houses in the London area, often ill and depressed but still writing poetry and reading widely.

In the summer of 1901 Masefield left his office job and became a freelance writer. His poems were being published regularly in the 'Tatler', 'Speaker' and 'Pall Mall Magazine'. His first major work, 'Salt Water Ballads', was published in 1902 and attracted favourable attention. It has been suggested that the poems showed the Kipling touch, but Masefield denied that he had been thus influenced; he disliked Kipling's verse intensely, he said. Strangely enough, several of the 'Salt Water Ballads' treat subjects that have no connection whatsoever with the sea. One of these is 'Tewkesbury Road':

It is good to be out on the road, and going one knows not where,
Going through meadow and village, one knows not whither nor why;
Through the grey light drift of the dust, in the keen cool rush of the air,
Under the flying white clouds, and the broad blue lift of the sky;

And to halt at the chattering brook, in the tall green fern at the brink
Where the harebell grows, and the gorse, and the foxgloves purple and white;
Where the shy-eyed delicate deer troop down to the pools to drink,
When the stars are mellow and large at the coming on of the night.

O! to feel the warmth of the rain, and the homely smell of the earth,
Is a tune for the blood to jig to, a joy past power of words;
And the blessed green comely meadows seem all a-ripple with mirth
At the lilt of the shifting feet, and the dear wild cry of the birds.

This first book of his poetry was dedicated to three women. One was his godmother Ann Hanford-Flood, whom he had visited as a boy at Woolas Hall on the slopes of Bredon Hill, a Cotswold outlier. Another was a cousin, Helen Heane, who had once befriended him. The third dedicatee was Constance Crommelin, whom he had met at a dinner party given by the poet Laurence Binyon, Masefield's friend and a great influence on his writing. Constance came from Cushenden in County Antrim, Northern Ireland, and had studied mathematics, classics and English Literature at Cambridge. She was eleven years older than Masefield, but he was soon in love, and in 1903, not long after Masefield's first visit to the Ashbees at Campden, the couple were engaged. John Masefield and Constance Crommelin were married in London on July 23rd 1903.

Their daughter Judith was born in April 1904; in later years she would illustrate some of her father's books and help with his dramatic productions. (It indicates the friendship between the Masefields and the Ashbees that soon after Judith's birth her father took Charles Ashbee on a visit to Cushenden, where the Masefields had rented a disused coastguard station near Constance's birthplace.)

Later that year Masefield and his wife gave up the flat which they had been occupying in Marylebone Road and moved to a semi-detached house in Greenwich. Almost at once Masefield was offered an editorial job with the 'Manchester Guardian', and for five months he commuted between London and the North. Janet Ashbee visited the Masefields' new home and had, it seems, a warm reception in a very cold house.

Despite travelling, and with a wife and baby to claim his attention, Masefield was still writing poems as well as short stories and plays (though most of the latter from this period appear to have been lost). He loved Campden, and in the spring of 1905, at about the time he resigned from his Manchester job, he took Constance and Judith to the Cotswolds to stay with the Ashbees.

When he returned to Greenwich, Masefield wrote to Janet Ashbee. He thanked her for their 'delightful holiday' and included a short poem:

> When I from Campden town depart,
> I leave my wits, I lose my Art,
> A melancholy clouds my face
> I feel as though I fell from grace.
> With morals sapped and manners gone
> Sing willow, willow willow.
>
> But when I come to Campden town
> I've adjectives for every Noun.
> I tire pretty patient Con
> With brilliant conversa-ti-on.
> My virtues beam from every pore
> I feel myself a man and more
> Sing all a green palm bough shall be my garland.

Charles and Janet Ashbee were at this time planning a book of Cotswold Ballads, to include poems by, among others, A. E. Housman, Masefield and the Ashbees themselves. It was to be called 'Giles Cockbill', commemorating a local nineteenth century farm worker whose photograph as an old man had captured Charles Ashbee's imagination. Masefield eagerly submitted a poem to Janet for inclusion:

> On Campden Wold the skylark sings,
> In Campden Town the traveller finds
> The inward peace which beauty brings
> To bless and heal tormented minds.

O still it is in Campden Town
Man lives and works, and hates and likes,
The beech leaves drop and rustle down
The bells chime when the Church Clock strikes.

The plough teams jangle to the field,
By rick and stack the straying kine
Munch wisps of the fat acres' yield,
The golden wind-vanes swing and shine.

And there is beauty everywhere,
In that grey curving English Street,
The man who goes a-wandering there
I think his blood doth quicker beat,

And no man walks her lovely ways,
And marks the shifty wind-vane's gleam
But thinks of noble deeds and days,
And builds a town of Troy in dream.

For there those elemental fires,
Set hearts aflame like glowing coal,
To build and guild the carven spires,
To crown the city of the soul.

Rather surprisingly, neither this poem nor the preceding 'thank-you' poem to Janet Ashbee was ever given a title or published through the normal channels. The Ashbees' 'Giles Cockbill' anthology appears never to have seen the light of day.

Masefield soon began work on the first of his plays to receive public performance, 'The Campden Wonder'. In August 1660 one William Harrison, steward to Juliana, Lady Campden, disappeared while collecting rents. John Perry, Harrison's servant, confessed to murdering Harrison and implicated his brother Richard and their mother Joan Perry. The three were found guilty by a jury, and hanged on Broadway Hill, though Harrison's body had not been found. Two years later Harrison turned up, saying that he had been attacked and robbed, taken to Deal in Kent and forced aboard a sailing ship which was later captured by Turkish pirates. He claimed that he had been sold into slavery but escaped and made his way to Lisbon, from where his passage home was paid for by a friendly merchant. Soon after Harrison's return his wife committed suicide, causing speculation that she knew more about the matter than she had admitted.

The mystery of the 'Campden Wonder' remained unresolved. What really happened to William Harrison? Why did John Perry confess to a murder which hadn't taken place, and why did he implicate his mother and his brother? What role did Harrison's wife play? The story intrigued Masefield, and his play received eight performances at the Court Theatre, London, between January 8th and February 1st 1907. It was not a success, possibly because the audience had spent the first half of the evening watching trivial comedy and was not in the mood for tragedy.

Masefield was soon at work on 'The Tragedy of Nan', which was performed at the Royalty Theatre, London, in 1908. He was not at this time in good health, and he longed to be away from the city. Publishers and editors were demanding his attention, however, and he and Constance perforce had to live in the capital, though the sea and the Cotswolds were surely in his thoughts. He moved his family to a more central location near Paddington, and found his diversions at the theatre, or with literary and artistic friends such as John Galsworthy or the artist William Rothenstein. (Rothenstein first met the poet when Laurence Binyon came to supper at the home of a mutual friend, "bringing a stranger, a quiet youth, with eyes that seemed surprised at the sight of the world, and hair that stood up behind like a cockatoo's feathers ... Masefield - this was the young man's name - spoke in a deep and solemn voice; a serious and romantic youth, I thought; and I got to like him ...")

In 1909 the Masefields at last had a place in the country, a farmhouse in the Buckinghamshire Chilterns near Great Missenden; here the poet could walk in the fields and woods and gather inspiration. Constance was soon pregnant again, and Lewis Crommelin Masefield was born on July 4th 1910. In that year 'Ballads and Poems' appeared, but a more significant work was 'The Everlasting Mercy' of 1911. This was Masefield's first major poem. If Masefield had hitherto been at all unsure of his true vocation the acclaim which 'The Everlasting Mercy' received left him in no doubt. In the years following, narrative poem followed novel and narrative poem from Masefield's pen. He was wined and dined by the London literati, who reviewed his work with excitement, and the public recognised that a major writer had arrived among them.

1912 saw the Masefields move their London home from Paddington to a large house in Hampstead. The poet's spirits were raised by the promise of good walking on the (then) rural Heath, though the Chiltern farmhouse was for the time being retained.

In the summer of 1914 the Buckinghamshire house was sold, and the Masefields purchased Lollingdon Farmhouse in the Thames Valley south east of Didcot. John was thirty six and Constance forty eight; Judith was ten and Lewis four. Their happiness in their new house below the Berkshire Downs and the scarp of the Oxfordshire Chilterns was to last for just a few months; hostilities had begun all over Europe and on August 4th 1914 Britain became embroiled when it declared war on Germany. Masefield was too old for battle, neither did he earn the sobriquet 'war poet', though he wrote one 'war poem', 'August 1914', from the relative security of his Thames Valley home. However, his emotions were as stirred by the Great War as were those of Edward Thomas, Wilfred Owen, Rupert Brooke and the others. During the first months of the war Masefield, in poetry and prose, alluded to the conflict in bitter and patriotic terms. In February 1915 he volunteered as an orderly with the Red Cross and went to a hospital in Northern France. The work was, of course, hard and bloody, but Masefield spent his home leave in the spring by fund-raising for the field hospitals. After returning to France he went to Gallipoli, where, amid hellish conditions, he organised a motor-boat ambulance to take the wounded to the Aegean island of Lemnos. He would later write of this disastrous and abortive Dardanelles campaign, describing the effort of the British troops in romantic terms. (The hostilities, which were intended to outflank the Turks and capture Constantinople, led instead to the evacuation of British forces from Gallipoli).

On a visit to America in 1916 he met in New York the Wall St. banker Thomas W. Lamont and his wife Florence. With the latter, who became a close friend of the Masefields, the poet began a voluminous correspondence which started even before he left the United States in March 1916 and ended only with Florence's death in December 1952. This correspondence, which has been collected and edited by the Lamonts' son Corliss and grandson Lansing, is, for biographers of Masefield, an important source.

In 1916 appeared a one-act play in verse, 'Good Friday'. Although this was but the first of several religious plays which Masefield would write (there followed 'The Trial of Jesus' in 1925 and 'The Coming of Christ' in 1928), he did not at any time appear to be a devout Christian. Perhaps he rationalised too much, though throughout his life he retained a degree of spirituality which was not far from religious belief.

Soon after returning from America Masefield was in France again, assessing the practical help which the Americans were giving to the war effort by way of ambulances, hospitals &c. He was particularly affected by his visits to the Somme battlefields. "...in all that vast expanse of death, destruction and corruption", he told Florence Lamont, "there is no life, no sign of home, nor trace of man's joy or man's quiet, no complete trees, almost no living blade of grass, but an awful tossing of mud and dirty water, with the passing and the coming of death..."

Meanwhile, Constance was busy moving house. Zeppelin raids made Hampstead dangerous and the remote and rather cheerless farmhouse in the Thames Valley was in need of repair, so the Masefields had already decided to find a new home. In April 1917 Constance, with the two children, settled into a brick-built house, 'Hill Crest', at Boars Hill, four miles south west of Oxford. This would be the Masefields' home until their move to the Cotswolds sixteen years later.

In January 1919 Masefield was at last able to settle down with Constance and the children at Boars Hill. Until now he had not been able to regard 'Hill Crest' as "home" because of his frequent travelling, though he did make use of a shack in the grounds as a study. The area was on the edge of open countryside, and the Masefields were happy there. The poet found a renewed zest for writing, and on January 24th 1919 he told Florence Lamont that he was "sitting in my shack here. I used to hear the guns in France all day long, & now they are silent. They must have been over 100 miles distant". In that year appeared one of Masefield's finest works, 'Reynard the Fox'. This was the first of several long narrative poems which Masefield wrote in the years immediately after the Great War, but he was not a recluse. 'Hill Crest' received visitors from home and abroad. Poets, university staff and undergraduates came and some settled in Boars Hill and the Masefields soon had a large and valued circle of friends. In November 1919 the Gloucestershire poet and composer Ivor Gurney (p.165) wrote to his friend John Haines:

> On Saturday... we visited Masefield in his proper haunt at Boars Hill. He was extremely nice, a boyish, quiet person with a manner friendly enough and easy to get on with ... Boars Hill is not pretty as we know prettiness but it isn't bad - 4 miles south of Oxford and (so they say) within a few hundred yards of a great view, which we did not see...

In the 1920s Masefield was, perhaps, at the height of his invention and the peak of his popularity. As well as poetry he wrote novels and plays, speeches and articles; he loved children and his 'The Midnight Folk' (1927) - written for "children of all ages" - became a classic. In addition to the honorary Doctorates

44. John Masefield (Plaque given by the John Masefield Society to Preston Church Nr. Ledbury to commemorate Masefield's baptism in the church on 1st July 1878.)

which he had received from Yale and Harvard in 1915, his achievements were now recognised with honorary degrees from the universities of Oxford, Aberdeen, Glasgow and Manchester. (Liverpool, St. Andrews and Wales followed in the 1930s).

The Masefields were at this time enthusiasts for amateur dramatics, both at Boars Hill and elsewhere. (The poet would not have forgotten Ashbee's productions at Campden). In spite of the work needed to stage the plays at 'Hill Crest' Masefield found time and energy to organise annual voice-speaking competitions in the University, which became known as the Oxford Recitations.

On April 21st 1930 the Poet Laureate, Robert Bridges, died. On May 10th King George V appointed Masefield to the Laureateship. The choice was not an obvious one - there were several worthy contenders - but Ramsay MacDonald's recommendation met with little dissent, as Masefield's poetry was accessible to most people. In the thirty seven years when he was Poet Laureate Masefield wrote a great deal of poetry, not all of it of a high standard. Royal deaths and coronations, of course, required verses from him, but his best work came when the effort was voluntary.

In 1932 the Masefields decided to leave Hill Crest. Constance had been diagnosed as having a brain tumour. An operation in London early in the year was successful, but she could no longer help in her husband's theatrical productions. Buildings had been going up in Boars Hill for some time and the village was becoming a suburb of Oxford. An RAF aerodrome had recently opened at Abingdon, two miles to the south. The first bombers arrived in October that year, and a move to pastures new was clearly indicated for the poet and his family.

It seems likely that Masefield may have visited his friend William Rothenstein while the latter lived at Far Oakridge and fell in love with the area. Perhaps as a consequence, in April 1933 the Masefields became the tenants of Lord Bathurst at Pinbury Park near Sapperton, where Ernest Gimson and the Barnsley brothers had once lived and worked (Chapter 8). On May 2nd Masefield told Florence Lamont "This is certainly a heavenly place, & time slips away fast, there are so many things to do and so little time", and in anticipation of a visit by Florence to Pinbury he told her on May 18th:

> I think you will like this place although the garden is not yet ready for you. We are slowly learning its old & romantic history, & are enchanted to learn that it was once Anne Boleyn's, & probably sent dues of some sort to her, though she may never have seen it .
>
> ...I am so happy, that I have just seen here a wild dormouse, a rather rare & charming little beast that few see out of cages; there are also wild duck, such as I wrote the verses about; & so it only needs you to be perfect.

Perhaps it was Diana Awdry (later Mrs. Bernard Oldridge) who brought Masefield back to the south Cotswolds. She had met him while she was an undergraduate at Oxford in the 1920s, and now lived at Kings Hill, Dursley. Diana Awdry was the organizing secretary of the Stinchcombe Hill Music Festival, and at her invitation Masefield had attended a meeting at Stinchcombe Manor near Dursley on January 21st 1900, where he suggested, perhaps thinking of his 'Oxford Recitations', that the Festival should include a Verse-Speaking Competition. On February 13th he was at Dursley to explain his idea to the public, and later that year the Festival's first Verse-Speaking Competition was held; Masefield, of course, was one of the judges.

Masefield was at this time hoping to raise funds for the projected Gloucestershire Home for Wayfarers at Pauntley Court, near his home town of Ledbury. Diana Awdry was the Honorary Secretary of the Appeal, and after the Home opened in 1933 became chairman of the management committee. By giving poetry readings throughout the county Masefield raised most of the £800 needed for the purchase of the house. The recreation room at Pauntley Court was restored and equipped with the help of an amateur dramatic group at Uley, near Dursley, who raised nearly £50 by performances of Masefield's 'The Tragedy of Nan'. In recognition of the poet's efforts on behalf of the Home, the new recreation room was named "The John Masefield Room".

The Masefields went on a long holiday to America in 1933, but were glad to get back to Pinbury. On November 29th the poet told Florence Lamont.

The place is as lovely as ever, now that the leaves are off. The jasmine & the violets are out: the berries are scarlet on shrubs and trees, & the storm-cock loudly sings, & marvels that no American beauty tries to catch his notes on the piano.

But life at Pinbury was not as comfortable for the Masefields as they would have wished. In May 1934 the poet told Florence... "It is bitter cold here: 17 May: ice in the open air & snow yesterday". On September 7th there was both good news and bad: "C. [Constance] is slowly pulling up out of the illness into health: is now much stronger and heartier. Then we have had rather a plague of rats, which have not yet entered the house but have thriven in the hen runs...".

In 1935, on the occasion of King George V's Jubilee Birthday Honours, Masefield received the Order of Merit. This would have pleased him immensely; some thirteen years earlier, when a holder of the Order had just died, he told Florence

...An O.M. is an Order of Merit. Old Albert Edward instituted the order & made it very select for the very choice & the very famous & the very old. ...generally it is the last order you can receive before you die. It is the only Order here which means anything at all. If you are any of the other orders it may only mean that you have given good dinners enough to the right people, or subscribed enough to charity, but if you are an O.M. it means that you are one of 12 picked souls, of which only about one at any time doesn't quite deserve it, & therefore it is about 11 to 1 that you are a real dog. I don't know quite what the Order is; but it is probably same ugly little star.

The Poet Laureate was, of course, expected to carry out professional duties. The death of George V in 1936, the accession of Edward VIII, and, following the Abdication, the Coronation of George VI, all brought lines from Masefield. He referred to Edward VIII in a letter to Florence Lamont written on Christmas Eve, 1936:

Well I liked and love the way the king, my master, whom may God preserve, stood up for the woman he loved. He is such a man as has not been promised to our throne for 300 years, when the young Prince Henry died . ... Well, he has gone; and we have the ministers and we have the archbishop, and a great soul and the woman he chose are chucked aside.

In July 1937 Masefield and Judith spent three enjoyable days with the Lamont family at the latter's holiday home on Loch Lomond, but the poet was glad to return to Pinbury, his 'heavenly place'. He shared with Lewis a love of animals, and the fields and beechwoods above the Golden Valley were of constant interest. He had, though, made few close friends in the area. At heart he was a conservationist, not a huntsman (in his

'Reynard the Fox' the quarry escaped), and a workman, not the squire. Some of his later novels portrayed the upper classes in such a poor light that it was clear that the family could not expect, in spite of Masefield's royal accolades, to be accepted into their circle.

The Masefields' Cotswold period came to an end when they moved from Pinbury early in 1939. The poet told Florence that in the event of war he would prefer to be near Oxford, but there was surely more to it than that. By the end of the year the family was ensconced at Burcote House, Clifton Hampden, near Abingdon. This old house by the Thames, with its views to the Chiltern scarp on the one hand, and Wittenham Clumps on the other, would be their last home.

Soon Judith was at Oxford helping the war effort, while Lewis enlisted in the Royal Army Medical Corps and was posted to the Middle East. John and Constance lived quietly at Burcote, he writing in a shed in the garden and both of them tending the vegetables and poultry. "I suppose", he told Florence, "the Germans will have a crack at us pretty soon; and then we shall know more about it".

Some of the books and poems which Masefield wrote at this time dealt directly with the war; his own experiences on the battlefield a quarter of a century before allowed him to empathize completely with the young men fighting in Europe and elsewhere. This could not, though, alleviate the pain and the grief when John and Constance learned in 1942 that their son, their own Lewis, aged thirty one, had been killed by artillery fire in North Africa.

Such 'freedom' as came with the ending of the war allowed Masefield to travel - to Sheffield, for example, in 1946 to receive an honorary degree at the university, and to London in 1947 for a similar purpose. His exchange of letters with Lamont continued until her death in 1952, but he was now corresponding with other women, and through these letters maintained many close friendships.

Masefield's writings were hampered by severe illness in 1949 when he was seventy-one. He slowly recovered, but very little work was now published. An exception was his literary autobiography 'So Long to Learn', which tells of his early attempts at writing.

Constance Masefield died at Burcote on February 19th 1960, aged ninety-three. Such entertaining as her husband did after this time was with the help of Judith and a series of housekeepers. Masefield continued his duties as Poet Laureate and in spite of his advancing years attended official functions, including awards of literary honours, whenever he could.

John Masefield died on May 12th 1967 at the age of eighty-eight. His ashes were laid, with due ceremony, in Poets' Corner at Westminster Abbey. In his poem 'The West Wind' Masefield wrote

It's a warm wind, the west wind, full of birds' cries; I never hear the west wind but tears are in my eyes. For it comes from the west lands, the old brown hills, And April's in the west wind, and daffodils.

The 'daffodils' are clearly the wild flowers for which the woods around the poet's birthplace are famed. Perhaps the 'old brown hills' were the Cotswolds?

Chapter 12 - FURTHER READING

Babington Smith, Constance: *John Masefield, a Life*. Oxford University Press (1978).,

Handley-Taylor, Geoffrey (comp.): *John Masefield O.M., The Queen's Poet Laureate. A Bibliography and Eighty-First Birthday Tribute.* The Cranbrook Tower Press (1960).

Lamont, Corliss,and Lamont, Lansing (eds.): *Letters of John Masefield to Florence Lamont* Macmillan (1979).

Macarthy, Fiona: *The Simple Life*: *C. R. Ashbee in the Cotswolds*. Lund Humphries (1981).

Masefield, John: *So Long to Learn*. Heinemann (1952).

Rothenstein, Sir William: *Men and Memories* (Vol. 1). Chatto & Windus (1978).

13. MUSIC FROM THE COTSWOLDS
(i) Holst and Vaughan Williams

GUSTAV HOLST (1874 - 1934)

The village of Wyck Rissington lies in a fold of the hills three miles south of Stow and just over a mile east of Bourton-on-the-Water. The church of St. Laurence is of Norman origin and has work from most centuries since. Above the organ, a plaque commemorates Gustav Holst, who as a young man was organist and choir master here; it was on this instrument that he played. Although much of his subsequent life was spent away from this area Holst visited Wyck Rissington and Bourton whenever he could return to the Cotswolds.

Gustav Theodore von Holst was born on September 21st 1874. His name derived from his grandfather Gustavus and his great-uncle Theodore. Gustavus had been born in Riga, Latvia, and on this side of the family there was Scandinavian, Russian and German ancestry. Gustavus was brought to England at the beginning of the nineteenth century by his parents. Like his father, Gustavus von Holst became a composer and a pianist; after a time spent playing salon music for rich patrons in the London area he left the metropolis and settled as a music teacher in Cheltenham with his English wife. Their son Adolph grew up in the musical tradition of the family; he became a gifted pianist and a busy piano teacher. Adolph von Holst gave recitals and conducted chamber concerts in Cheltenham. He was music teacher at Pate's Grammar School and organist at All Saints Church, Pittville. In 1871 he married one of his pupils, Clara Lediard, and in 1874 their son Gustav was born at Pittville Terrace (now 4 Clarence Road, the Holst Birthplace Museum). He was a weak child, but neither his asthma nor his poor sight received much attention. As for music he took readily to the piano but hated practising the violin. He learned the trombone in an attempt to cure his asthma.

In 1887 Holst entered Pate's Grammar School, where he was soon reading Berlioz's 'Orchestration', which prompted him to try his own hand at composition. Adolph had hoped that his son would become a professional pianist, but Gustav was troubled by neuritis in his right arm which made such a prospect unlikely. He applied to Trinity College, but failed the scholarship examination, so on leaving the Grammar School he went to stay with his maternal grandmother at Oxford, where he studied counterpoint with the organist of Merton College, George Frederick Sims. From Oxford Holst applied for a music scholarship at the Royal College of Music. He was unsuccessful, and after four months with Sims he returned to Cheltenham and threw himself into the local musical scene, helping his father with the practicalities of staging concerts in the town. He even composed the music for a two-act operetta, 'Lansdown Castle'.

In 1892 Holst was appointed organist and choirmaster at St. Laurence's Church, Wyck Rissington at a salary of four pounds a year. In her biography of her father Imogen Holst said

> The organ had been put in a prominent position in the middle of the tiny chancel, in full view of the whole congregation, and at first he found it difficult to appear absorbed in the sermon while keeping an anxious eye on the behaviour of his choir boys. But he got on very well with them, and several of them remained his friends for over forty years.

The appointment also required Holst to conduct the fifty-strong Choral Society at nearby Bourton-on-the-Water. For an aspiring composer of seventeen years of age this was all good experience, and Holst tackled the work eagerly. He had, of course, to make the best of what instrumental players were available. A lady harpist staying in the neighbourhood was persuaded to take part in the 1893 performance of John Farmer's oratorio 'Christ and His Soldiers'. There was no harp part, but Holst showed her on the piano what it was he wanted, and she suggested to him how it would sound best on her instrument. "Apparently", said Imogen Holst, "the result of the part that he wrote for her made a deep impression on the audience". The local newspaper reviewed the concert and remarked that " Great praise is due to the talented young conductor, Mr Gustav von Holst, whose enthusiasm seemed to be shared by every member of the Choral Society".

There were no trains from Cheltenham to Bourton on a Sunday, so Holst travelled up on a Saturday and stayed in Wyck Rissington until the Monday (in the last cottage on the left as one leaves the village on the Stow road). The walk between Wyck and Bourton was across the fields and, said Imogen Holst, while walking between the two villages "there grew in [her father] a deep love of the Cotswold Hills. He seldom spoke of it, but it was always to remain one of the most precious things in his life". During these weekends in the Cotswolds, Holst gave piano and organ lessons, and in later years these former pupils were among the friends he visited when he was in the area.

During the week Holst would be in Cheltenham assisting his father with concerts at the Rotunda or the Corn Exchange, or working on 'Lansdown Castle'. In 1893 this was performed at the Corn Exchange to much acclamation. Adolph was so impressed that he borrowed a hundred pounds from one of his relatives and sent his son to study at the Royal College of Music in London.

His teacher at the R.C.M. was Charles Villiers Stanford. Although Holst was a conscientious student he did not appear to Stanford to have particular talent, though on his third attempt in 1895 he won the open scholarship for composition.

By now the earlier influence of Arthur Sullivan had been replaced, as Holst's experience widened, by a respect for the works of Wagner and Bach. His career, though, had reached a turning point: it had become clear that because of the cramps and pains which he was suffering in his right arm, he would not become a professional pianist. He turned instead to the trombone; at least he could earn some money, and with his meagre income and occasional help from his father this was essential if he were to continue at the College, where his scholarship did not cover his board and lodging. Thus it was that the summer vacation would see Holst playing his trombone in a pier orchestra at one English resort or another, while in the winter he would be in the orchestra pit at some London theatre for its current pantomime.

In 1895 began a friendship which would last for the rest of Holst's life. Ralph Vaughan Williams returned to the R.C.M., which he had left in 1892 to study music at Trinity College, Cambridge. Like Holst, Vaughan Williams was Gloucestershire born, and he was no more than two years Holst's senior. Holst did not lack friends in the College, but his new acquaintance was profoundly to affect his life and work. Each listened while the other played his latest - unfinished - composition, and in later years Holst insisted that the opinion he valued more than any other was that of Vaughan Williams.

He became interested in Socialism, read a number of William Morris's books and joined the Hammersmith socialists who met at Kelmscott House (p.75). He valued their companionship, though he was never politically active. Holst had a high regard for Morris, and when, a few years after Morris's death, he was composing his 'Cotswolds Symphony', he wrote as the slow movement an Elegy 'In Memoriam William Morris'. Holst conducted the Socialist Choir at Hammersmith, and it was while he was rehearsing at Kelmscott House that the impressionable twenty year old met a young soprano, Isobel Harrison. He was soon in love. In due course the couple were engaged, but it was not until 1901 that they could afford to marry.

In 1898 Holst became first trombonist and rehearsal assistant with the Carl Rosa Opera Company. He had to leave the College, but the work meant an end to poverty and gave him the chance to broaden his musical experience.

Between his playing engagements Holst found time and energy to pursue his own interests. He taught himself a little Sanskrit and with difficulty translated some Hindu literature into English. He even began writing the libretto for a three act Indian opera, Sita, though this was not completed until 1906.

He was now working, too, on what Imogen Holst suggested was "his most ambitious effort" to that time, his 'Cotswolds Symphony'. Holst was touring with the Carl Rosa company when he finished it, and the last page is inscribed '24 July 1900 (Skegness)'.

There were the usual four movements, which were Allegro, Adagio (the Elegy), Scherzo and Finale. The first public performance was on April 24th 1902 at the Winter Gardens, Bournemouth; the Bournemouth Municipal Orchestra was conducted by Dan Godfrey. Early that morning the Holsts set out from London to be at the final rehearsal. Vaughan Williams went too; after all, this was the first professional performance of a work by his friend. The rehearsal did not go well; there were mistakes in the parts and frequent queries from the conductor. Holst was naturally nervous. He need not have worried: as the rehearsal proceeded Vaughan Williams leaned over and murmured "I like this". Remaining difficulties were resolved, and the performance seems to have gone well. According to the programme note;

There is much picturesque and romantic music in this symphony that is bound to make a good impression. The first movement is written in usual symphonic form, except that there is no repeat. It is short and unpretentious. The Elegy is a more important movement. We take it that the composer means us to bear William Morris, poet, art worker and friend of Burne-Jones - a wonderful man Morris was - in mind when listening to this movement. To those who have never read the 'Earthly Paradise' by Morris, we can promise a treat. It is a masterpiece. The Scherzo is an extremely clever composition, and is perhaps the best of the work. The Finale is vigorous, and shows the composer to be well skilled in the subtle art of orchestration.

'The Times' wondered about 'The Cotswolds' as a title.

...what the composer exactly means us all to understand by this is not very clear. There is evidence of much musicianly writing and considerable talent for melody, and this is the more noticeable in the slow movement, the best thing in the work. The first movement is very weak and lacking in originality. The audience seemed pleased with the symphony and gave it a good reception.

Early in the following year Holst and his wife went to Germany for a much needed holiday. When they returned Holst decided that he would give up the trombone and spend his time on composition. There were, though, no such things as performing rights or gramophone royalties, so composition generated little income; in any case, such music as he did send to publishers met with one rejection after another. His earnings, were barely sufficient for the needs of his wife and himself. He accepted with gratitude the offer of a post as singing-teacher at James Allen's School in Dulwich, and soon afterward he became music teacher at the Passmore Edwards (later the Mary Ward) Settlement. In 1905 Holst was appointed Director of Music at St. Paul's Girls' School in Hammersmith and he remained there for the rest of his life.

It was at about this time that he 'discovered' folk music. Vaughan Williams had been collecting folk songs, and with his help, and inspired by the work of Cecil Sharp, Holst began to write music based on English folk tunes.

The Holsts' lives were now based firmly in London. In 1907 their daughter Imogen Clare was born, and in that year, too, Holst took a post as Director of Music at Morley College for Working Men and Women in South London. He was now commuting between his home in Barnes and teaching posts in different parts of the capital. He managed to find time for composition, though, and his music began to be more widely heard. A Somerset Rhapsody was first performed in 1910 and the suite Beni Mora followed in 1912. During the war years Holst spent much time on his large and complex symphonic suite The Planets, which remains his best known composition.

In 1919 Holst was appointed to the staff of the Royal College of Music (to Vaughan Williams's delight, no doubt), and as a part-time music teacher at the University College, Reading (now Reading University). He did not enjoy the work as he doubted his ability to teach adequately at this level, but he seems to have been successful, holding his students' attention through his unusual and often humorous approach.

The years after the War were a productive time. The comic opera The Perfect Fool was given its first complete performance in 1923, the Choral Symphony in 1925, and the orchestral tone-poem Egdon Heath in 1928.

An accident at Reading early in 1923, when he fell from the rostrum and was concussed, did not prevent Holst and his wife from spending two months in America. He was now at his most popular as a composer, but he had not recovered fully from the concussion and was nearing a breakdown. A year's 'rest' was required, but even now Holst could not put composition entirely to one side.

Early in 1925 Holst was elected a Fellow of the Royal College of Music. He was gradually resuming a 'normal' life and in these years he lectured in Switzerland, and at the Universities of Glasgow and Liverpool. In 1927 his home town of Cheltenham honoured him by organizing a Holst Festival. The City of Birmingham Symphony Orchestra gave a concert in the Town Hall under Holst's baton, and Imogen Holst recalled that there were choir boys from Wyck Rissington there, as well as old Grammar School friends and violinist colleagues of Adolph. In the interval he was presented with a painting by Harold Cox of Venus, Jupiter, Saturn and Neptune seen from the Cotswolds. It now hangs in the Birthplace Museum. Holst described the evening as "the most overwhelming event of my life... a colossal success".

Although he was not strong now, Holst still enjoyed walking in the open country for preference but in the streets and parks of London if necessary. At Easter 1926 he walked from Bristol to Dorset to visit Thomas Hardy and to walk on Egdon Heath. He rambled on the hills of Shropshire, the moors of Yorkshire, and in the lanes of Suffolk and the beech woods of Sussex. Abroad, he went to Munich, Vienna and Prague. In 1929 he was in Italy and Sicily, and later that year in New York. Best of all, though, were the walks in the Cotswolds whose morris dances had given him tunes for 'At the Boar's Head', an opera based on the tavern scenes in *Henry IV* which he composed in 1925.

Holst continued to teach at St. Paul's Girls' School, but relinquished his other appointments to give himself more time for composition. In 1930 the Royal Philharmonic Society awarded him its Gold Medal, but despite such accolades Holst had become exhausted and lethargic. Returning from a holiday in Normandy, and perhaps seeking some comic relief, he tried his hand at film music, but for a variety of reasons the project was unsuccessful. More seriously, he went to the vacation school of the English Folk Dance Society at Malvern and to the Three Choirs Festival at Gloucester, where his Choral Fantasia was given its first performance. Vaughan Williams was there and found the work moving.

The start of 1932 saw Holst well enough to travel to America to take up a lecturing post for six months at Harvard University and to conduct his own music with the Boston Symphony Orchestra. He went to see his brother Emil, who had been working in the USA for many years as an actor. He conducted in Montreal and lectured in Washington; and suddenly he was ill. He was rushed to hospital with stomach bleeding, and for a time his condition was grave. He stayed in hospital for two weeks while his condition improved; after a convalescence Holst was well enough to conduct his music again before he returned to England in June.

Soon after arriving back in England Holst had news that Emil would be coming over for a short stay. Here was an opportunity for the brothers to visit the Cotswolds together. Accompanied by Imogen they travelled north-west from Oxford to the hills that Holst loved. Inevitably they went to Wyck Rissington and Bourton, and on to Cheltenham. At Cirencester, where the tour ended, they

45. Gustav Holst (portrait by Martha Stern, taken shortly before he died).

walked in the Park and in the churchyard they found the grave of one of their mother's family - a Lediard. They had been away for a week. "It was a good holiday", Imogen recalled. "One of the last, and one of the best".

At the end of the year Holst was taken ill again. Gastritis and internal bleeding had weakened him, and he was forced to spend some time in a nursing home. When he could, though, he continued to compose. The Brook Green Suite and the Lyric Movement for viola and orchestra are from this period. He even did a little teaching and conducting, but much of the time had to be spent resting. The portrait of him (plate 45) was taken at about this time.

In May 1934 Holst underwent a major operation. His body proved unequal to the challenge and he died on May 25th. On June 24th 1934 his ashes were interred in Chichester Cathedral at the request of his friend Bishop Bell.

Shortly before his operation Holst went to a concert in Oxford. It was to be his last, and, fittingly, the programme consisted of folk music from the Cotswolds.

RALPH VAUGHAN WILLIAMS (1872-1958)

Come down, O Love divine,
Seek thou this soul of mine,
And visit it with thine
Own ardour glowing.

O Comforter, draw near,
Within my heart appear,
And kindle it,
Thy Holy Name bestowing.

This well-known hymn first appeared in 'The English Hymnal' in 1906. The words are by Bianco da Siena (d. 1434). It was set to music by Ralph (Rafe) Vaughan Williams, who named the tune 'Down Ampney' after the Cotswold village of his birth.

Down Ampney lies in the flat country of the upper Thames south east of Cirencester. Though near the busy A419 and the gravel pits of the Cotswold Water Park it is a place of peace. It was not always thus, though: in the north wall of All Saints Church a stained glass window commemorates the men who flew Dakotas and gliders out of RAF Down Ampney for the D-Day and Arnhem landings in World War II, and who brought back wounded from the battlefields of France.

The village is in Gloucestershire (just). The Ampney Brook flows past the church and the opposite bank is in Wiltshire. Upstream are three other Ampneys, St. Mary, St. Peter and Crucis. Ralph Vaughan Williams was born in the Old Vicarage, (plate 46), on October 12th 1872. He was the younger son of the vicar, the Rev. Arthur Vaughan Williams, and his wife Margaret (née Wedgwood). His parents had lived at Down Ampney since 1858. Ralph's mother was the great-granddaughter of Josiah Wedgwood the potter, and the great-niece of Charles Darwin. The male side of Ralph's family was of Welsh descent, his great-grandfather having been born near Carmarthen. This man became a King's Sergeant, and Ralph's grandfather and an uncle were judges. Another uncle as well as Ralph's father entered the Church. It would, therefore, not have been at all surprising for Ralph to have become a lawyer or a clergyman. We are fortunate that his life took the path it did.

Ralph's father died in 1875, when Ralph was two years old. He is buried near the porch of All Saints' Church and in the church there is a memorial window to him.

Following her husband's death Margaret took the children to live with her father and sister at Leith Hill Place in Surrey, which had been bought by her father in 1847. It was here that Margaret had met Arthur Vaughan Williams; Arthur's father had taken the tenancy of Tanhurst, a house near Leith Hill Place, and the families were close friends. It was while he was living here that Ralph wrote his first composition, a four-bar piece for piano called 'The Robin's Nest'.

Ralph was educated at Rottingdean preparatory school and Charterhouse. In 1890 he went to the Royal College of Music where he studied composition with Parry and the

46. Down Ampney Vicarage (Vaughan Williams' birthplace).

organ with Alan Gray. In 1892 he went to Trinity College, Cambridge, but continued with weekly lessons at the R.C.M. He graduated Mus.B. (Cantab) in 1894 and took a second class history degree in 1895. Returning to the R.C.M. he took lessons in composition with Charles Villiers Stanford. (" ...Stanford was a great teacher, but I believe I was unteachable"). On his return from Cambridge Vaughan Williams began his friendship with Gustav Holst (p.152). On their regular 'field days', as they were called, the two men studied and criticized each other's compositions. "I think he showed all he wrote to me", recalled Vaughan Williams, "and I nearly all I wrote to him. I say 'nearly all' advisedly, because sometimes I could not face the absolute integrity of his vision, and I hid some of my worst crimes from him. I regret now that I did not face even his disapproval". One assumes that the rehearsal of Holst's 'Cotswolds Symphony' in 1902 (p.152) was not Vaughan Williams's first acquaintance with the work. His comments on this uneven score are a matter of speculation.

On October 9th 1897 Vaughan Williams married Adeline Fisher of Brockenhurst, Hampshire, whom he had known since he was a boy, when the Fisher family took their summer holidays at a house not far from Leith Hill Place. After a honeymoon in Germany the couple moved into a house in Barton Street, Westminster.

Vaughan Williams obtained his Fellowship of the Royal College of Organists in 1898 (he had been organist of St. Barnabas, Lambeth, for several years, though he did not enjoy the job, calling the church 'this damned place'). In 1899 he passed the examination for Mus.D. (Cantab), but did not take the degree until 1901. For the rest of his life he sought no form of address other than 'Dr.' or 'Mr.' Vaughan Williams.

In 1903 he discovered a new interest: folk music. He began to collect tunes from the villages around Leith Hill Place and elsewhere, encouraged by Cecil Sharp, and gave lectures on folk music in various parts of England.

It was Sharp, with Canon Scott Holland, who recommended Vaughan Williams as the music editor of a new hymn book, to be called the English Hymnal. A group of clergy, dissatisfied with the revised edition of Hymns Ancient and Modern which had just appeared, had decided to produce a new collection of about 150 hymns. In 'The First Fifty Years, a history of the English Hymnal', published in 1956, Vaughan Williams recalled a visit in 1904 by the Rev. Percy Dearmer when he was asked to accept the music editorship.

> I protested that I knew very little about hymns, but... the final clench was given when I understood that if I did not do the job it would be offered to a well-known Church musician with whose musical ideas I was much out of sympathy... I thought it over for twenty four hours and then decided to accept, but I found that the work occupied me two years and that my bill for clerical expenses alone came to about two hundred pounds... The truth is that I determined to do the work thoroughly, and that, besides being a compendium of all the tunes of worth which were already in use, the book should, in addition, be a thesaurus of all the finest hymn tunes in the world - at all events all such as were compatible with the metres of the words for which I had to find tunes.

Vaughan Williams brought together tunes from the 16th and 17th century psalters, from the pens of Tallis and Orlando Gibbons, from psalm books, carols and traditional music of the 18th century and from the 19th century. "While trying to include all the good tunes", he recalled, "I did my best to eliminate the bad ones". Some of the tunes were English folksongs, such as those for 'He who would valiant be' and 'O little town of Bethlehem'. In some cases the verses had unusual metres for which it was necessary to compose new tunes. A number of composers were invited to contribute melodies, including, of course, Gustav Holst, who wrote three tunes. One of these has Cotswold associations - the tune 'Cranham' for the Christmas carol 'In the Bleak Midwinter' (words by Christina Rossetti (plate 47)[1]. "I also", wrote Vaughan Williams, "contrary to my principles, contributed a few tunes of my own, but with becoming modesty I attributed them to my old friend, Mr. Anon".

Thus it was that Vaughan Williams immortalised his birthplace in the Cotswolds as hymn number 152, 'Down Ampney' (plate 48). In his biography of Vaughan Williams (1953) Percy Young says that "'Down Ampney' is strictly concerned with graciousness, possesses a conspicuous fluidity of movement formed within three bar periods, and has the same effortless charm which attaches to similar works by Gibbons".

THE CHRISTIAN YEAR

25

CRANHAM. (Irreg.)

In moderate time ♩ = 100.

G. VON HOLST.

[The metre of this hymn is peculiar. The music as printed is that of the first verse, and it can easily be adapted to the others.]

Verses 2 and 3 run:

Our God, heaven can - not hold him Nor . . earth sus - tain;
E - nough for him, whom Che - ru - bim Wor - ship night and day,   A

Heaven and earth shall flee a - way When he comes to reign: In the bleak mid-
breast - ful of milk, And a man-ger - ful of hay;   E - nough for him, whom
&c.

44

47. Hymn Tune 'Cranham' (to Christina Rossetti's words 'In The Bleak Midwinter...')

THE CHRISTIAN YEAR

DOWN AMPNEY. (66. 11. D.)
Moderately slow ♩ = 88 (𝅗𝅥 = 44).

152

Anon.

Bianco da Siena, d. 1434. *Tr. R. F. Littledale.*
Discendi, Amor santo.

COME down, O Love divine,
Seek thou this soul of mine,
And visit it with thine own ardour
glowing;
O Comforter, draw near,
Within my heart appear,
And kindle it, thy holy flame bestow-
ing.

2 O let it freely burn,
Till earthly passions turn
To dust and ashes in its heat consum-
ing;

And let thy glorious light
Shine ever on my sight,
And clothe me round, the while my
path illuming.

3 Let holy charity
Mine outward vesture be,
And lowliness become mine. inner
clothing;
True lowliness of heart,
Which takes the humbler part,
And o'er its own shortcomings weeps
with loathing.

4. And so the yearning strong,
With which the soul will long,
Shall far outpass the power of human telling;
For none can guess its grace,
Till he become the place
Wherein the Holy Spirit makes his dwelling.

216

A - men.

48. Hymn Tune 'Down Ampney' ('Anon' was Vaughan Williams).

In 'A Musical Autobiography' (1950), Vaughan Williams recalled that he started work on the English Hymnal with reservations about the wisdom of embarking on such a project. "But I know now that two years of close association with some of the best (as well as some of the worst) tunes in the world was a better musical education than any amount of sonatas and fugues."

Vaughan Williams was travelling far afield at this time in his search for folk tunes - to Wiltshire, Kent and to Norfolk, but a new interest soon engaged him. Musical festivals were beginning to be held in various parts of the country, and it was decided that one should be held at Leith Hill Place. The founders were Lady Farrer and Vaughan Williams's sister Margaret ('Meggie'). The Leith Hill Festival duly took place on May 10th 1905, with Vaughan Williams conducting the evening concert. Thus began a major music festival which attracted musicians of world renown, one with which Vaughan Williams was deeply involved as conductor and organizer for over fifty years. He was busy, too, at Morley College, helping with the performances which Gustav Holst, as Musical Director, had arranged.

In November 1905 Vaughan Williams and his wife moved from Barton Street to a house in Cheyne Walk overlooking the river, where, no doubt, they made the acquaintance of their neighbour C. R. Ashbee. They remained at Cheyne Walk until 1929, when they moved to Dorking, Some of his most substantial works were written during these years, including three symphonies, two operas and a violin concerto.

In the years of the Great War Vaughan Williams served in the R.A.M.C. in France. In 1918 he was commissioned as a lieutenant in the Royal Garrison Artillery and was demobilized in 1919. In that year he received the honorary degree of D.Mus. from Oxford University and was appointed Professor of Composition at the Royal College of Music. He worked there for more than twenty years.

Vaughan Williams had been associated with the London Bach Choir since 1903, and in 1920 became its conductor, taking over from the director of the R. C. M., Hugh Allen (later Sir Hugh). The Leith Hill Musical Festival, which had been interrupted by the War, resumed in 1920, and Vaughan Williams busied himself with rehearsals. One visitor was Diana Awdry of Dursley, who organised the first Stinchcombe Festival in 1920, enlisting the help of the Leith Hill committee. Vaughan Williams went to Stinchcombe to help with the new venture and to judge the competitions. Ten years later, at John Masefield's instigation, verse-speaking would be included. (p.146).

Vaughan Williams visited America for the first time in 1922, to conduct his Pastoral Symphony in Norfolk, Connecticut. Back in England, he immersed himself in composition. 1924 saw him revising a romantic opera, Hugh the Drover, which he had written before the War. The librettist was a Gloucestershire journalist, Harold Child (1869-1945). In the second scene of the opera, a village is portrayed on May Day morning. "Ralph", wrote Ursula Wood[2] "wanted the sound of bells chiming a tune as they do at Northleach... (which was the sort of village in which he imagined the story to be set...)". In 1950 Maurice Jacobson, who had been a pupil of Gustav Holst, adapted the opera as a cantata for tenor, soprano and baritone, A Cotswold Romance.

The Oxford University Press were preparing a new hymn book, Songs of Praise, in 1924. As with the first edition of the English Hymnal the Rev. Percy Dearmer edited the words and Vaughan Williams the music, assisted this time by Martin Shaw. Down Ampney and the other hymn tunes which he had written for the English Hymnal appeared again in Songs of Praise, together with five tunes which Vaughan Williams had written specially for the new book; this time he acknowledged the tunes as his own. He was pleased with Songs of Praise, saying that there was not a single tune in it of which he was ashamed.

The accommodation at 13 Cheyne Walk was shared for a time by R.O. Morris, a musician who had married Adeline's sister Emmie. In 1925 a young man, Gerald Finzi, became one of Morris's pupils. It was inevitable that Vaughan Williams and Finzi met. Their friendship developed, and lasted until Finzi's death in 1956. At the Bach Choir's spring concert in 1928 Vaughan Williams conducted the first performance of Finzi's Concerto for Violin and Small Orchestra.

After the move from London to Dorking in 1929, Vaughan Williams could no longer spend time with the Bach Choir, though he continued to commute to the R.C.M. He was still busy with composition and, of course, the annual Leith Hill Musical Festival claimed his attention. An honour rare among English composers came to him in 1930 when he was presented with the Gold Medal of the Royal Philharmonic Society. Soon after, it was awarded too to his friend Gustav Holst.

Three major English composers died in 1934: Edward Elgar in February, Gustav Holst in May, and Frederick Delius in June. Following Elgar's death he was offered the post of Master of the King's Musick, but refused it. He was at Worcester in March for Elgar's Memorial Service; he had already been rehearsing 'The Dream of Gerontius' for Leith Hill and the performance duly took place.

Holst's death was a great loss to him. "My only thought", he wrote, "is now which ever way I turn, what are we to do without him ... what would Gustav think or advise or do...". Vaughan Williams was, of course, at Chichester Cathedral for the burial of Holst's ashes, when the Whitsun singers sang, among other items, the Kyrie from Vaughan Williams's Mass in G minor.

In 1935 Vaughan Williams was invested with the Order of Merit by King George V. He had refused most honours hitherto, but the O. M. was one which he felt bound to accept.

During the years at Dorking Vaughan Williams wrote four symphonies, a piano concerto, an oboe concerto and much other music, including, during the War years, patriotic music and several film scores. The Fifth Symphony is of particular interest: ten years after it was first performed, Percy Young wrote (1953) "the symphony is an epic moulded by a lifetime of experience and emanating from the lyrical epitome of Down Ampney".

Vaughan Williams returned to his birthplace in 1948. He and Adeline had been to the Three Choirs Festival at Worcester with their friend Ursula Wood. In her biography, Ursula recalled that "after lunch we drove back through Gloucester and Birdlip, familiar country to us both, and then to Down Ampney where we stopped and where Ralph showed me the house where he was born and the dark, laurel-shadowed path that was his earliest recollection."

Adeline Vaughan Williams died in May 1951, aged eighty. Vaughan Williams continued to live in the house at Dorking for two more years. Following his wife's death he busied himself with conducting engagements, visits to festivals (the Three Choirs and Leith Hill in particular), attendance at operatic productions at Covent Garden, and orchestral concerts all over England. The University of Bristol awarded him the honorary degree of Doctor of Music in December 1951. It was conferred by the Chancellor, Winston Churchill.

On February 7th 1953 Vaughan Williams married his friend of some fifteen years, Ursula Wood, the widow of an Army officer. Later that year the

49. Vaughan Williams (portrait by Sir Gerald Kelly painted towards the end of his life).

Dorking house was sold, and Vaughan Williams and his wife settled at Hanover Terrace, Regent's Park in London. 1953 was, of course, Coronation Year, and for the service in Westminster Abbey Vaughan Williams wrote the anthem 'O Taste and See,' and made an arrangement of the Old Hundredth psalm tune 'All People that on Earth do dwell', in which the congregation was able to take part.

Substantial compositions were continuing to appear. A Tuba Concerto was written in 1954. His Eighth Symphony received its first performance in 1955 and his Ninth in 1957. It was in 1957 that he paid his last visit to Gloucestershire, when he attended the Cheltenham Festival. His London Symphony was played by the Hallé Orchestra under Sir John Barbirolli. The portrait shown in plate 49 dates from about this period.

Ralph Vaughan Williams died suddenly on August 26th 1958, aged 85. On September 19th his ashes were laid in Westminster Abbey. The music included some of his own works. As the casket was placed in its niche the congregation sang 'Come down, O Love Divine' to his tune 'Down Ampney'. At the last, Vaughan Williams's birthplace in the Cotswolds was remembered.

Chapter 13 - FURTHER READING

HOLST
Holst, Imogen: *Gustav Holst, a Biography*. Oxford University Press (1969).
Holst, lmogen: *The Music of Gustav Holst and Holst's Music Reconsidered*. Oxford University Press (1986).
Short, Michael: *Gustav Holst the Man and his Music*. Oxford University Press (1990).

VAUGHAN WILLIAMS
Day, James: *Vaughan Williams*. Dent (1961).
Foss, Hubert: *Ralph Vaughan Williams, a Study* (contains *RVW's A Musical Autobiography*). Harrap (1950).
Howes, Frank: *The Music of Ralph Vaughan Williams*. Oxford University Press (1954).
Vaughan Williams, Ralph: *The First Fifty Years, a History of the English Hymnal*. Oxford University Press (1956).
Vaughan Williams, Ursula: *'R V W'*. Oxford University Press (1964).
Young, Percy: *Ralph Vaughan Williams*. Dent (1970).

[1] Interestingly attributed to 'G. von Holst'. Holst dropped the 'von' by deed-poll in 1918.
[2] Vaughan Williams' second wife. See p.163.

14. MUSIC FROM THE COTSWOLDS
(ii) Gurney, Finzi and Orr

IVOR GURNEY (1890-1937)

'Cranham, Crickley, Cooper's, Cotswold' - the names often appear in Ivor Gurney's poetry, for he loved the county of his birth perhaps more than anything else, and when he was forced to be away from Gloucestershire his longing to come again could be seen in some of his best writing. Severn, May Hill, Dymock, Maisemore and Framilode are there too, for he ambled all over the county, often accompanied by John Haines (p.124) or his old school friend Will Harvey, and painted it in words and music. Gurney was a keen observer of nature, and his poetry has therefore been compared with John Clare's. Like Clare, his style is direct and simple, but, particularly in his later poems, lapses in punctuation and missing words sometimes obscure the meaning. Images could become jumbled, as if his thoughts came tumbling out faster than he could write. This was probably indicative of the mental illness which would confine Gurney to a mental hospital for the last fifteen years of his life. It is only in modern times that he has become recognised as an important English poet.

To be a genius in one field of human endeavour is rare. To be so in two is exceptional, for as well as his verse Gurney wrote over two hundred songs, nearly half of which have been published. His poems numbered nearer a thousand, and in his poetry there are evocative portraits of Cotswold, Severn and Dean, but until recently it was as a composer that Gurney was better remembered.

On August 28th 1890 Ivor Bertie Gurney was born in the city of Gloucester. His father hailed from Maisemore, on the Severn near the city, and his mother from Bisley, high in the Cotswolds near Stroud. At the age of eight Gurney became a chorister at All Saints Church in Gloucester, and at eleven he moved to the King's School and the choir of the Cathedral. Gurney's biographer Michael Hurd says that there are indications that Gurney was writing music by the age of fourteen. A crucial influence on the boy at this time was his godfather, Canon Alfred Cheesman, who gave Gurney access to his library of English poetry and prose. The Cathedral organist, Dr. Herbert Brewer, arranged organ lessons for him, and thus it was that Gurney's literary and musical genius was given the room it needed to develop to mature expression.

It was at the King's School that Gurney met F. W. (Will) Harvey, who would, like Gurney, become a significant War poet. He also became a friend of Herbert Howells, another of Brewer's pupils and himself destined to be a composer. John Haines, too. was a companion. Haines, a solicitor of Hucclecote, Gloucester, and a poet and amateur botanist, was a relative of Catherine Abercrombie, wife of Lascelles Abercrombie, and it was probably through Haines that Gurney met the Dymock poets.

In 1911 Gurney won a scholarship to the Royal College of Music. He went to London, as Herbert Howells put it, "with his wallet bulging with works of many kinds. There were piano preludes thick with untamed chords; violin sonatas strewn with ecstatic crises; organ works which he tried out in the midst of Gloucester's imperturbable Norman pillars ... In 1911 he had enthusiasm enough to write anything".

The interviewing panel at the College included Sir Hubert Parry and Sir Charles Villiers Stanford. According to Harry Plunket Greene

> Parry was greatly excited over Gurney's MS composition and was pointing out to his colleagues the similarity in idiom and even in handwriting to Schubert, when Gurney was called. As he walked into the room Parry said in an awestruck whisper "By God! it is Schubert".

Greene went on

> Those who knew Gurney can well believe it. Totally unselfconscious, untidy to a degree, lost in the clouds, he walked in a poet's dream. His MSS were in a permanent state of hopeless confusion, a second fiddle part of a string quartet tucked away with the trombones of an overture or maybe not written out at all. He would talk of Schubert by the hour and might have been his reincarnation.

At the College Gurney met the musicologist Marion Scott, who would remain a friend for the rest of his life. (In later years she collected all his poetry and music manuscripts, though it was Gerald Finzi who, according to Howard Ferguson, undertook the major part of the work involved in cataloguing it and arranging publication. Although Finzi did not know Gurney personally he greatly admired his work).

Marion Scott describes meeting Gurney in May 1911.

> ...I saw coming toward me along a corridor in the Royal College of Music a figure which, even in that place of marked individualities, appeared uncommon. For one thing the boy was wearing a thick, dark blue Severn pilot's coat, more suggestive of an outdoor life than the composition lesson with Sir Charles Stanford for which (by the manuscripts tucked under his arm) he was clearly bound. But what struck me more was the look of latent force in him, the fine head with its profusion of light brown hair (not too well brushed!) and the eyes which, behind their spectacles, were of the mixed colouring - in Gurney's case hazel, grey, green and agate -which Erasmus once said was regarded by the English as denoting genius. "This", I said to myself, "must be the new composition scholar from Gloucester whom they call Schubert".

Stanford subsequently told Herbert Howells that Gurney was "potentially ...the most gifted man that ever came into my care. But he is the least teachable".

At this stage Gurney had not begun to write poetry in earnest, though he was reading widely; his first important musical work was the five Elizabethan songs - settings of Campion, Fletcher, Nashe and Shakespeare - which he composed in 1913/14, (his five "Elizas"). "He never rested till he made me see them", said Marion Scott. She added "The tremendous hold Gloucestershire had upon his thoughts and affections was apparent from the first. Filial and attached though he was to his parents, one nevertheless felt that Gloucestershire was his foster-mother.

He could not settle at the College, though, and for a while returned to Gloucestershire, before taking a post as church organist in High Wycombe, where he was befriended by a local family, the Chapmans.

When the Great War broke out, Gurney volunteered at once, and after initially being rejected because of his poor sight he joined the army in 1915. On October 6th he wrote to Marion Scott from 'The Band', D Company, 2nd-5th Gloucestershire Regiment at Chelmsford.

As my health and spirits improve, so within me I find a store of poetry, an accumulation of pictures - dead leaves, Minsterworth Orchards, Cranham, Crickley and Framilode reach. They do not merely mean intensely to me; they are me, points from which my soul, as our armies at Lens and Champagne, will make irruptions and declare as I hope Music to be as much English as a German art.

In the spring of 1916 Gurney had five days' leave, and went home to Gloucester. One day he cycled over to see Lascelles Abercrombie at Ryton near Dymock, but his friend was away "munition making in Liverpool", so Gurney spent six hours with Catherine and the three children.

The Glosters were soon in France with the British Expeditionary Force. On October 8th he ended a long letter to Marion Scott

50. Ivor Gurney.

There's a great Autumn wind raging outside, and freezing my face in this barn.
...A day to love, and to walk the Cotswolds in.

How the leaves must be flying on Cranham, and up and down and round in swirls on Portway! Painswick Beacon will stand as high and immovable as ever, and Birdlip too; I can do without them. But oh for the wild woods and the leaves flying!

Gurney was soon in the Somme trenches. Even now musical composition did not cease, but more and more he was writing poetry, and sending it to Marion Scott when he could. She typed it and returned it, but kept carbon copies and arranged the publication of Gurney's first volume of poetry, 'Severn and Somme', in 1917. When he was wounded at Vermand, Gurney was transferred to Rouen for recuperation. Gloucestershire was, as ever, not far from his mind, and from Rouen he wrote to Marion Scott in April 1917:

Last night after lights out I had a long talk with a Cotswold man lying next to me - of his ambition to be a gardener; of Cotswold gardens; of the beauty of those churches; of certain jolly old masters-of-life there; of old songs; of the joy of life there in those homely and friendly-seeming houses of grey stone with so wonderful an array of flowers round each. I could hear music that I should make mixt with the older music respiring from his talk - language of Shakespearian comedy - and set myself to wait a little longer, and perhaps not so very long either.

and in August

Curse the weather! Is it going to change again? Ah, but were it Autumn and I in England! Such golden-pathed days I remember, on Cranham; wading knee deep in rustling leaves, or exulting in some miraculous sombre-passionate sunset over Wales, and in such peace as nothing but the very presence of God may give.

Poetry continued to flow. Thirty seven poems, sent to Herbert Howells, appeared in 'War's Embers', Gurney's second volume of verse (1913). One of these poems was written when he believed (wrongly) that Will Harvey had been killed. It begins

He's gone and all our plans
Are useless indeed.
We'll walk no more on Cotswold
Where the sheep feed
Quietly and take no heed.

It would seem that, out of the battle line, Gurney spent his waking hours reading. (Housman's 'A Shropshire Lad' was his constant companion), or writing. Like his comrades, Gurney pined for home ("...To see grey stone and Cotswold gardens", he told Marion Scott, "To be continually drinking tea, and playing Bach of evenings...").

In the event, he was gassed at Passchendaele on August 22nd and sent home, first to the Edinburgh War Hospital and then to hospitals in Warrington and St.Albans. After a month or so he returned to the Army, but was not fully recovered and was discharged a few weeks before the war ended. He went back to Gloucester, of course, but the conditions he found there did not help the depression from which he was suffering. His mother was caring for Gurney's terminally ill father, and his brother Ronald was unsympathetic and unwelcoming. Gurney spent much of the time wandering, walking in the Gloucestershire countryside, often with John Haines or Herbert Howells (p.165) In the 'Gloucester Journal' (January 5th 1935) Haines recalled Gurney as

> ...a fierce, tall, stooping but athletic figure with bushy eyebrows and most piercing eyes, a kind of combination of Don Quixote and D'Artagnan, gallant, intractable, kindly, ferocious, and distressingly lovable. With blazing eyes, he would pour forth an endless stream of talk on the English country, or on English poetry...

Gurney described one such walk to Marion Scott in April 1919:

> Yesterday brought me that rare sight - the ground end of a rainbow. I could see the hedges through it - a wonderful sight. Under Crickley it was, under the Roman camp - such a ridge, such a sky, such a rainbow, and (afterwards) such a sweeping scud of storm - a wonderful glittering curtain of rain sweeping across the valley.

He had, said Haines,

> ...many friends; some local friends, such as ...myself, who could only just compete with him in terrific walks over the Cotswolds, the Forest of Dean and the Black Mountains, and lend him the books he desired to read, books which brought him in touch with the work of Edward Thomas and Gerard Manley Hopkins, the two modern poets he most admired and those who contributed most to his literary technique.

He was well enough now to resume his scholarship at the Royal College of Music. For a time he studied composition there under Ralph Vaughan Williams. He lived in poverty before moving back to High Wycombe and playing the organ in a local church.

This was Gurney's happiest and most creative period. 'War's Embers' appeared in 1919, and more poetry (perhaps his best) was to follow, though it would not be published in his lifetime. He could not stay away from Gloucestershire and walked there - often at night - because, according to Marion Scott, he had no money for the train fare.

Typical of this period is his poem 'Cotswold Ways' (published in its original form in the 'London Mercury' as 'Encounters').[1]

One comes across the strangest things in walks:
Fragments of Abbey tithe-barns fixed in modern
And Dutch-sort houses where the water baulks
Weired up, and brick kilns broken among fern,
Old troughs, great stone cisterns bishops might have blessed
Ceremonially, and worthy mounting-stones;
Black timber in red brick, queerly placed
Where Hill stone was looked for - and a manor's bones
Spied in the frame of some wisteria'd house
And mill-falls and sedge pools and Saxon faces;
Stream-sources happened upon in unlikely places,
And Roman-looking hills of small degree
And the surprise of dignity of poplars
At a road end, or the white Cotswold scars
Or sheets spread white against the hazel tree.
Strange the large difference of up-Cotswold ways;
Birdlip climbs bold and treeless to a bend,
Portway to dim wood-lengths without end,
And Crickley goes to cliffs are the crown of days.

When Gurney was not writing poetry he was writing music. In 1920 the composer Gerald Finzi heard a Gurney song, ('Sleep', from the 'Five Elizas'). He immediately became a champion of Gurney's music and with the help of Howard Ferguson and Marion Scott he began to collate, catalogue and prepare for publication Gurney's songs and poems from wherever they could be found. Between 1917 and 1920 most of his songs were settings of the Georgian poets, "of which body", said Vaughan Williams , "he is himself a distinguished member". Certainly, a number of the poets who appeared in the five volumes of 'Georgian Poetry' which were published between 1917 and 1920 were his friends (Abercrombie and de la Mare, for example), and in some cases it is arguable that Gurney's poetry was better than theirs. On April 19th 1921 he told Marion Scott "...Lord Sandwich is trying to land me in the next Georgian", but this was not to be. Edward Marsh did not include Gurney's work in his anthologies. It would have scarcely mattered if he had; Edward Thomas, after all, was not harmed by his own exclusion.

The Royal College saw less and less of Gurney. He slept rough on the Embankment, or earned a night's lodging by singing in some country inn on his way to or from Gloucestershire. He obtained work for a few months at Dryhill Farm, Bentham, just below Crickley Hill. "An old gray-stone rambling array of building under a Roman camp near the site of a Roman villa where many things have been from time to time discovered. A place of thorn, oak, ash, elm, clear streams, a 500 feet-up place where one gets a sight of the Severn Sea, May Hill, and on clear days of the Welsh Hills, by looking out of a window merely or wandering out of a gate". He returned to the College, and found digs in Earls Court, but despite the company of friends, including Edmund Blunden and Wilfrid Gibson, he was desperately homesick. On February 9th 1921 he told John Haines "This is a beastly life, this houses and drain-pipe streets life - this is the afternoon for Cranham or the Adam and Eve, or by Stinc[h]combe to end up at Bisley, where Roger Bacon might have been born, and my mother was...".

Gurney's scholarship ended in 1921 and he went home - not to Barton Street but to his aunt at Longford, not far from Gloucester. He wandered the countryside, and in May 1922 spoke to Marion Scott of "the chief luck of living out at Longford where the neighbour meadows are matchless - such arrangements of trees, such light, and levelness never known. Nevertheless one sight of Coopers Hill woods beats all."

In his state of increasing mental instability Gurney did what odd jobs he could find; de la Mare obtained some money for him from Edward Marsh, and he found a post as pianist in a cinema in Bude, Cornwall. When he lost this position Marsh helped him to obtain employment in the Gloucester Income Tax Office. His behaviour was becoming increasingly eccentric, though friends rallied to help him. Marion Scott did what she could to enlist support. (He composed and wrote "almost incessantly" she said. "Twenty-four hour spells of work were not uncommon"). Several prominent singers gave public performances of his songs, but Gurney declined to such a degree that in 1922 he was certified insane. He injured himself while attempting to escape from a Gloucester mental hospital and was transferred to the City of London Mental Hospital at Dartford, Kent, where he stayed for the rest of his life.

In about 1932 Marion Scott wrote to Helen Thomas, explaining her friendship with Gurney and how he "passionately loved" Edward Thomas's work. She suggested that the two women visit Gurney at Dartford. In 'Time and Again' Helen Thomas describes her experiences. She talked with Gurney of the countryside which she and Edward knew and which Gurney knew too. He wanted more than anything to go back to Gloucestershire, but for his own safety this was disallowed. Helen had an idea: on her next visit she took with her her husband's well-used ordnance maps of the county.

This proved to have been a sort of inspiration, for Ivor Gurney at once spread them out on his bed and he and I spent the whole time I was there tracing with our fingers the lanes and byways and villages of which Ivor Gurney knew every step and over which Edward had also walked. He spent that hour in revisiting his home, in spotting a village or a track, a hill or a wood and seeing it all in his mind's eye...

At Dartford Gurney languished, writing poetry which was sometimes good, and occasionally unclear, but always demanding attention.

The High Hills

The high hills have a bitterness
Now they are not known
And memory is poor enough consolation
For the soul hopeless gone.
Up in the air there beech tangles wildly in the wind -
That I can imagine
But the speed, the swiftness, walking into clarity,
Like last year's bryony are gone.

In 1937, when Gurney was seriously ill with tuberculosis, Marion Scott, Gerald Finzi, and Howard Ferguson suggested that an appreciation of him should be published in the quarterly Magazine 'Music and Letters'. A symposium was duly arranged with contributions from several of the leading musicians and writers of the day, though it did not appear until after Gurney's death. Finzi and his friends also arranged for the publication of two volumes of Gurney's songs by the Oxford University Press, and when Gurney heard of this he could only say 'It is too late'.

Ivor Gurney died on December 26th 1937. He was buried at Twigworth, near Gloucester, the service being conducted by his godfather and lifelong friend Canon Cheesman, who was now Vicar of Twigworth. Herbert Howells was the organist and the music included Gurney's songs 'Severn Meadows' and 'Sleep'. Perhaps the latter would have reminded Finzi, who was at the church, of first hearing the song seventeen years earlier when he realised Gurney's worth.

Gerald Finzi was anxious to see more of the songs and a selection of his poems in print, but the war intervened.Two more volumes of the songs had to await publication until after the war.

In 1954 a book of seventy-eight of Gurney's poems was published with a biographical foreword by Edmund Blunden, and in 1973 a further selection of poems appeared, edited by Leonard Clark. In his foreword Clark wrote:

For Gurney, beauty and strangeness in all things was everything, and it is this adoration of the sublime which illuminates many of his strange themes. His poems sing the praises of his county of Gloucestershire. They are full of his zest for Beethoven, Schubert and Bach...

A selection of some 300 poems, edited by P.J. Kavanagh, was published in 1982, and this volume was regarded by Gurney's biographer, Michael Hurd, as of first importance in enabling Gurney's worth as a poet to be recognised.

Gurney's letters to his old friends the Chapman family were edited by Anthony Boden and published in 1986 as 'Stars in a Dark Night'. The volume includes Gurney's essay 'The Springs of Music', in which he attempts to survey the musical scene from

Bach to Schumann. Although Gurney has been called 'The English Schubert' it was in the music of Robert Schumann that for him, the essence of the Cotswolds was to be found:

> Firelight is infinitely strong on us all, but on Schumann pre-eminently. One would think that man to have known Cotswold, and to have sheltered from its winter air in a house built of the stone most worthily used for cathedrals, and as perfectly built. To have watched the dance and interlacing of shadows on the dim walls, but most to have gazed and lost himself in the deepest heart of the log-fire roaring upwards towards the vast chimney and the frosty stars...

GERALD FINZI (1901-1956)

We cannot be certain why Gerald Finzi chose, as a young man, to settle in the Cotswolds. Perhaps it was serendipity; he came on holiday with his mother in the summer of 1920, when they stayed in Churchdown, at the foot of Chosen Hill - a Cotswold outlier near Gloucester. The area was evidently to their liking as they returned in the following March, lodging this time at Chosen Hill Farm. Perhaps Finzi was attracted by the region's rich associations with the arts: William Morris had, after all, selected a Cotswold manor as his 'retreat', C.R. Ashbee had chosen Chipping Campden for his Guild of Handicraft, and just across the hills from Churchdown Gimson and the Barnsley brothers had made their homes at Sapperton. Dymock was not far away, but poetical associations were literally on Finzi's doorstep: Ivor Gurney, from Gloucester, walked on Chosen Hill with his friend Herbert Howells (p.169).

Gerald Raphael Finzi was born in London on July 11th 1901, the son of a ship broker, John Finzi, and his wife Eliza. He was educated privately. He was taught music by the composer Ernest Farrar. When Farrar was killed in action Finzi studied for four years with the organist of York Minster, Sir Edward Bairstow. Finzi's father had died when Gerald was eight. This, and the loss of three older brothers, made him realise that life is sometimes short, and that time must be used effectively to achieve one's aims.

Even as a young man Finzi was aware of Gloucestershire's links with music. He went with his mother to Vaughan Williams' birthplace at Down Ampney during their 1921 holiday (before he had met the great man). The names of Gurney, Howells, Holst and Parry were also familiar to him. He had championed Gurney's music since hearing 'Sleep', from the 'Five Elizas' in 1920, and Finzi and his wife would, years later, work to ensure the publication of Gurney's songs (p.172).

It is not certain when Finzi met Herbert Howells. It may have been in 1920 when Howells was courting a Churchdown girl (whom he married that year). Finzi's wife later suggested that they could have met when Finzi was staying at Chosen Hill Farm in 1921. Howells and his wife were then living in London, but were regular visitors to Churchdown, and Howells may have found a convenient lodging at Chosen Hill Farm. He and Finzi came to know each other well, but were, it seems, never close friends.

In 1922 Finzi and his mother moved to King's Mill House, on the Painswick stream just south of Painswick village. It is the lowest of a series of mills along the brook; a mill had existed on this spot since the end of the fifteenth century. King's Mill House itself was built in the seventeenth century and subsequently extended. In 1870 it was used as a pin factory. When Finzi moved in it was a large and attractive house and for a few years at least, he could write music in relative seclusion. Finzi settled into village life and soon founded the Painswick Music Club.

By now he had begun setting poems by Thomas Hardy, and a setting of six songs for baritone and string quartet, called 'By Footpath and Stile', was published in 1923. It was performed that same year at the Contemporary Music Centre. Finzi's friend Edmund Rubbra wrote "...the words are not forced into a musical framework; they are left to sing themselves in their natural rhythm, which is usually quite separate and distinct from that of the accompaniment." This early work (Finzi was only 22 at the time) already indicated, as the critic C.M. Boyd put it, "a personal turn of melody, a fastidious regard for craftsmanship, and a rare ability to identify himself closely with the thoughts of the poet."

It is likely that many of Finzi's much later works were conceived at Painswick. His friend Howard Ferguson recalled that "the habit of spreading the composition of a work over twenty or twenty-five years was feasible only because Finzi's style (like Ravel's or Elgar's) changed comparatively little during his lifetime."

'By Footpath and Stile' turned out to be the first of many settings of Hardy's poetry which Finzi composed. Boyd, referring to Hardy's 'idiosyncracies of language', commented

> ...although no-one would deny his verses a certain lyrical quality (Hardy himself called them 'songs'), we see in them, more than anything else perhaps, his unceasing regard for the 'craftsmanly art' - Hardy the stonemason. In his settings Finzi has matched these qualities with music which is lyrical when the text permits lyricism and which shows a craftsmanly heightening of the words when it does not.

The writer on music Diana McVeagh further explored the affinity between Finzi and Hardy when she wrote in 1980

> Hardy watches the small eternal country things, the old man and his horse, the little bonfire of couchgrass, the pairs of young lovers... Finzi took the thought a little further, to make the poem and the poet himself that which will last through change and wars and man's folly...

Gloucestershire, of course, abounded in these 'small eternal country things'. ("One comes across the strangest things in walks", wrote Gurney). Dr. Herbert Sumsion, who became organist of Gloucester Cathedral in 1928, recalled that Finzi "...took the keenest interest in flowers, fruit trees and almost everything that had life and growth, and many is the walking tour that I have had with him. He was the ideal companion, for his memory was so vivid and his knowledge so wide".

Finzi was indeed a keen walker. At various times he tramped the Welsh hills, East Anglia, the Isles of Scilly, the Ridgeway of Berkshire and Wiltshire and, of course, Hardy's county of Dorset but, said Sumsion, "...for Gloucester and the Gloucestershire countryside he had a deep affection... he has told me many a time that his heart was in the Severn Vale and the country around May Hill."

It was almost inevitable, then, that while he lived at Painswick Finzi would write a 'Severn Rhapsody' (1923, for chamber orchestra). At Painswick, too, he composed a Requiem da Camera for small chorus (or four soloists) and chamber orchestra, dedicated to the memory of Ernest Farrar. An orchestral prelude precedes settings of words by Masefield (from 'August 1914'), Hardy ('In time of the Breaking of Nations') and Wilfrid Gibson ('Lament'). The orchestration of the Requiem was completed posthumously by Philip Thomas, who discovered the Hardy setting, in draft form, in the Bodleian library in 1982.

As has already been said, Finzi was deeply conscious of his own mortality. "This thought was constantly through his mind", said his friend Howard Ferguson, "like a ground-bass to his whole existence". The metaphor is appropriate: Finzi wrote strongly for basses, not allowing their line to be lost in the general effect. Perhaps his empathy with Hardy's poems gives an inkling of the darker side of Finzi's nature; Ferguson was certainly aware of it:

> Anyone who met Finzi personally will remember his bubbling sense of fun, his humour and his electric nervous energy. As I picture him in conversation he is always striding restlessly about the room, never seated at rest. Fewer will know that beneath this incisive, buoyant exterior lay a deep and fundamental pessimism.

Finzi's main musical influences are generally regarded as Elgar and Vaughan Williams, but the Painswick years saw him already developing a personal idiom. He had become interested in eighteenth century music and would later imitate its style in his Fantasia for Piano (1928). Folk song, too, had captured his attention: even before the move to Painswick Finzi had written to Cecil Sharp, and now he was writing to Vaughan Williams for permission to use a folk song in his own work.

A close friend of Finzi at Painswick was the architect Detmar Blow, a direct descendant of the composer John Blow (1649-1708). Detmar Blow had been an architectural assistant in London in the 1880s, and later assisted Ernest Gimson on several buildings. Two miles from Painswick, on the Cotswold edge near Harescombe, Blow had built himself a house, 'Hilles'. According to Stephen Banfield, Blow and his wife "took Gerald under their wing in the 1920s to the extent of becoming virtually his surrogate family". Finzi was often to be seen at Hilles; his passion for folk culture and the social ideals of Winifred and Detmar Blow were entirely compatible.

The last work which Finzi wrote at Painswick was a setting of W.H. Davies's poem 'Days Too Short'. Davies was already a visitor to the Cotswolds, and would soon move there himself.

By the end of 1924 Finzi had decided that for reasons of professional advancement he would have to leave Painswick. On the advice of (Sir) Adrian Boult he moved to London and King's Mill House was put up for sale. His mother, meanwhile, went back to Mrs Champion at Chosen Hill Farm, near Churchdown. Finzi arranged a short course of lessons on counterpoint with R.O. Morris and commuted to Churchdown when he could. At Morris's home, 13 Cheyne Walk, Finzi met Vaughan Williams and began a friendship that would last for the rest of his life. At Morris's home, too, he met Howard Ferguson, Edmund Rubbra, and several other musicians who became part of his circle.

In 1925 Finzi decided that he would become independent of his mother and would settle in London. He moved in January 1925 into 21 Caroline Street, near Sloane Square, which had been found for him by his friend Detmar Blow. "For the next eight or nine years", recalled Ferguson, "...Finzi and I managed to meet about once a week, either at his home or mine. We went through each other's compositions, talked, and made music ceaselessly". (One is reminded of Vaughan Williams' and Holst's 'field days'). Finzi had, at last, the freedom and stimulus which he had been seeking. Concerts, operas and plays were, of course, accessible, and he could build up his (already large) collection of books. "He was unusually [well] read" said Ferguson, "and, large as his music library was even then, there were many more books in the house than there was music".

It was almost inevitable that during his years at Painswick Finzi would have met John Haines (p.124). Finzi, having left his mother in Gloucestershire without permanent accommodation, was relieved, on December 11th 1927, to be able to tell Haines that she "has at last got a house. Having searched for all these years in the West, she has found one near Clare, Suffolk".

Despite the trauma of moving house and his concern for his mother, Finzi continued to compose. Between 1925 and 1927 appeared 'New Year Music' and a violin concerto. Finzi later scrapped the first and third movements, but the second (an Introit) - "the most beautiful of the movements" said Rubbra, "a piece of rare and grave sweetness" wrote Diana McVeagh - was revised and later published.

The years 1930-1933 saw Finzi teaching composition at the Royal Academy of Music. In 1933 he married Joyce ('Joy') Black, an artist and a warm, practical person - his ideal companion. Ralph and Adeline Vaughan Williams were delighted by the match and went to the wedding. In 1935 the Finzis moved from London to Aldbourne in Wiltshire. They were extremely busy now: not only were they planning their permanent country home but both were working with Vaughan Williams, Howard Ferguson and Marion Scott to bring the Works of Ivor Gurney to the attention of a wider public (p.172) though Finzi never met Gurney in person.

He was in demand, too, as an adjudicator at musical festivals which had sprung up all over the country. The Stinchcombe Hill Festival, held at Dursley, was increasingly popular, and in the 1933/34 Report the organizing Committee was able to announce that the Festival had been extended to three days. Finzi does not seem to have been involved until 1938, when, on March 30th, he was one of two judges in the competition for choral societies. (The other was Imogen Holst). On April 2nd Finzi wrote to Diana Awdry (now Mrs Bernard Oldridge)

> ...there was a happy feeling behind it all. Certainly something positive of that kind is about the only thing to keep one sane, with all these crucifixtions [*sic*] going on around us, East v West... We shall certainly meet without the usual Festival rush, for Joy and I intend to abduct you, and make you lazy for a few days in the sun, when the new house is built.

In March 1939 the Finzis moved into their new home at Ashmansworth, high in the hills south of Newbury in Berkshire. The setting, with its long vistas, was idyllic, and they had the space they needed - for their young sons Christopher and Nigel as well as themselves. From choice, their lives were simple but wholesome: Finzi tended his orchard, bought yet more books, founded the Newbury String Players and composed (or, often, worked on some long-written fragments). Joy, meanwhile, sketched and sculpted, and together they entertained their many friends.

1939 was to have seen the first performance, at the Hereford Three Choirs Festival, of what has been regarded as Finzi's finest work, 'Dies Natalis', a cantata for soprano and strings to words by the seventeenth century poet Thomas Traherne, The Festival was cancelled when war was declared, and it was not until January 1940 that the work was performed, at the Wigmore Hall in London. Finzi was by instinct a pacifist, but saw the war as a 'damnable necessity', and from 1941 to 1945 he worked at the Ministry of War Transport.

Finzi's involvement with the Newbury String Players had revived his interest in eighteenth century English music. He edited volumes of works by composers of that period and with his amateur players presented it to a public most of whom were hearing such music for the first time. All this left little time for composition, but when the war was over Finzi's music started to be published again. 'An Ode for St. Cecilia' appeared in 1947 and a clarinet concerto in 1949 - the latter for that year's Hereford Three Choirs Festival. The soloist was Frederick Thurston.

51. Gerald Finzi.

Music festivals everywhere were struggling to survive in the post-war years of austerity. Stinchcombe Hill was no exception; the 1948 festival was cancelled, and on April 17th Finzi commiserated with Diana Oldridge:

...It's a miserable business... and a part of the general inertia which seems to be creeping over things - not exactly helped by transport conditions - which needs killing. All the same, I'm absolutely convinced that, given the right Captain, the ship can always be sailed...

The Stinchcombe Festival was in fact revived in 1950.

Finzi's setting of Wordsworth's poem 'Intimations of Immortality', for tenor, choir, and orchestra, had, like many of Finzi's works, been long in gestation, but it was ready for the 1950 Three Choirs Festival at Gloucester. It was performed, too, in the 1951 Worcester Festival which also included his 'Farewell to Arms', for tenor and small orchestra.

Finzi continued to write music - and to champion the causes of other composers whose works he felt were neglected - though he knew that he had, at the most, ten years to live; leukemia had been diagnosed. In spite of his illness and the necessary treatment, he wrote at the request of Sir John Barbirolli a major work for the 1955 Cheltenham Festival - a cello concerto. Christopher Bunting was the soloist and Barbirolli conducted the Hallé Orchestra.

Finzi's last major composition was the choral work 'In Terra Pax'; he was at Gloucester to conduct the work on September 6th 1956. The whole Finzi family and many of his friends, including Howard Ferguson, were there, and on the following Sunday, recalled Ursula Vaughan Williams, "the Finzis drove us out to Chosen Hill and Gerald described how he had been there as a young man on Christmas Eve, at a party in the tiny house where the sexton lived, and how they had all come out into the frosty midnight and heard bells ringing across Gloucestershire from beside the Severn to the hill villages of the Cotswolds..." According to Howard Ferguson, it was the memory of this occasion that inspired Finzi to write 'In Terra Pax'.

They proceeded to explore the country around Chosen Hill and visited the sexton's cottage, where they found children playing. It was probably here that Gerald Finzi caught chicken pox; his immune system had been weakened by the leukemia treatment and the virus spread to his brain. He died on September 27th 1956, aged 55.

C.W. ORR (1893-1976)

Orr's music is not well known today but the quality of some of his songs was undoubtedly high. His settings of the poetry of A.E. Housman are of first importance.

Charles Wilfred Orr was born in Cheltenham on July 31st 1893. He was a pupil at Cheltenham College, but ill health, in particular the persistent eczema which had developed following a childhood vaccination ("that foul Jenner" Orr cried, though in the event Jenner was not to blame, as the eczema was constitutional), forced him to leave at the age of fourteen; for a similar reason he was discharged from the Coldstream Guards in 1917. Orr moved with his family to Wimbledon in 1914, where he discovered the music of Frederick Delius. He introduced himself to the composer and showed him some of his music. Delius replied

> I find you have what to me is the most important quality in music, 'emotion'. There is a warm feeling over your music & I should certainly advise you to devote yourself entirely to it & work very hard...

When Orr considered training at the Guildhall School of Music, Delius advised

> Go by all means to the Guildhall School of Music for a while & see how you profit by it - But do not get hold of a professor who teaches you little 4 or 8 bar counterpoint exercises & little harmony exercises - trust your own ears & try to express your emotions in any way you can . ...

There is little doubt that without Delius's support Orr would not have persevered. "He was", wrote Geoffrey Hoare, "...to bombard Delius for comment and encouragement on his early attempts at composition... the influence, artistry and name of the famous and established composer Delius... provided the impetus so desperately sought". Hoare met Orr in 1961 and remained a friend until Orr's death in 1976.

Another source of advice and encouragement was the composer Philip Heseltine ('Peter Warlock'), whom Orr met in 1918 at the Hampstead flat which Delius was renting from Sir Henry Wood.

Orr spent one term at the Guildhall studying ensemble playing and composition. He left in January 1919 and, for a short time, took lessons in counterpoint with Edward Dent, Professor of Music at Cambridge. It was in this year that Orr encountered the poetry of A.E. Housman, when he chanced to hear Graham Peel's setting of 'In Summer Time on Bredon'. His life changed. He read everything which had been written about Housman, and in 1921 began setting Housman's verses to music. He was not the first composer to do so; before the Great War Butterworth, John Ireland and Ralph Vaughan Williams had all written songs to Housman texts, and Orr studied these settings carefully,before beginning his own. 'The Carpenter's Son' (1922) was dedicated to Philip Heseltine. Of the thirty-six songs which Orr wrote, twenty-four were Housman settings, though it seems that the poet and the composer never met. (Geoffrey Hoare has traced 44 composers who have used Housman texts, but Orr was the most prolific.)

Housman will, of course, forever be associated with one county, but Geoffrey Hoare maintained that

> ...with few exceptions many of the poems comprising 'A Shropshire Lad' (not Housman's title, anyway) should have, or could have, been set in the Cotswolds. For

'A Shropshire Lad' was a completely imaginary character. There were no ties with Shropshire, in fact he only visited that county long after the poems were written... Even by 1936 he stated "I do not know Shropshire well, only Wenlock and Ludlow".

Hoare pointed out that most of the poems in A Shropshire Lad "can be altered or modified to Cotswold country", giving examples of acceptable substitutions of names. Housman certainly knew the Cotswolds: his mother was born in Stroud in 1825, the daughter of the Rector of Woodchester, and married Edward Housman at Woodchester in 1858. She died when Housman was twelve years old, but in his twenties he often visited friends in the area, including the Rothensteins at Far Oakridge.

Orr became ill with tuberculosis in 1923 and took some time to recover. In 1925 his mother died. For the next five years he lived in London, writing newspaper articles and composing. In 1929 he became engaged to Helen Tomblin, who was working in London as a secretary after two years at Newnham College, Cambridge. He was still troubled by tuberculosis, and a doctor advised a move out of London - to South Africa or at least to the country.

After their marriage in 1930 Orr and his wife moved to the Cotswolds. They bought Church House, an old house next to St. Mary's church in Painswick, and renamed it 'Clevelands'. Soon after moving in, the attic was converted into a music room. (The name has since reverted to 'Church House').

It was not, though, a good time to be writing songs. The 'wireless' was replacing 'songs around the piano' as home entertainment (Dick Russell was beginning the mass production of wireless cabinets for Murphy), and the gramophone had become popular. 'Talking pictures' were enticing people from their homes and more people were owning a motor car.

In his attic room at Painswick Orr continued to write songs, with Housman's texts to the fore. The Cycle of Seven Songs from A Shropshire Lad was completed in 1931. Philip Heseltine, who would certainly have given advice, had died in December 1930. Orr sought opinions from three other friends, the conductor Eugene Goossens, Walter Legge and Arnold Bax. Replies were favourable but publishers were reluctant to accept the songs. They were, it was claimed, too difficult for amateurs to sing or to play, and Orr was forced to pay to have the songs printed. The cycle was published in 1934, the year that Elgar, Holst and Orr's friend Delius all died. Goossens suggested that some of the songs should be orchestrated. Instead, Orr wrote a short piece, Cotswold Hill Tune, which was orchestrated for small string orchestra by Philip Heseltine's copyist. Orr dedicated it to Goossens.

At Painswick Orr was setting more Housman poems. A performance by Robert Rowell at London's Wigmore Hall on July 15th 1935 received critical acclaim. A 'Times' critic considered them "true songs in which a just balance is maintained between the claims of sheer melody, verbal fidelity, and suggestive accompaniment". When three of Orr's settings from A Shropshire Lad were published in 1940 they were dedicated to Gerald Moore, who had been Robert Rowell's accompanist at the 1935 recital.

Orr was a familiar figure in the area. "Most days", his friend and G.P. Dr. Jim Hoyland recalled, "his upright 'de Gaulle-like' figure would be seen walking over the Painswick Beacon, sporting an Old Cheltonian tie and a long cigarette holder. He was greatly respected and his friends delighted in his sense of humour".

Orr stopped composing when war broke out in 1939 and wrote no further music until 1952. He and Helen stayed in Painswick until 1941, when they moved to London. After the war they returned to Painswick, and Orr became manager of a Stroud bookshop. Six songs which he wrote in 1952 included his last setting of a Housman text; Orr's last published work was 'Midsummer Dance' for cello and piano (1957). He died at Painswick on February 24th 1976, and his ashes were placed in the churchyard.

52. C.W. Orr.

Chapter 14 - FURTHER READING

GURNEY

Boden, Anthony (ed.): *Stars in a Dark Night - Letters of Ivor Gurney to the Chapman Family.* Alan Sutton (1986).

Hurd, Michael: *The Ordeal of Ivor Gurney.* Oxford University Press (1978).

Kavanagh, P.J. (ed.): *Collected Poems of Ivor Gurney.* Oxford University Press (1982).

Moore, C.W. : *Ivor Gurney, Poet and Songwriter.* Triad Press (1976).

Thornton, R.K.R. (ed.): *Collected Letters of Ivor Gurney.* Carcanet Press (1991).

FINZI

Banfield, Stephen: *Gerald Finzi : an English Composer.* Faber & Faber (1997).

McVeagh, Diana: *Gerald Finzi.* Article in Grove's Dictionary of Music and Musicians, Macmillan (1980)

ORR

Hoare, Geoffrey: *Charles Orr - Master of English Song.* 'Cotswold Life' Magazine (July 1976)

Palmer, Christopher: *In Memoriam C. W. Orr.* Delius Society Journal, Vol. 55 (April 1977).

Wilson, Jane: *C.W. Orr, the Unknown Songwriter.* Thames & Hudson (1989).

[1] The poem as printed here agrees in wording and punctuation with the version given in Kavanagh's edition of the Collected Poems (1982).

ACKNOWLEDGEMENTS

ACKNOWLEDGEMENTS FOR ILLUSTRATIONS - COLOUR

Front Cover. By kind permission of the Robert Dover's Games Society.

II. © Stroud District Museum Trustees, Museum in the Park, Stroud.
IX. By kind permission of The Chapter of Bradford Cathedral.
X. The William Morris Gallery, Walthamstow, London.
XI. By permission of the Society of Antiquaries of London.
XII. By kind permission of Viscount Sandon and the Burnt Norton Trust.

ILLUSTRATIONS - BLACK & WHITE

1. The Architects' Journal 2. Essex House Press, courtesy of Felicity Ashbee.
3,7,8. Bodleian Library, University of Oxford, Refs: G.A. Glouc.b.2, Gough Glouc.5,
& J.J. Drayton. e. 74.
4. The Gloucester Record Office. 5,6. By permission of Lord Bathurst and the
Photographic Survey, Courtald Institute of Art (Private Collection).
11. The Reader's Digest Association Ltd.
12. By kind permission of Mrs. Elizabeth Murray.
13. By courtesy of The Methodist Publishing House.
14. By courtesy of the National Portrait Gallery, London.
15. The Gloucester Record Office: photograph by H.G.W. Household, with permission.
16. The Warden and Fellows of Keble College, Oxford. Photo © Woodmansterne.
18. © Tate, London 2002. 19. The William Morris Gallery, Walthamstow.
21,23. From *Ernest Gimson, His Life and Works*, by permission of Basil Blackwell.
22,24,26. Cheltenham Art Gallery & Museums.
27,28,30. Guild of Handicraft Trust, Chipping Campden.
29. V & A Picture Gallery.
31,32. By kind permission of Felicity Ashbee.
33,34. Cheltenham Art Gallery & Museums.
35,36. Cheltenham Art Gallery & Museums.
37. By kind permission of the Gordon Russell Trust.
38,41,43. By courtesy of the National Portrait Gallery, London.
39. By kind permission of Myfanwy Thomas. 40. Lens of Sutton. 42. By permission
of the Estate of John Drinkwater. 44. By permission of the John Masefield Society
and the Churchwardens of Preston Church. 45. Cheltenham Art Gallery & Museums.

46. © Crown copyright: National Monuments Record.

47, 48. From The English Hymnal by permission of Oxford University Press.

49. By courtesy of The National Portrait Gallery, London.

50. By permission of the Gurney Archive, Gloucester Library.

51. By permission of the Finzi Trust: photograph by Herbert Lambert.

52. From the collection of Geoffrey Hoare.

Map II. Reproduced from Ordnance Survey mapping on behalf of The Controller of Her Majesty's Stationery Office © Crown Copyright. 100037129.

ACKNOWLEDGEMENTS FOR QUOTATIONS

CHAPTER 7.

Morris, May: *William Morris - Writer, Artist and Socialist*. (2 Vols) Basil Blackwell (1936). By permission of Basil Blackwell.

Shaw, George Bernard: Two quotations by permission of the Society of Authors on behalf of the Bernard Shaw Estate.

CHAPTER 8.

Lethaby, W.R., Powell, A. H., & Griggs, F.L.: *Ernest Gimson, His Life and Works*. Shakespeare Head Press & Basil Blackwell (1924). By permission of Basil Blackwell.

Verey, David: *The Buildings of England - Gloucestershire: The Cotswolds* (Ed. Pevsner). Penguin (1979). By permission of Yale University Press.

CHAPTER 9.

Ashbee, C.R.: *Craftsmanship in Competitive Industry*. Essex House Press (1908).

Ashbee, C. R.: *The Last Records of a Cotswold Community*. Essex House Press (1905). Both by kind permission of Felicity Ashbee.

Ashbee, Felicity: Address at unveiling of commemorative plaque at the Old Silk Mill, Chipping Campden (1988). By kind permission of Felicity Ashbee.

Bury, Shirley: *An Arts and Crafts Experiment - The Silverwork of CRA*. V & A Museum Bulletin Vol III No. 1 (1967). By permission of the Victoria & Albert Museum.

CHAPTER 10.

Russell, Sir Gordon: *Designer's Trade (an autobiography)*. Allen & Unwin (1968). By kind permission of Mrs. Kate Baynes and the Gordon Russell Estate.

Russell, Sir Gordon: Address to the R.S.A. (1978). By kind permission of the Royal Society for the Encouragement of Arts, Manufacture & Commerce.

Gloag, John: *Gordon Russell and Cotswold Craftsmanship*. Architects Journal 15 Aug. (1928), by kind permission.

Pevsner, Nikolaus: *Patient Progress Two: Gordon Russell*. Studies in Art, Architecture & Design,

Vol. 2. Victorian and After. Thames & Hudson (1968), by kind permission.

CHAPTER 11.

Thomas, Edward: *Collected Poems*. Faber & Faber (1958). By kind permission of Myfanwy Thomas.

de la Mare, Walter: Foreword to *Collected Poems*. By permission of the Literary Trustees of Walter de la Mare and the Society of Authors as their representative.

Thomas, Helen: *Under Storms Wing*. Carcanet Press (1988). By kind permission of Myfanwy Thomas.

Davies, W.H.: *The Complete Poems, with an Introduction by Osbert Sitwell*. Jonathan Cape (1963). By permission of Mrs. H.M. Davies Will Trust.

Sitwell, Osbert: *An Introduction to the Complete Poems*. By permission of David Higham Associates Ltd.

Drinkwater, John: *Cotswold Characters*. Oxford University Press (1921). By permission of Samuel French.

Eliot, T.S.: *Collected Poems*. Faber & Faber (1954). By permission of Faber & Faber.

CHAPTER 12.

For 'Tewkesbury Road': see Masefield's *Collected Poems*. Heinemann (1923).

For the 'Ashbee' poems: see Fiona MacCarthy's *The Simple Life - C. R. Ashbee in the Cotswolds*. Lund Humphries (1981).

All Masefield's poems and prose by permission of the Society of Authors as the Literary Representative of the Estate of John Masefield.

CHAPTER 13.

Holst, Imogen: *Gustav Holst, a Biography*. Oxford University Press (1969). By permission of G.& I. Holst Ltd.

The English Hymnal: O.U.P. (1906).

Vaughan Williams, Ralph : *The First Fifty Years, a History of the English Hymnal*. O.U.P. (1956). Both by permission of the Oxford University Press.

CHAPTER 14.

Kavanagh, P.J. (ed.): *Collected Poems of Ivor Gurney*. Oxford University Press (1982). By kind permission of the Ivor Gurney Trust.

Haines, John: *The Gloucester Journal*. Jan. 5th (1935). By permission of Gloucestershire Newspapers Ltd.

McVeagh, Diana: *Records and Recording* (1980). By kind permission of the author.

Hoare, Geoffrey: *Cotswold Life*. Aug. (1973). By kind permission of the author and editor.

INDEX